What Next?
Recollections of an Inveterate Voyager

What Next?
Recollections of an Inveterate Voyager

CP Sharma

Vij Books India Pvt Ltd
New Delhi (India)

Published by

Vij Books India Pvt Ltd
(Publishers, Distributors & Importers)
2/19, Ansari Road
Delhi – 110 002
Phones: 91-11-43596460, 91-11-47340674
Mob: 98110 94883
e-mail: contact@vijpublishing.com
web : www.vijbooks.in

ISBN: 978-93-90439-56-0 (Paperback)
ISBN: 978-93-90439-57-7 (ebook)

*Dedicated to my parents Capt Faqir Chand and Sital Pyari
for always supporting me and giving me the courage
to chase my dreams.*

Contents

Preface

Some people write books on the spur of the moment, while some write after years of contemplation. Some like me fall somewhere in between. The book was on my mind for a long time, but there seemed to be no time after work and other responsibilities. But most unexpectedly there was suddenly an abundance of free time when we were stuck at home due to restrictions imposed during the COVID spread in the country. I started on my MS which was completed in about three months. It was a truly great learning experience for me.

I started my career with the Indian Navy, and this experience was enhanced by joining the Merchant Navy and then venturing out to run a travel business. A major lesson that I have learnt over the years is that when you are passionate and honest in whatever you do success will follow. Because of this I have had a smooth transition from government to public sector, to private sector. Certainly being an entrepreneur is most challenging and satisfying. As we know each individual is different in nature and attitude, but if one is ready to enjoy his work the means and ends are the same. A question that I have been asked a number of times is which job was better. I have always found it difficult to give an answer because the truth is that I enjoyed them all.

Some people think that I am a risk-taker, something I would deny. There has certainly been a bit of a risk factor, especially when one ventures out on one's own to leave a stable job and the sense of security that it brings. Whatever I have done in my life at every stage is something that I have been passionate about. I always tell people that I have never really "worked" and anything and everything I have done was treated like a hobby.

For me events in life have been the way I dreamt them to be. It is one life and I thought one might as well live and do things the way one likes, rather than just going through routines. Of course my life has had its share of ups and downs, highs and lows, peaks and troughs, ebbs and flows. It is something that I have learnt to take in my stride and move on. As Walt Disney once said: "All our dreams can come true, if we have the courage to pursue them."

The biggest satisfaction of being an entrepreneur, apart from the different challenges, innovation, providing employment and doing what I really wanted to do, was being my own boss. This is very important to me and this freedom is something I greatly prize. But with this freedom also came responsibility which one cannot shirk.

After leaving the Navy I did explore some options but then zeroed-in on to the travel business. There was this bug for travel in me which I cannot deny. I did not know the intricacies. I thought from day one I would be travelling, but it was not so for many years. As of today I have travelled to over seventy countries and to some of them a number of times. I still yearn to travel more, meet interesting people and explore and learn about so much that is available and on offer in the world. Because of my travels I have made numerous friends all over the world, met fascinating people, and came in contact with quaint cultures.

In this book I have covered my early childhood, various aspects of my life and my travels in particular. This book is perhaps more of a travelogue as it covers my travel experiences, beautiful and exotic places, and peoples and cultures I came in contact with; readers would be amazed how bewilderingly diverse the world is. I made friends with people while walking on the roadside, in a bus, cycling, sailing in yachts and boats and cruise ships both on rivers and on the sea, on flights, and while visiting small quaint villages and also the usual touristic sites. I have written about some exotic countries and places that I have visited which would give an insight about travelling to these places. In most cases I have given a brief introduction of the place and in some cases a bit of its past history. I have written about some places that people would probably have on their travel wish-list and the book should motivate them more. But there are some places covered which are not so popular for various reasons including the perception of danger and risk. But I could not cover everything in just one book and I had to be selective! Maybe I would do it at a later stage.

I have also included a photo section and hope it will trigger a desire in readers to travel. There is a postscript that highlights the impact of the

COVID-19 pandemic on our lives and especially on the travel trade business.

Throughout my adult life I have often thought of the less fortunate in our society. However, I could actually concretize my inner desire to give back to society after many years and after some exposure to institutional charity work as a Rotarian. Neptune Foundation was established at the end of 2006 making the year a milestone year in my life. I have devoted a small section to it. The Foundation's work has given me immense satisfaction and joy to be doing something worthwhile which has brought smiles on the faces of hundreds of deprived children.

CP Sharma
New Delhi
31 October 2020

Acknowledgements

I would like to express my gratitude to my brother Col V.P. Sharma, my wife Neeru, my son Dhruv and his spouse Aditi, my daughter Arooshi and her spouse Ritin; they have been a strong support in all aspects of my life. My granddaughter, Diya has been a source of much joy.

Mr R.S. Mani, my Principal at King George's School left a great impact on all of us in the school. He was a true educationist and the most important mentor in my formative years.

I owe a lot to several of my seniors from the Navy and Merchant Navy who left an extraordinary influence on me. They are: VADM Harinder Singh, RADM N.N. Anand, VADM H. Johnson, ADM Sushil Kumar who passed away recently, Admiral Ronnie Pereira who passed away in 1993 and Capt P.C. Alexander from the Shipping Corporation of India.

My heartfelt thanks I owe to friends who helped me start my business and guided and supported me. Special mention needs to be made of Cdr R.S. Pujji who passed away recently, Swamy my first Bank Manager, Shailendra Agarwal, Kuki Chawla, Gagan Uberoi, Amit Dhir, Thomas, Harsh Vardhan –Managing Director- Vayudoot, Kiki Skagen Munshi, Papli (Mrs V.P. Singh) who passed away recently, Adriana Miori and many others who I may have inadvertently missed out.

I remember with fondness Mr Sudarshan Agarwal former Governor of Uttarakhand and Sikkim who passed away recently in 2019 for introducing me to Rotary and Pulin Trivedi who passed away in 2012 for bringing me back to Rotary after a year's break.

Organizations and individuals that have been associated with and supported Neptune Foundation and charity polo matches are: Rotary Club of New Delhi, Army Polo and Riding Centre, Doordarshan, Sanjeet from Travtalk, Christine Mukharji - Director of Austrian National Tourist Office, Khun Runjuan Tongrut, Director of Tourism Authority of Thailand, Medhavi Pande of Kumarakom Lake Resort, Captain Ravee from Fireball, Sanjay

Chawla from Cotton Harbour, Ms Priyanka Nijhawan from Constance Hotels, Manu Mehta, Kailash Mishra who passed away recently, my friends from the print media and a large number of well wishers. I owe a deep debt of gratitude to them all.

I am grateful to Inder Raj Ahluwalia for opening the world of writing to me and Roxani Oikonomou for motivating me to write this book.

Finally, I wish to express my deep appreciation to Tapan K. Ghosh, my consultant editor, who took me through the whole editorial process with patience and understanding born of years of experience. His inputs and lessons would be invaluable for me in any future endeavour with the written word.

Chapter 1

Growing Up and Memories of School

I was born in 1952 in the Base Hospital in Delhi Cantonment. I grew up in a large family. We were five brothers and three sisters. I was the seventh child.

I missed out seeing my grandparents except for my maternal grandfather Pandit Durga Dass. I have a hazy memory of him, as he had passed away when I was quite young. He ran a sweet shop in Phagwara and the tradition even today is continued by my cousins. My paternal grandfather Pandit Kanshi Ram was an accountant with Punjab Transport Department in Hoshiarpur and hailed from Bajwara.

My father Faqir Chand started his career as a civilian with Remount Veterinary hospital in Mhow. Before the beginning of the Second World War, he was given an option to become a combatant, which he accepted. He took part in the Burma campaign in the British colony of Burma during the war. He retired as a Captain. He was an excellent role model as a parent. He ingrained in all his children qualities such as politeness, honesty and humility.

My mother Sital Pyari was popularly known as Sita. She was a very gracious, strong lady and was a pillar of strength to the large family. She was a lady of frugal habits. Although she had only studied in school up to a few classes, but she was always proud and said that this was the best a girl could have done in her locality in Phagwara in Punjab in those days. She took pride in teaching her grandchildren, specially the Punjabi version of "Jack and Jill" nursery rhyme which she had studied in school.

Both our parents complemented each other and brought us up well in spite of the limited resources with them and a large family that they had to take care of. They did not leave any stone unturned in giving us the best of education and bringing us up to be good human beings. We never felt the shortage of any requirements when growing up.

I was 22 years younger than my eldest brother, Om Prakash. He started practicing as a physician in 1952, the year that I was born. My parents worked hard and ensured that he could complete his medicine. He did repay his debt to my parents by supporting our family in later years. Vishwa retired as a civilian officer from the Ministry of Defence and Ved as a colonel from the Corps of Signals from the Indian Army. My younger brother Surya started his business as a chemist but later closed shop and joined me in my enterprise. My sisters Swarna, Prem and Sneh, being much older, took good care of me as a child and then married and settled down. With a large family we had a natural support system to help each other in times of need.

Early School Days

All of us have fond memories of initial growing up and school days.

I spent the early part of my childhood in Meerut and subsequently in Saharanpur. I do not remember much about Meerut, where my father was posted.

My first school was in Saharanpur and was called Sophia Girls School; boys were only allowed in junior classes. I have vivid memories of going to school in a Tam Tam (a horse driven cart).

I do remember that the sisters (nuns) and teachers were very affectionate. They took good care of us and have left sweet memories.

One day I complained to the class teacher and asked why I was not being taken to the church. Since I insisted, I was taken there and given some statues for polishing. This kept me happy and later my father was told that I had been only taken there because of my insistence. It was a small and wonderfully beautiful church.

I recall a play in which I acted. In this play, I was a student in the class and was drawing some cartoons on my slate and the teacher (another student) seeing me inattentive, picked up a stick to beat me for not doing classwork. I was supposed to throw the slate away towards the teacher, my classmate. When I threw the slate the sharp edge of the slate hit his back and hurt him. He did not complain about it, even though he was in pain. Years later, I came to know that he was from the family of Nawabs in Saharanpur.

Tam Tam would always be there to pick me up on time. Once it got delayed and I lost patience waiting. I decided to walk back home and took the wrong route and reached the local courts. I was crying and was lost. One of the lawyers called up my father who later came to pick me up. It was then I was given strict instructions to always wait to be picked up from school.

My father was transferred from Saharanpur to Ahmednagar around July 1961 and we were transiting through New Delhi. I was eight years old then. I was waiting at the Railway Station with the baggage to be loaded and to embark on the train. When the train was approaching the platform for passengers to embark I was fast asleep. Probably in my half-asleep state I thought the train was already there and while trying to embark fell on the railway track. There was a lot of commotion and noise on the platform. My parents heard people shouting that a child had fallen in front of the moving coaches, but they had no clue it was me.

I can only recollect that I was lying across the track and I could see some coaches moving past. A coolie, a good Samaritan, had jumped down to save me by pushing me across the track. Once the coaches stopped moving, the coolie brought me to the platform and handed me over to my parents. But for the selfless act of the coolie, I may not have survived. I was brought safe and sound to the coupe. There was an elderly gentleman travelling in the same coupe who told my father that I had survived because of the selfless brave act of the coolie.

In Ahmednagar, I went to the Armoured Corps School for a short duration, from July 1961 to December 1961.

At King George's School (January 1962-April 1969)

In Ahmednagar, I got selected for King George's School. Due to the transferable job of my father, out of five brothers, four of us went to boarding schools. Three went to the same boarding school. My father gave importance to education, discipline and humility. Despite many constraints, he did the best for us. My mother was a strong lady who worked hard and left no stone unturned in bringing us up and building our character. She was a very humble lady.

There were tests conducted in a number of places to join King George's school and the names of those who got selected were announced on the radio. I remember the family glued to the radio and the joy once my name was announced. In January 1962, I joined King George's School in Belgaum in standard five. Belgaum is a city in the state of Karnataka located in its northern part along the Western Ghats. It is known for its scenic beauty and enjoys a cool and pleasant climate throughout the year. Surrounded by lush green forests, rivers, and mountains, Belgaum is breathtakingly beautiful and attracts tourists from all over the country and far off places. Belgaum also has a strong historical background which dates back to the late 12th century AD when it was formed. The Belgaum fort, a massive structure that occupies its position in the centre of the town was built in 1519. The fort houses some mosques that are several centuries old and a Jain temple, Kamal Basati, which has an idol, Neminantha, made of black stone. The idol dates back to 1204 AD.

King George's school was founded on 30 December 1945 as a Boys school. It was then called King George VI Royal Indian Military College. On Republic Day 1950, the school was renamed King George's Military College. In July 1952, the school was reorganised along the lines of residential public schools. The school was simultaneously renamed as King George's School. The school was renamed as Military School in 1966. On 25 June 2007, the school got its present name "Rashtriya Military School". Our school has several of its alumni occupying high positions in the Armed Forces, the bureaucracy, corporate world, businesses, politics and in other sectors and are doing stellar service.

My elder brother Ved was already in the school. My parents came to leave me at Ahmednagar railway station, I went and took my seat; for me it was like taking any other train journey. My mother a few years later told me that I did not give a feeling at all of going away from home. May be I was so secure because I was travelling with my brother. My father always made it a point to see me off and receive me on every train journey if he was in town. Later most journeys I undertook were from New Delhi. Whenever I have travelled by train and even now, the memory of my father coming to see me off is still etched in my mind. I can visualize him standing there, wistfully looking toward me, as the train slowly began moving. I remember going to school in a Damni from Belgaum Railway Station. Damni was a nicely decorated cart driven by an ox. It was not before long we saw all kinds of mechanized vehicles for transportation in the city.

During the first assembly of school and beginning of the academic year, new entrants had to introduce themselves. As the shorts of my uniform that was stitched for me was loose, I would keep pulling it up every few minutes even as I talked animatedly. Everyone had a good laugh and would always recall this incident whenever we reminisced on our early school days.

As things turned out I was the roommate of my brother, Ved, who was the House Captain as well. I had to pay the price for being his roommate; it was three of us in the room, Keshab a classmate being the third occupant. Morning wake up call would be at six in the morning; being his room mates we had to get up fifteen minutes earlier. The only wake-up alarm that we could hear was the shout "Keshab, CP get up!" We would both jump out of our beds and rush out of the room simultaneously towards different bathrooms. I lost touch with Keshab, after leaving school. Much later I came to know that he became a Naxalite and died in one of the encounters with the security forces.

Ved was a strict disciplinarian. He wanted everyone to learn English; in case we were caught speaking in Hindi, we would have to write a few hundred times, "I will speak in English". Most of our schoolmates remember the punishment even today and realize how it helped them in later years. Fortunately, I did not have go through this exercise as I had studied in an English medium school.

Our rooms were inspected daily and we were given marks for cleanliness and tidiness, etc. We really had to work hard to keep our rooms in tip-top condition. We did well on this part, being the House Captain's room. We had to keep everything spick and span. Ours was the first room and that also at the entrance of the hostel.

A normal day would start with physical training in the morning, followed by breakfast, classes, lunch, afternoon prep classes and finally evening sports period. We had prep classes at seven in the evening also when we revised various subjects and completed our home work. In the evenings I would always be rushing for the class and there was no question of being late as prefects would punish us. I seemed to be always running, with a comb in my pocket, blazer in my hand and tie in the blazer's pocket. Even today a comb is always there in my pocket as a matter of habit though I am not sure if I really need one with hardly any hair left.

We always looked forward to celebrating our birthdays in school. It was a big event, being away from home. Our hostel superintendent, signed a chit for more sweets than we could normally buy to be distributed to classmates. Mr Nambiar was very sharp and had a wonderful memory. Once when Somnath, my classmate was getting the chit signed from him the fourth time for his birthday in the same year, Mr Nambiar asked him "Somnath, how many times were your born this year?"

The journey to school and back home by train was always a memorable experience, specially the long train journeys. Most trains had steam engines; by the time we finished our journey, there was enough coal in our hair and clothes which would turn black. Heat, coal, travelling in ordinary class did not bother us, since it was fun. For some places we would have a whole coach to ourselves; in that case travelling by train was most of a private affair. This coach would be attached from one train to other and shunted in railway yards. Students came from close by and distant places. Talar Doye was from NEFA (North Eastern Frontier Agency) and since he came from the interiors it took him on an average eight to ten days to travel to and from school. But when the mighty Brahmaputra was flooded, he would reach in a month. Years later it was nice to see him on the television, as the President of ruling party of Arunachal Pradesh. Because of this we established contact again, during his visit to Delhi. It was the same boy who would have a book in front of him and could sleep with his eyes open.

With plenty of playgrounds, our school produced some outstanding sports persons. It was a very good environment to grow up in. National Hockey Team Olympians Laxman and Bandu Patil would practice on our school grounds. Moto of our school was "Play the game". We were taught to follow this in real life apart from sports. We played all sports in school like hockey, football, cricket, basket ball, volley ball, water polo, kabaddi, athletics and of course not to forget our locally improvised game only peculiar to our school. It was called "Jhar Bandar" meaning "tree monkey", where one would be selected to pick up a stick thrown away. Meanwhile, others would climb up on trees. He had to climb up the tree with the stick and touch someone. The one who was touched had to follow the same procedure of the stick being thrown and getting up the tree to catch someone.

We had regular swimming classes. It was probably one of the few swimming pools in Belgaum. Much against the rules we would at times go quietly swimming at night, despite many ghost stories in that area. There was a famous story of an individual who had hung himself on a tree and died. At night his ghost would swim in the pool. Some of us claimed to have heard a noise at night of someone swimming in the dark. One of the youngest teachers who joined the school was an enthusiastic swimmer. A few days after joining he jumped from the three metre diving board to the one metre diving board, thinking that he would get extra spring action to dive into the pool. In the bargain, he fractured his leg.

Pithoo was another game that we would play. This was played by forming two teams and making a pile of seven flat stones. If the first team successfully knocked over the stones, the game would begin. The second team would get the ball and try to hit players from the opposing team who would try to rebuild the pile. However, if they failed to do this and all players were out, the defending team would gain the point and they would have a turn to hit the pile of stones. Other games we played were Stapu and Gilli Danda.

Our school did produce some good athletes. We would go running to the sports grounds and it was a normal routine to go around Laxmi hill.

The students at the school were placed in different houses, namely, Ashok, Shivaji, Pratap and Ranjit each under a housemaster. We kept moving from one house to other while changing classes from 5th onwards. For sports and other extra-curricular activities we were divided in sets called Todas, Nagas, Gonds, Santhals and wore colours Green, Blue, Red and yellow respectively. Mr Mani believed that children were like tribes and needed nurturing, hence the names of sets were given names of tribes.

To teach us discipline and make us self-reliant and dependable we were made Cubs in junior classes. Later we became Scouts. After that we all had to join National Cadet Corps, which is the youth wing of Indian Armed Forces, and depending on our interest we could join Army, Navy or the Air Wing.

I joined Navy Wing. We were taught about Navy, seamanship, handling of boats and naval drill. We would go for NCC Camps to various places and meet cadets from different states. This was a great opportunity to interact with others. I remained Petty Officer cadet for a long time.

In senior classes some of us were selected to go for adventure course which was held in different places of the country every year. I went to Mayo College located in Ajmer. We were made to take part in adventure activities like cross country trekking, rock climbing and rappelling.

The course organizers were very happy with our school and only ten of us had gone to attend it. They were very impressed with our dress, identical kit bags and nicely painted trunks of the same size. This gave a very good impression when the officer went on rounds of the accommodation we were put in. During the rounds we would outshine other participants when our kit was on display. One night when the officer was taking rounds, he saw that everyone was sleeping covered in the blanket head to toe. He had some suspicion and lifting up one blanket, he found some clothes and pillow had been kept inside. Most had gone out to watch a movie in Ajmer.

We were reprimanded the next morning. I think we got off lightly for our nocturnal escapade!

Mr Jack Gibson who was the Principal of Mayo College gave us a presentation of his mountaineering expeditions. He was a renowned academician and a well-known mountaineer. He had also served as Principal of the Joint Services Wing, which is now the National Defence Academy. He is widely credited to have brought Mayo College to national prominence.

On and off there would be educational tours organized to various places be it factories or visit to other places. Maratha Light Infantry Regimental Centre was adjoining our school. The Maratha Light Infantry was raised in 1768, making it the most senior and decorated light infantry regiment in the Indian Army. We would be taken to see how the recruits were trained; this was in the outskirts of the city. They would be crossing trenches, with heavy light machine gun firing a few inches above them and mortar shells being dropped over the bunkers they were in. There was a danger area marked and out of bounds for us spectators. I do remember the officer conducting the training telling us to remain outside the danger mark, as he "would not like to waste a bullet!"

School picnics would be organized on some farms, where a landlord named Mr Deshpande was always there to welcome us and we could pluck all kinds of fruits and eat them. Some of us went on a school trip to Goa soon after its liberation. In those days Goa still had the fresh Portuguese ambience; we could see all kinds of imported vehicles. It was like visiting a foreign country.

The prestigious Commando School is also located close to the school. For nearly 50 years, this eminent Commando School has produced the fittest and finest Ghatak Commandos who have fought the most notable wars of our generation.

Maratha Light Infantry Regimental Centre and the Commando School, which was established later gave the students an insight about the Army and has always been a great source of motivation.

We would get short winter breaks and long summer holidays, something that we all looked forward to. During winter breaks (about two weeks) those who were not staying far went home and others who had come from distant places stayed back in school. Those staying back kept themselves busy with various activities as there was no regular routine. There was more time to play, including our innovative sports. Rest of the time was used to pluck sugar canes, wild berries and fruits that grew in staff houses around the campus. Since some sugar cane fields were close to the school it was an adventure to pluck sugar cane, although it did not have the farmer's approval. One night some farmers laid a trap to catch the intruders and some students were caught. They told the landlord that the people who were plucking sugar cane had been caught and locked up in a room. Most convenient outfit for adventures like this was sports wear and sports shirts of red, blue, green and yellow colour. The landlord recognized the dress and asked the farmers to let them go and told them that the students should not be caught again whilst plucking sugar cane. The landlord happened to be a senior from school. Some teachers had papayas and guavas growing in the backyard. Once Mr K.N. Subbaramaiah (or KNS) caught someone plucking guavas. KNS was always fond of us but he said: "Even if you had asked me I would not have let you pluck them ". He did not believe in the old adage on stealing: "Why did you have to steal; in case you had asked for it, I would have given it to you."

During the summer holidays we all went home. There were some students coming from places as far as Darjeeling and not to forget Talar Doye who would come from NEFA (North East Frontier Agency) now known as Arunachal Pradesh. Summer holidays were always a great time to spend with our parents and rest of the family. Ours was a big family and we would all get together, including our nieces and nephews. We would go for picnics, swimming, read books and get a chance to laze around, and enjoy food at home. Unlike for children today where a lot of homework is given during holidays, we did not carry any books and no homework was given to us. We literally had no local friends when we came home. It was only a few of us who would meet on and off. In the bargain it gave us more time for spending with the family. The only means to keep in contact with school mates was by writing letters. Since the breaks were for almost two and half months, after some time we would all be looking forward to going back to school and meeting friends to talk about our adventures during the holidays. These holidays are fondly remembered; we often discuss the good times we had with family and friends.

We had excellent teachers like Mr Kaul, Mr Rege, Mr Vaid, Mr Nedungadi, Mr Desai, the matron Mrs Mudhaliar, Mr Chaube, Mr Mahatam Rai, Mr Poonekar, Mr Satyan, Mr Nithurkar, Mr Roberts, Mr Nagesh Rao, Mr Upadhyay and Mr Nambiar, among others.

Mr Roberts was our English teacher who was jovial, an excellent footballer and was also a National Football Referee. In case he caught us reading comics in the class, he never reprimanded us but took them with him for reading !!! Mr Rege was a great motivator. He would tell us that there were a lot of other professions that we should look at, and not just think of becoming military officers, engineers or doctors. He also had a family business of running a printing press. Mr Mahatam Rai, our Hindi teacher would always make the class very interactive; his teaching of the subject was unparalleled and mesmerized the class with his overpowering voice. Mr Gopalakrishnan, although the laboratory in-charge, was fluent in English; he would train us for debates and made some of us good orators.

It was the Principal Mr R.S. Mani, however, who left a great impact on all of us in the school. He was a true educationist.

Before taking over as the Principal, Mr Mani was an instructor in National Defence Academy and did a short stint at Raj Kumar College. There the students came from royal families; he moved out very soon from there, thinking that he was not the right person to teach there. It was more of a show by members of the royal /affluent families and there was no real focus on education.

A living legend for anyone who was a student under him, even today his memory lives with everyone in the school.

Initially, when he took over the school he did rusticate one student. He regretted having done that. He always thought that as a true educationist, he had to make every child an honest and a successful human being. He always told us with pride that he had all kinds of students, who reached various pinnacles in life though some did not. There were instances when he took students who were rusticated from other schools, so that he could reform them. He made one of them even stay at his home.

He would say in generic terms that he had produced from the school many officers, doctors, engineers and others who were not too disciplined and were later caught for wrong doings. He never disowned any student even if he lacked discipline and was poor in studies.

Every festival in school was celebrated with same gusto and spirit, be it Eid, Deepawali, Christmas, Guru Nanak's birthday to name a few. During Eid celebrations we would get Qawals to sing, at Deepawali would be the priest doing the prayers, at Christmas we would have a priest from the local church for our assembly and on Guru Nanak's Birthday would have a Granthi read the Sri Guru Granth Sahib. He would always say that he was a Burmese by birth, Hindu by religion, Buddhist in faith and Christian in action. On being invited as the Chief Guest at the local Gurudwara for their silver jubilee, he donated his one month's salary, though he had no savings.

A Dog and an Old Man

There was a stray dog in school; we named it Laika, after the famous Soviet space dog who became one of the first animals in space, and the first animal to orbit the Earth. This dog was a favourite of all of us; we would quietly feed him, getting food from the dining hall by hiding it in various ways. Laika would follow us for the morning assembly, classes and sports. Since it bit a student, it was sent to a farm, away from school, but with so much of love from all of us he found his way back. Rarely would Mr Mani use a cane for the students as a punishment. During one assembly in the morning, a student was to be caned. Mr Mani picked up the cane, but before he could do anything, Laika pounced and caught the Principal's hand. Typical of him, all he said was: "Look at the affection of the animal for all of you". No one was caned. Since Laika bit another student, finally it had to be sent away. We all missed Laika.

There was an old man who would stay in the shooting range, and students would feed him. He was never asked to leave the school premises. One morning he was outside the Assembly Hall in tattered clothes and he told Mr Mani that it was too cold. Mr Mani took off his Shark skin coat and put it on his half naked body. This did leave a great impact on all of us.

We were from various backgrounds, some of us from middle class and some from very affluent families. But there was no difference and we all grew up with great bonhomie and camaraderie in an atmosphere where everyone in school was committed to the growth of others.

Mamas and our Matron

We were served meals in the dining hall and there was an adjoining anteroom, which was used for small functions. We addressed the waiters, cooks and other support staff as *mama* (maternal uncle). We were taught to give them utmost respect and were punished in case someone was rude to them, which rarely happened. If it was in the dining hall he had to eat separately in the anteroom for a few days as punishment. This taught us to respect elders and people who served us. One of the parents once told Mr Mani, that he had two sons, studying in different boarding schools; the one studying in our school was always very respectful to servants whereas the other was very rude with them.

Mrs Mudhaliar the matron was a religious and a pious lady. She was in charge of the dining hall and made sure that each one of us was looked after like her own children. On festivals some special preparations would be made. The tradition of being called Pande Ji (title for Brahmin) started with my elder brother. I was in a junior class; I wished her and it being one of the festivals, she assumed I was fasting and told me to go to the anteroom where fruits were kept for us. In the evening there was a special elaborate menu for us since we were on fast and did not have proper lunch. From then on, I volunteered to go on fast.

Mr Mani always said that in case the results of any school showed all students passing, then there was something drastically wrong. He would say that all your parents would say that they came first in their class and they would not be able to show their marksheets! He added with a wry smile that no one should ask him for his marksheet. It is not that he did not want students to do well in studies. His endeavour was to turn students into good human beings.

Chicken pox—the silver lining

Once, a chickenpox epidemic spread through the school. Many of us were segregated but the numbers kept increasing. Those segregated could not take part in any activities or attend classes. It would start with segregation of a particular room for 21 days. We were later put in a separate segregation ward. In case anyone in the ward got chickenpox, all were segregated for a period of 21 days. I landed up spending almost 50 days in segregation. Even then fifteen more days remained for completing the segregation period. It had to be finally called off since it was only a few of us who were now in a small segregation ward and there was no more spread.

Due to the chicken pox epidemic a number of us missed classes and obviously academic performance may not have been upto the mark. It was the last assembly in school before the start of the holidays and ending of academic year. Before the assembly could start with any prayers or a talk by the Principal, he announced that the whole school was being promoted to their next class. There was a lot of cheering and shouting. Imagine the smile on the faces of those who had failed.

Belgaum although not a very big city had plenty of cinema halls and when we got an out pass, we would not miss an opportunity to watch a movie. There were some movies like "*It's a Mad, Mad, Mad, Mad world*", "*Sangam*", where the whole school went to watch them. The complete cinema hall would be reserved for us. Also on Thursdays at night there would be some documentaries or movies shown in the Assembly Hall, but if it was not interesting we all caught up on sleep. There were some who would skip and watch movies at night without permission. It was an adventure of a kind. Mr Nambiar who was one of our hostel superintendents learnt to read Hindi from the many posters that were there in town. If ever he caught someone in town watching a movie or outside the school premises, he never reported it to the Principal, but would ask us to go back to school. Once, one Ganguly decided to skip school and go out for a movie at night. As described by Mr Nambiar there was someone walking in front of him with a blanket wrapped around the shoulders with a cigarette in his hand; as he got closer the person started walking faster. Below the blanket, Mr Nambiar could see Oxford pattern shoes and flannel trousers, and as he went closer he could see the school blazer from the side. The person in front was still walking fast, till the time he reached the cinema hall and was at the counter about to purchase a ticket. No one ever could outsmart Mr Nambiar. Before Ganguly could buy the ticket, Mr Nambiar came up and whispered in his ear: "Ganguly, please go back to school".

We had a lot of mango trees. Before Mr Mani took over as Principal, these were given out to contractors for the season and the school made some money. Students would still pluck mangoes or get them down by throwing stones. When he saw some students doing that, he also picked up a stone to get some mangoes. That was the last time, these were given on contract.

In the sixth standard, we had a debate for and against movies. I spoke in favour emphasizing good points of watching movies and stressing that movies could be a great source of education. One would not need a passport, visa or spend a lot of money, to travel; we could see many places on the screen. Well, I won the debate; little did I think then that one day I would be running a Travel Company.

I do remember the death of a classmate, Sunil Kekre, due to meningitis. He was the smallest boy in the class. It took us a long time to recover from his loss.

After passing out from school, we all moved to various places and took different disciplines for further study. Some of us joined the National Defence Academy, others pursued study to become doctors, engineers, artists, commercial pilots, or joined businesses.

There were five such schools in the country in Chail, Ajmer, Dholpur, Bangalore and Belgaum. Occasionally we would have a combined get-together in various cities, specially the major cities. On one occasion some of us met in Mumbai. One senior from our school by the name of Pusalkar suggested that we should make a bust of Mr Mani and put it in school; another old student from another school did not appreciate the idea. He probably had no idea who Mr Mani was and what he meant to us. The senior from my school was quite upset. He said that Mr Mani meant to him more than his father and one had no reason to question a small thing like putting a bust of him. The love and regard that echoed in Pusalkar's voice as he said that the amount and much more would be transferred in remembrance of the late Principal, really touched a chord with us all.

Even today when we meet old schoolmates, we are proud to be called Mani's Georgians. Indeed, the school days were the best years of our lives.

Chapter 2

At the National Defence Academy

After passing out from school, as for every young person, there were several people to advise on the career path be taken. Maybe to an extent I was a bit confused. But my father, in particular, told me that I should do what I liked most.

Having been a science student somehow I did not want to pursue science for higher studies. I thought that the best thing would be to take a diploma in Automobile Engineering and subsequently start a workshop. My satisfaction was short-lived; my elder brother VP, who has always been my guide and mentor, told me that I should finish my graduation first and pursue anything that I liked thereafter. I was in a peculiar situation. Colleges in Delhi had already started their academic year and there was no chance of getting any admission there.

I had earlier filled up my form for the written test for National Defence Academy (NDA) while in school. One had to appear for the Union Public Service Commission examination. As I had expressed my desire to my father regarding my plans, he advised me that I should go and appear since the fees were already paid, even if I did not ultimately join NDA. I did go and appear in the examination.

As admissions to Colleges in Delhi were over, I moved to Belgaum, where I had done my schooling. Here I took Humanities and joined Lingaraj College. It was something I wanted to pursue.

After passing out from a boarding school, the college routine was a bit too relaxed. I was used to a routine where the day started at six in the morning and we were kept busy till late at night. In college, the first class would be at eleven in the morning and it was all over by four in the evening, with decent breaks in between. If the first period was not attended, it was more like a holiday. I was enjoying it to an extent, with subjects that I wanted to study, making new friends, but was not happy with so much of spare time on my hands.

Since my school was also in Belgaum, some juniors who met me told me that I had passed in the written test for National Defence Academy. It was great news for me; I had given my first choice as Navy and second choice as Air Force. This would give me an opportunity go to the Services Selection Board in Bangalore and then to Mysore for the Pilot aptitude battery test. I took this opportunity as a chance to travel.

The final interview was taken by the President of the Services Selection Board. Apart from other questions, he asked me what I would do in case I was rejected. My prompt reply was: "I would take the first possible train and go home." He said, "in that case you are not interested in joining the services?" I replied: "Sir, you have given me an option and I have accepted it. In case I do not make it, I will look at other opportunities." The final result was out and I was selected. Later, when I related this to my father, who was also an army officer, he retorted: "The Colonel who selected you, must be a crazy man!"

As some time had passed, I thought I should ask my father, regarding the Merit List for NDA. In those days sending letters by post was the main means of communication. A few days later I got a reply from him: "My dear son, congratulations, you have made it in the Merit list. However, it is mandatory on your part to let your father know as to what you are doing."

I Join the Academy – early days as a Fresher

In January 1970, I took the train to Pune from Delhi to join the Academy where I was going to stay till end of 1972. To start, it was a nice and interesting experience after arrival, from the allotment of numbers, cabins, squadrons and issue of kit. First termers had to report a few days before for orientation and to get into the system. Some guidance from some seniors from our school who had joined the Academy came in handy. The main guidance point was to look as dumb or innocent as possible, so that any senior would take pity and one could get away from any kind of ragging which was quite common then. Not that it always worked, even this could go against one.

I was carrying my brother's NDA blazer and wore it initially, but that went against me. I was told by seniors that my brother must have already briefed me about the Academy. Soon I put the blazer back in the box.

The first- termers or freshers were given brand new uniforms and were an easy prey to some seniors who would like to take the new stuff from them and give the old one. But freshers had their own tricks to get around this problem. When someone asked for shoes, prompt came the reply, "Sir, I have been issued two shoes only for the left foot" or for other outfits, the usual reply would be "have not yet been issued" or "have returned it for the correct size".

Bicycles are allotted to all the cadets at the beginning of the term. This is the main and only mode of transport in the Academy. In a way it was an identity mark as well; all bicycles issued to every cadet had the squadron and number painted on it, which was specific to every cadet. It was like a number plate on the car that traffic police note down. But the cycles were our most reliable companions.

Bicycles were used for movement between periods, going from one place to another and whenever we had to change ie from Classrooms to PT Grounds , Drill square, Equitation lines, etc. Cadets were expected to move with full speed, with only a few minutes in between to do so, and that too without any accidents !

All the movement on bicycles had to be in squads of minimum four cadets, with one cadet leading and two abreast following and maintaining proper distance. Cycling out of squad ie not in formation was a punishable offence. You had drill instructors monitoring at every nook and corner. Immediate punishment would be the order to dismount and run with bicycle in one hand. In case it was Prem Singh Rai and Tashi Bhutia from Sikkim, in the squad we were definitely in for trouble; they had never seen bicycles before and learnt to ride them on joining the Academy. They would go all over and that was good enough for the drill instructors to punish us. But these two did more than that - from riding into other squads, over the pavements and hitting others. If you did not form a squad with the required number you could not mount the bicycle and had to run with it. Being asked to lift up the bicycle and run with it was a normal punishment.

I do remember going to Peacock Bay for sailing as a Naval Cadet. We always had to move around in squads on bicycles. I was cycling alone and was crossing Deputy Commandant's (Dep Com) Ronnie's house. I heard him shout: "Why are you going solo? You should have been an air force cadet!" Air Force cadets had to clear their tests flying solo in a glider. Anyway, it was a relief not to be punished.

Since there were only a limited few who could be in the polo team, most of us played cycle polo on the concrete ground in front of the squadron using hockey sticks.

Mid-term breaks were something that we looked forward to. It basically split the term in two parts and gave us a break as well. Some of us stayed back or trips would be organized to places close by. We all looked forward to the term finishing and going home end of the term. On the blackboards in each class room we would write DLTGH ie *Days left to go home.*

At the end of the term most of us travelled home by a special train called NDA special, exclusively booked for cadets by the Indian Railways. It was a great experience. Train would start from Kirkee Railway Staion; the first leg of the journey was to Mumbai. Being monsoons the scenery en route was breathtaking with all round greenery, waterfalls and the experience of the train passing through tunnels. I had undertaken this train journey a number of times. Ashok Sirohi, my coursemate was excited to enjoy this fascinating train journey being his first time. I was fast asleep; he woke me up to show me the scenery. Irritated, I shouted back at him. He even remembers this today. The train would have limited stops. Once whilst travelling the chain was pulled at least thirty times, causing unscheduled stops. It was fun then, but the railway authorities complained to the Academy.

After our vacation, all those who had travelled by this train were given a punishment to go to Sinhgad Fort on six hikes. *Hike* in the Academy parlance was a punishment and not a leisurely walk or trek. We had to wear FSMO (Full Service Marching Order), meant carrying of battle load and Jap Cap in style. We would start at six in the morning, after assembling in the PT grounds and had to be back by noon, failing which we would have to do another one in lieu. We ran most of the way and had to go on top till Sinhgad Fort, collect a token and give it back on return. It was definitely a decent punishment for forcing unscheduled stops of the train. Sinhgad hikes were awarded for various other misconducts as well. Dep Com would hand out Sinhgad hikes like these were gifts.

Since I had already done a couple of hikes I had become quite an expert. On an occasion another coursemate of mine who was not really up to it, decided to follow me for the hike. It was raining and we were absolutely drenched. With the sky overcast with clouds one could barely see the Fort. I kept motivating him all through that it was an easy run and would be completed in comfort. For him the run was never ending till the time we had to climb up the mountain. When I told him that we were almost on the top, he lost his cool and told me that I was fooling him. Anyway, he made it to the top and we collected the tokens.

One morning, the Div-O, in-charge for conducting the hike, announced that those not interested in going should raise their hands. This sounded a bit fishy to us. We were in a bit of a fix. We dared not say that we did not want to go, in case some other sort of punishment was in store for us. Two cadets, however, raised their hands and to our amazement were asked to go back to the cabin and their hike was marked completed!!

During the war with Pakistan in December 1971, we travelled home by the NDA Special Train and were looked after by people at all stops with food and hospitality. We told them that we were cadets and going home and not to the border. They told us: "Every one going to the war tells us the same thing. We need to look after all of you".

Since it is a tri services Academy, cadets before joining give their choice of service ie Army, Navy or Air Force. We had to undergo rigorous academic and physical training. My service was Navy; the main purpose for selecting this service was that I thought I could go around and see the world. Being a Naval cadet, one had to take up technical subjects, something I had detested. In my fifth term, I applied for change of service to Army. Although it was something that was not easily granted, but due to my perseverance, I was given the change of service. I was happily back in my squadron, but soon one of our Divisional Officers, Lt D.M. Lal came to know of this. He spoke to me for a few minutes, asking me why I did not want to join such a wonderful service where I would get a chance to travel around and meet interesting people. In a few minutes, I was convinced and withdrawing my request for change of service. Luckily it was accepted.

Commodore Ronnie Pereira, who took over as Deputy Commandant left a tremendous impact on all the cadets. Mrs Phyllis Pereira was a mother to all of us.

Ronnie was omnipresent; he could be seen all over the Academy almost at the same time. We all dreaded him; being caught doing anything wrong would certainly lead to punishment with restrictions, hikes, relegation, which meant a loss of seniority and often joining with the next course. It could also lead to spending part of the break in the Academy in case one was given restrictions towards end of the term.

As much as we were scared of him, we loved him probably more. At heart he meant good for all of us. Ronnie and Phyllis were parents to all the cadets in the Academy. They had no children of their own.

Many of us had encounters with the Deputy Commandant. I would like to make a mention of some personal ones. It was in my 6th term. I remember, I was going alone on a bicycle to the Naval Training Team. Since I was alone Dep Com appeared from nowhere and asked me to go running to the Khandwa Gate and back as punishment, which was more than two kilometres one way. He being his good self stopped his car and asked me, if there was an examination that I had to go to? I told him there was none. So he said: "Well son, might as well keep running then!" This point I would like to stress; one could only see how concerned he was that he stopped to confirm about the examination.

Just a few days prior to passing out parade, being a member of riding display team, one morning I was walking in my riding rig towards equitation lines which were about three km away. Suddenly Dep Com's car came to a screeching halt next to me and he called me. I thought in my mind that I had been caught for an offence, as I was alone and not in a squad. I saluted and stood at attention; he asked me why I was walking alone. I told him, "Sir, I am going to the Equitation Lines for display rehearsal and my cycle has been returned to MT Lines". He asked me to hop into the car and said "do you mind in case I pick up my uniform from Sudan Block?" He then dropped me in his car all the way at the Equitation Lines.

He later on became the Chief of the Naval Staff. There would be a number of officers and instructors, who would have trained us well and left an impact on us. But it was Admiral Pereira who left an impact on all cadets of NDA and they still worship him for the way he touched their lives.

Years later, after I had left the Navy and started my travel agency, once Mrs Pereira called up our office while she was in Delhi to book some flight tickets. My wife had no clue who it was, but the name meant something. My wife tentatively enquired whether the caller was Admiral Pereira's wife. She definitely was. So much was the influence of Admiral Pereira on us. They both had a long chat thereafter.

In the Academy, we had various people who trained us and so to say we learnt a lot from them. List is endless from Dep Com, Battalion Commanders, Squadron Commanders, Divisional Officers, Physical Training Officer, Equitation Officer, Adjutant, Drill instructors, Riding instructors, Physical Training Staff and others attached to the Naval Training Team and Air

Force Training Team. Some of our academic instructors who were the backbone of education, were always held in high esteem and I can still recall Mr Bhandari, Mr Bhawnani, Mr Savardekar, Mr Prem Singh, Mr Paul and Mr Keshwani, all of them dedicated faculty members.

If Ronnie was an idol for all of us, Drill Subedar Major Kanshi Ram was not far behind. Drill is the bed rock of any military training. It imbibed in us discipline.

After joining NDA, one of the first things that any cadet wants is to pass the Drill Square Test, which entitles him to take off the arm band which has the academy number on it, and has to be worn all the time with the uniform. But once a cadet clears the test he gets to wear the Lanyard and go out on Liberty. The test has to be cleared under the keen eye of the Adjutant and Drill Subedar Major.

Kanshi Ram could fail you for anything from poor brass work, shoes not being polished ("dirty leather work", in his parlance), shoelace twisted, improper hair cut to uniform not up to the mark and beret not being worn properly. Then there are the drill movements from saluting, turning, marching and swinging of hands. One is likely to go wrong somewhere. While giving stern looks, he would say, "Cadet you are over all dirty." The result was obviously known. His fleet of drill instructors followed him to check us.

The drill periods were hectic, the cadets being made to do all kinds hyper activity in 40 minutes. Drill instructors (*Ustaads*) were supercharged to keep cadets on the go. These Ustaads go through a stringent selection process before being appointed. They would be monitoring cadets of their squadron with loud commands under the leadership of Kanshi Ram. All drill instructors would carry pace sticks, which is a symbol of authority and as an aid to drill. Pace sticks measure fixed distances, corresponding to various lengths of marching pace, such as "double march", "quick march", "step short", etc. They would smartly twirl the stick for various paces.

Noticing any laxity or flaw in drill, Kanshi Ram would come charging towards the cadets or squads with full speed and gusto, twirling his pace stick smartly, which was good enough to keep everyone on their toes. Drill Ustaads played a major role in grooming us. I cannot imagine where we got the energy to do triple outdoor, starting with PT Class, ET (endurance test) run in battle order followed by the drill period. Ustaads would not be bothered about the weather or such things and we had to do our best. In one of the drill periods, our instructor made us run around the drill square in squads; there does not have to be any reason, it is the instructor who decides. Ustaad Waryam Singh shouted that each step should be of 30 inches. I already had had enough and shouted back that each step should be of 40 inches. Before I knew it was Waryam Singh charging at me and he marched me upto Kanshi Ram. I was given a long lecture on being respectful to the drill Ustaads.

Horse riding was compulsory for all cadets. Equitation officers were Major Suhag and Major V.P. Singh, who were highly decorated in equestrian sports. V.P. Singh was the highest handicap player of polo after Independence of India. Here again riding instructors who are good horsemen are posted to impart training. Cadets are given preliminary knowledge of horses and stable management and vet aids. The idea was to get closer to the horses and get to know about their habits in the stables. The methods of training involved theory classes, practical training and exposure to various disciplines of equestrian events like Show Jumping, Cross Country, Riding, Hack Riding, Tent Pegging events, Dressage, Polo and other adventures in equestrian sport. I got an opportunity to ride and excelled in riding. It included taking part in riding displays, stunts on horseback, show jumping and polo. There were a number of cadets who were petrified of riding. In any case, we all had to pass basic riding tests.

Very few us would be part of the riding display team. With this, we were excused from attending Passing out Parade rehearsals and the final POP. There was no choice for me in the sixth term, to take part in the riding display since it was compulsory to be participating in the parade, in the passing out term from the Academy.

There were various inter squadron and inter battalion competitions, mainly of sports, drill and entertainment. I would regularly go for practice for a Qawali (song) to be part of the competition. I had two reasons for my interest in taking part; one being one skipped all punishments and other that I wanted to be a part of it. One day before the competition, my senior told me that it was nice that I had been practicing hard. I was to be there in the competition but would not be singing, as my voice was not in sync with others. Just before the final performance, I was asked to play the harmonium. He pressed two notes and I was told to pump the back with one hand, which is joined to the bellows that blows the air. Suddenly the two notes popped up; I had no idea which one were these. All kinds of noises started coming from the harmonium. My squadron commander on the side of the stage asked me to stop playing and my senior wanted me to continue playing. Anyway, I kept doing what I thought was right, knowing quite well that I would land up in trouble once the song was over. Luckily we won the competition. This was my first and last encounter with singing and music.

Till fourth term all the cadets followed an identical routine. From fifth term onwards, service-wise training started. We were taught service subjects in the Army Training Team((ATT), Naval Training Team(NTT) and Air Force Training Team(AFTT) . Instructors were qualified to teach subjects pertaining to each service.

Army cadets were taught subjects such as Tactical Training, Weapon Training, Map Reading, Military Writing, Field Engineering, Organization and Administration and Radio Telephony. A lot of emphasis is laid on outdoor training and handling of weapons.

Naval cadets were taught Navigation, Seamanship and Communication. Practical seamanship training is conducted at Peacock Bay including sailing and motorboat handling. Lt Cdr Sushil Kumar was the officer in charge of NTT, who was a renowned polo player as well. I had the privilege of playing under his guidance. He later became the Chief of the Naval Staff.

Air Force cadets were taught basics of military aviation through ground training and flying training on gliders.

After passing out depending on the service that we had opted for, we were all ready to join Indian Military Academy, Training ships and Air Force Academy, before being commissioned.

Come what may, we never missed any movies being screened in the Academy on Saturdays and Sundays. After watching the movie, MLs (moral lectures) from the ACA (Academy Cadet Adjutant) was a routine. These were not pep up lectures but were to tell us what we had done wrong. There were plenty of reasons for punishment whether it be being part of some particular squad, course or squadron. Reasons for being punished could be many, and would include any kind of conduct which was not appropriate in the eyes of ACA. Sixth termers were never part of it; they could comfortably enjoy the movie and move for dinner.

In case in the eye of ACA there was an exemplary conduct by some cadets, they would not be punished and asked to proceed for dinner. There was no set pattern, but it was great fun; movie could not be skipped at any cost. It was once after the screening of a movie captioned *"Paraya Dhan"*, that the ACA announced that all cadets from the school where the hero Rakesh Roshan had studied were to "fall in" outside separately. The rest of us marched back for dinner. Cadets belonging to the school did not turn up for dinner and came much later sweating. We were curious to know what had happened. The ACA had punished them stating that their school could not even produce a good actor!

Three years in NDA passed by and we all marched out of the Quarter Deck of Drill Square, with the band playing the song 'Auld Lang Syne' meaning 'old long ago', which can be translated as 'days gone by' or 'back in the day', written by Scottish bard Robert Burns. We all passed out with camaraderie and were now ex-NDAs, a stamp earned by us for the rest of our lives in the Army, Navy and Air Force.

Chapter 3

Ahoy Sailor - My days in the Indian Navy and thereafter

After passing out from the National Defence Academy, I joined Training Ship, INS Delhi in January 1973. This was formerly HMNZS Achilles a Leander-class light cruiser which served with the Royal New Zealand Navy in the Second World War, the second of five in the class. Originally constructed by the Royal Navy, she was loaned to New Zealand in 1936 before formally joining the new Royal New Zealand Navy in 1941. She became famous for her part in the Battle of the River Plate, alongside HMS Ajax and HMS Exeter and notable for being the first Royal Navy cruiser to have fire control radar, with the installation of the New Zealand-made SS1 fire-control radar in June 1940.

After the World War II service in the Atlantic and Pacific, she was returned to the Royal Navy. She was sold to the Indian Navy in 1948 and re-commissioned as INS Delhi. She was finally decommissioned in 1978.

In early 1973, we sailed for Kenya and Tanzania, covering a distance of 2403 nautical miles to Mombasa, our first port of call, a dream come true. Our ship belonged to the First Training Squadron of Indian Navy.

It was quite a culture shock to come to the training ship as a naval cadet from National Defence Academy. In the Academy, you had bearers to keep your uniforms ready and shoes polished and waiters and butlers to serve you in the Mess. Coming to the training ship, we had to serve food amongst us, wash the plates, polish shoes and practically do everything by oneself.

As part of the training we had to chip, paint and holystone the deck. Holystone is a soft and brittle sandstone used for scrubbing and whitening the wooden decks of ship. Whilst I was holystoning on the way to Mombasa our Commander Training, Cdr Ranbir Singh, looking at me cleaning the deck and obviously, he knew that no cadet would be enjoying doing it, he asked me whether I still wanted to go to Mombasa, my immediate answer was "I do not know !"

Capt Bindra who was TS1 (a nomenclature for senior officer of ships of 1st Training Squadron), kept all the ships of training squadron busy with various exercises, manoeuvres, RAS (replenishment at sea), a method of transferring fuel, munitions, personnel and stores from one ship to another while underway. This would be done with the other two ships of the training squadron on either side of INS Delhi. More often than not we would be at action stations. *Action stations* is an announcement made on a warship to signal that all hands (everyone available) onboard must go to battle stations as quickly as possible. This was in addition to various subjects that we were taught on board.

I joined the Navy hoping to see the world but I do remember one of the Divisional Officers telling me that "the world around was water when you were on a ship and sailing".

On the way we crossed equator. The "crossing-the-line" ceremony is an exclusive maritime experience from the days of veteran sailors aboard wooden ships courageously venturing out into the unforgiving environment of the open ocean.

The tradition holds that King Neptune, a mythical god of the sea, detects an infestation of "pollywogs" , ie those who have not crossed the equator before; he deems it necessary to take control of the ship to rid it of this plagued condition. A "shellback" is a sailor who has previously crossed the line, and the most senior shellback aboard the ship plays the role of King Neptune in the ceremony.

Master Chief Petty Officer Boatswain Mate, Yashpal, was dressed up as King Neptune and conducted the ceremony by initiating all the cadets. We had to take a dip in the pool prepared for this purpose. Later we were given certificates by him for "crossing the Equator".

After sailing for over 2400 nautical miles from Bombay, it was nice to see land and the beautiful city of Mombasa. Since it was an official visit, we were kept busy with duties on board and lot of official visits and activity. Over official reception on board the ship I made friends with Naresh Sharma, who was a friend of my uncle from Punjab. Later, I had Mr Naresh Sharma's car to take me around. I do recollect one of the officers meeting me in town and telling me that one African Sharma's driver was looking for me, as Naresh Sharma was a Kenyan.

We had to visit a farm, where lunch was organized by the local Indian community, whose ancestors came here as traders and craftsmen a few generations back. They have made enormous contributions to the economy of Kenya. A dinner was organized at Mr Naresh Sharma's palatial residence. Cdr Ranbir Singh was also invited and he came to his place with some cadets. He was quite surprised to see me there. One of my friend's told him that I was a personal guest of Mr Sharma. Later, having travelled so much, without doubt I can say that people in Mombasa are most hospitable and friendly.

Cdr Ranbir Singh was our Cdr Training of the Training Squadron. We called him Cdr Tourism, as whenever going ashore he would have cameras hanging around his neck.

With ships going abroad, it was always a great opportunity to buy items, mainly electronic, since at that time these were not available in India and if so, were very expensive. With three ships there, sailors bought lot of folding umbrellas, which was a novelty in India that time. Mombasa had run out of stock of umbrellas. I remember my friend Farooq, a local of Mombasa asking me, whether it rained a lot in India as no umbrellas were available in any shop.

From Mombasa we sailed for Zanzibar. It was a quiet and an under developed island. One could see the effect of the Zanzibar revolution. Arabs and Indians had left behind everything and Afro Shirazi Party occupied these homes, which were converted into public buildings. Idi Amin of Uganda had also created a lot of fear with his massive human rights abuses. Fear in the Indian community was so much that they were scared to talk. Some would open the door a bit when we were passing by their houses and ask us if ships had come to take them.

We were looked after very well, and some local parties and visits were organized. We were escorted all over by police jeeps. The common folk around us would bow to the entourage. I am not very certain whether it was out of fear or respect.

A parade was organized by the crew of all the three ships in the stadium, where the then Vice President Mr Aboud Jumbe took the salute. There were troops all around the stadium for his security. Those days it was a rare sight; today this kind of security is seen for any high profile dignitary.

There was a big applause from the crowd when the band from our ship played the National Anthems of India and Tanzania.

From Zanzibar, we sailed to Dar es Salaam, the principal port serving Tanzania. It was Tanzania's capital city.

As usual we had official functions to attend. The Asian community was not really up beat. Shops and business establishments were open. There were shop owners who were ready to give away items at throwaway prices since we were from India; they even gave things as gifts. Idi Amin had his ripple effect here as well.

It was very easy to exchange money and one could get almost three times the official conversion rate. Businessmen were so scared that a coursemate of mine, Fola Ayelabola could not exchange any money, since he was a Nigerian. People thought he could be from the police and they may land in trouble. I helped him out to exchange the amount. Then it was time to return home.

After a wonderful experience and visiting these ports we sailed from Dar es Salaam to Bombay covering a distance of over 3043 nautical miles through Indian Ocean and Arabian Sea. We spent almost 15 days at sea and finally we reached Mumbai. TS1 kept the training squadron busy with exercises on the way.

In July 1973, I joined Naval Ships Krishna and subsequently Mysore as a Midshipman. Midshipman is an officer of the lowest rank in the Navy. Here we received onboard training. Cdr Talibuddin, the Commanding Officer of INS Krishna for some reason developed a dislike for me. Once on the bridge on duty he asked me about our training as cadets on Training Ship INS Delhi. I gave him my views and suggested how certain things during the training could have been better. Little did I know that he had come from Directorate of Naval Training from Naval Headquarters. As Midshipmen we used to get a Task Book and it would go to him for signature. A coursemate of mine had copied it all from my Task Book. In his Task Book the remark entered was "Very good" and in mine "copied !"

Another task that I was given as an exercise was to organize a visit to Mazagon docks for foreigners. I made a couple of visits there and made a proper proposal with letters etc and the second was to interview Mr Gautam Khanna of Oberoi hotels, who was the son in law of Mr Oberoi, owner of Oberoi hotels. It was impossible to meet Mr Khanna. I met the Duty Manager, who gave me a brochure about Oberoi hotels. I prepared questions and answers, as if I had actually interviewed Mr Gautam Khanna. My Divisional officer remarked on my detailed proposal about the visit of foreigners to Mazagon docks that it could have been done on phone. For the imaginary interview that I had done with Mr Gautam Khanna, the remark was "very good". Interestingly, I met Mr Gautam Khanna years later and narrated this to him. He responded with a smile.

All in all it was good learning. Being a Midshipman is a great experience. One of the first ports we visited was Calcutta; this city always welcomed sailors. We had invitation from Hotel Hindustan International to go for dinner and watch a cabaret at a special rate. Bikky (a coursemate) and I had just got our first salary and what a great way to spend an evening. We reached the hotel and the General Manager, smartly dressed in a tail coat was kind enough to escort us to a table close to the cabaret performance. We were treated like VIPs and given a memorable service.

We went on a foreign cruise as part of our training programme and visited Penang and Colombo. There is always some reason to be punished; we landed in Cochin and were told not to proceed ashore. A movie *"Bobby"* had just been released. All of us decided to go and watch the movie, apart from one or two of us, who were on duty. Divisional Officer Lieutenant Wahi and Sub of the Gun Sub Lieutenant Bakshi were also there watching the movie. We wished them. They were also happy to see us there. Later, we realized that each was under the impression that the other had given us the permission to go ashore. Otherwise we would have been asked to go back. By then the damage had been done. Next morning they did not even talk about it.

It was a wonderful time to be a Midshipman, which would be for a period of one year. For our course the period was nine months, since for the next course it had to be reduced to 6 months. We did next three months on INS Mysore, a cruiser. INS Mysore was commanded by Capt M.P. Awati, an admirable personality. He looked a 'top Sea dog' with his trademark beard and a majestic gait. I was in contact with him even later for many years.

We all had our accommodation in the Gun Room (a junior officers' mess on a naval vessel). It was a couple of us here with bunks. Some of us would be preparing for Midshipman's boards, at the same time there would be others listening to loud music. This arrangement did not disturb any of us. We had a big fan at the entrance to blow out the air and prevent steam entering inside.

After being commissioned as a Sub Lieutenant on 1st April 1974, I went for Sub Lieutenant's course. Various subjects were covered, doing short courses. Whilst travelling from Cochin to Mumbai, I grew a beard, since Navy as a service allowed me to do so. One has to take permission for growing of beard; this train journey was a good excuse. I could tell at the new station that I had taken permission in the last station.

After completion of Sub Lieutenant's course, I went for watch keeping on INS Himgiri in February 1975. It was then the most modern and indigenously built Leander Class Frigate. From all officers to sailors everyone was picked up based on their performance. It was fully air-conditioned and there were 22 television sets on board; most ships then would not have even a single television. As the ship was new and operational we sailed most of the time and it was a professional and memorable experience. One could become a watch keeping officer in three months. Our Commanding Officer Cdr K.N. Zadu thought that it was a short period and I was given a watch keeping certificate after six months. It now meant that now I had total responsibility of safe and smooth navigation of the ship whilst on duty on the bridge. Later, Cdr Baby Anand took over command from Cdr Zadu. He was one of the best Commanding Officers that I have served with and was a great influence. One could easily get into a conversation with him on any topic and he was always receptive.

At that time it was one of the few ships of the Navy which had a helicopter on board. We were the first ones in the Navy to be qualified as Helicopter Controllers.

Mumbai as a city gave a lot of exposure and is cosmopolitan in the real sense. It gave me an opportunity to meet and interact with people from all walks of life. My friend Kunjur took me for a movie with his classmate from school, Rita Bhaduri, a budding actress. After the movie, we had planned to go for dinner in a restaurant in Colaba. She decided to go with me on my Lambretta scooter and not in Kunjur's car.

I would meet Col Tim Divecha at the United Services Club regularly. United Services Club has a great location next to the sea, with various sports facilities. It used to have a natural sea water pool for swimming. It was subsequently closed due to some accidents taking place. From here one could see the most beautiful sunset over the Arabian Sea. As I was a keen sailor, Col Divecha asked me to apply for the membership of Royal Bombay Yacht Club. After a couple of meetings, I was given the membership.

The Royal Bombay Yacht Club has a lot of history and was founded in 1846 as the Bombay Yacht Club with Henry Morland as club commodore and 30 years later - on the recommendation of Sir Philip Edmond Wodehouse and patronage of Queen Victoria became known as Royal Bombay Yacht Club. The club also has got a great maritime ambience. Here I had the opportunity of sailing with Jamshyd Godrej, Cama of *Mumbai Samachar*, Kishore Mariwala and others.

In November 1975 we went on a good will visit to Bahrain and Basra in Iraq. Bahrain was famous for oil, pearls, shopping arcades and world heritage sites. Even then it was a modern country. Bahrain was very popular amongst rich Arabs; they would fly down over the weekends. There were no restrictions on liquor and entertainment here. Arabs would not be bothered in case you walked into their stores for shopping. They had Asians working for them in the shops. A big reception was organized for us by the Indian community.

The next port of call was Basra. We anchored before entering Shatt Al Arab river. A pilot boarded, and since we had priority we sailed within a few hours through the narrow river. There were boats in the river both belonging to Iraqis and Iranians, since the river passed through both the countries. Only way of identifying them was by the flag they were flying.

Basra was founded in 636 AD along the waterway created by the joining of the Tigris and Euphrates. Basra became an essential stop for world travellers, such as the 14th century scholar Ibn Battuta. The city is one of the ports from which the fictional Sinbad the Sailor journeyed. The highlight of the visit was the meeting with some officers who had done their training in India and some seniors.

While visiting foreign ports a lot of educational visits were organized. One such visit was organized to the Date factory during the day and I had to take some sailors along. I requested Shibib, an Iraqi Naval course mate, who had done his training with us in India and was posted in Basra to get the timing changed for the visit to 0800 hrs and this was promptly done. This gave me time to go around to meet his relations and friends and take a quick tour of the city. One of his uncles had a shop in Burma Bazaar. He gave me dates as a gift to me and the family.

It was a busy day. In the evening he wanted to take me to Ali Baba Island to a fine restaurant. By the time we reached there it was closed. We were back in the city. You could only find some Kabab shops open. Being a vegetarian, all that I could get at that time were tomatoes being roasted with Kababs on the side in different rods. Locals were giving me strange looks while I was eating the tomatoes.

Basra reminded me of exactly the way people lived in India and similar economic strata although they had enough oil. A ferry just behind our ship was getting ready to take people across the river. We could see most of the girls taking off their burqas and putting it in their bags.

I spent a month with my father at New Delhi, who was not too well, before joining INS Katchall on 01 July 1976. The ship was based in Visakhapatnam in the Eastern Fleet. I did think of asking for a few days leave, but my father insisted that I should report on time. I took a flight to Hyderabad and spent the night there and took the next morning flight to Visakhapatnam. I had a dream in the hotel in Hyderabad that I was on a flight and the pilot had a heart attack. There was panic in the aircraft and I woke up with a jerk. I reached the ship around lunch time and a few minutes later my brother called me to say that our father had passed away in the morning at 0623 hrs. I could not attend his last rites. Since then I have made it a principle to be on time for work come what may.

INS Katchall was a Petya Class Russian Ship. It was quite a culture shock to be suddenly coming from a totally air-conditioned ship to a ship under repairs, forget about the air-conditioning. These were also ships with decent weapon capabilities and gas turbined. Visakhapatnam at that time did not have much of social activity. It gave me more time to go in for yachting, as and when the ship was under repairs or not sailing.

During sailing there was rationing of water. Water would only be available for a few minutes during the day. For all officers there was one bathroom. It is said that in one of the ships, when the Commanding Officer wanted to use the bathroom, action stations would be announced and everyone would be at their post, while he would quickly go and use the bathroom!

In December 1977, I was transferred to INS Mysore, where I had been on board as a Midshipman; this time not on training, but with additional responsibility. Although at this stage I was not a specialist, but I was given various responsibilities. The Commander of the ship gave me every possible job that he could, thinking that I would possibly falter somewhere and then be taken to task. Unfortunately, nothing untoward happened much to his disappointment. In brief, I had a smooth sailing.

Capt Punia was a very mature Commanding Officer who would listen to any suggestions; on my proposal he got the Command Orders amended.

He provided all the advice to meet the concerned persons. I recall on one occasion he was to go ashore by Captain's boat for an official appointment, and it took some time for the boat to come to the accommodation ladder. He was cool about it and only quietly asked me: "CP, why did it take so long for the boat to come?" I apologized for the delay. Once, I wanted a short break to go on a holiday to Delhi. This was on a Saturday. He told me that I should have the orders ready with all corrections; then he would let me go. It was a number of pages. In those days one had only typewriters. I got hold of a sailor who was good at typing and sat through day and night over the weekend. On Monday morning the papers were on his table. Even before I could ask him, he called me and told me I could go on leave as planned.

Apart from normal duties we had to look after the cadets who came on board for training. It was nice to train and interact with them.

In December 1978, I joined INS Nipat as Executive Officer, in effect as the second in Command. It was a small ship. With four officers ie Commanding Officer, Executive Officer, Engineer Officer and Missile and Gunnery Officer. It was a Vidyut class missile boat and part of the 25th Killer Missile squadron.

During the Indo-Pakistani War, the ship was part of the Operation Trident strike force. On the afternoon of 4 December 1971, the strike group made its way towards Karachi. Late that evening, off Karachi, Nipat identified a large target, MV Venus Challenger, chartered by the Pakistan Navy to carry US ammunition to East Pakistan. It had Pakistani naval officers and sailors on board. Nipat launched two missiles on MV Venus Challenger and sank it.

On one occasion Nipat had to go for loading of missiles at Karanja across the other side of Naval Dockyard in Mumbai. The same afternoon I was taking part in a sailing Regatta. Cdr Madan my Commanding Officer let me go for the Regatta instead and said that loading would be handled. The Jetty for loading was in shallow waters and in the process the ship ran aground. I was feeling bad for not being on board, but Cdr Madan never let me feel guilty at all for not being on board. We co-operated totally with the board of enquiry that was constituted, but nothing was proved against the Commanding Officer.

In January 1980 I joined INS Venduruthy for Long TAS Course. Basically it was to specialize as a Torpedo Anti Submarine Officer which mainly covered subjects on tracking, locating and destroying submarines and the weapons used for that.

After completing one year course, I got married in January 1981. Neeru and I dated for some time before getting married. I found her to be charming, very level headed and pleasant company.

Immediately after marriage, I joined INS Amba, a submarine tendership. Once on board I got the Sonar repaired and modified. We had cadets on board for training. As part of their training we visited Colombo and Male. I had the opportunity to serve with Capt Johnson, a pilot, the finest gentleman and officer that I could have met and served with. Our ship was in Cochin. I requested him for use of his car for some official work. Not many Commanding Officers would entertain such a request. He told me that he was going to call on the Commander in Chief and he would be back in a while and I could use the car. So I was in the naval base in his car and he was going on a bicycle. I have always remained in contact with him even after leaving the Navy.

When we came to Mumbai getting accommodation was difficult as expected. We landed in Borivili and stayed with friends Tushar and Asha for a few days. Then we moved into a friend's house in Navy Nagar who was going on leave. A few months later I got temporary accommodation in Naval Coast battery in Worli till the time we got our proper accommodation.

I joined INS Agnibahu in December 1981 for a few months before joining INS Bedi a Mine Counter Measure Vessel. Apart from the operational role, we carried out other major assistance like locating a naval aircraft which had ditched off Cochin. After spending almost eighteen months onboard I returned to INS Agnibahu as an instructor from November '83 to April '84.

From May 1984 to September 1986, I worked at the Naval Headquarters in New Delhi. Initially, I was posted as Assistant Director in Directorate of Combat Policies and Tactics. Since I had put in my papers to leave the Navy, I was posted to INS India and from there to look after the Naval Officers Mess, Kota House as Officer in Charge. It was an altogether different experience, but probably gave me bit of an exposure on what I would be doing on leaving the Navy. Not many would have thought of leaving this job, but I requested to be taken out of this duty and Directorate of Personnel posted me to the Directorate of Works as an Assistant Director. Here the main job was to look after the construction and accommodation requirements of the Navy. It was a different kind of an exposure.

Having been in one of the best Directorates, I was dissuaded at every stage by my seniors not to leave the Navy and keep moving ahead. I would tell them the bait would never end and in case I kept looking at promotions and doing more professional courses, I would then be double minded on leaving the Navy. As I was determined to leave, neither more courses nor promotions lured me. Those days all applications went to the Defence Minister for his approval on file. At that time the recommendations of fourth pay commission were to be announced. He put a remark on the file "In case the officer wants to leave even with the benefits of fourth pay commission let him leave." Finally, in February 1986 my request for premature retirement was approved.

Once this was done, the letter stated that I would be put on retired list from 06 September 1986 (Forenoon). This period was taking into account six months leave pending retirement. I thought this would give me enough time to settle down, but time just flew by. Meanwhile a lot of formalities had to be completed internally. My papers went for clearance to Radm N.N. Anand who had been my Commanding Officer on INS Himgiri; he called me and was quite annoyed. Although I had met him a number of times, I had never revealed my intention to leave. He did tell me that had I mentioned it to him even once, he would never had let me leave. Anyway, the damage was already done. If I always had seniors like him, may be thought of leaving would never had occurred. One thing that I had realized by then was that you can never choose your own boss.

With the Merchant Navy (July 1990 to February 1994)

This I would say was one of the most amazing experiences of my life. Although when I left the Indian Navy had no plans of joining Merchant Navy. But destiny has its way of taking you to places.

I had left the Navy with no specific plans, young and not really knowing the world that I was going to face. I met my senior from the Navy, J.S. Walia. I told him that I had started a Travel Company, which was in its infancy and would not mind doing something more to increase my employability. He advised that I should make a trip to Mumbai and explore.

I visited Mumbai in April 1990 and went to the office of Tolani Shipping. My uncle Captain Chopra was a Director with the Company. I met him to take his advise and also to see in case there was an opening for me in his company. He did explain the modalities and what would be the job like on board in case I decided to join them. He knew that I had served with Admiral Awati, in the Navy who was then the President of Tolani Shipping.

He made me meet him. It was a cordial meeting. He was aware of my interest in yachting and we had both been polo players. He was very happy to meet me and exchanged pleasantries. In presence of Capt Chopra he said that "Join my company and we will play polo together". Once we came out Capt Chopra who was a Master Mariner, told me to forget whatever the Admiral had said. "You would be on a ship and can forget about polo altogether. This was only on the lighter side," he added.

I did not pursue this any further, as this would entail my sailing for months together and my small enterprise would suffer which was still in its infancy.

I also met Mr P.C. Alexander, General Manager, Shipping Corporation of India. A pleasant and impressive personality, he told me in most explicit terms as to what I would be going through to take up a job on a ship in the oil fields. "Unlike the Navy, you would have no stewards to serve you and would have to do a lot of things of your own", he said. I never had any fear of the unknown. Since they had vacancies in the ships operating in the Bombay high oilfields, I took the offer. This would be a period of working for four weeks and getting an equal period off.

I sailed for four weeks on Samudra Nidhi, a Well Stimulation Vessel. It was a nice experience although not what I expected it to be.

I came back and met Mr Alexander again. I mentioned to him that I would like to join a Supply Vessel and not a Well Stimulation Vessel. He told me that I could be sent on a Multipurpose Support Vessel. I was not aware at that stage regarding the role of a Multipurpose Support Vessel in the oil fields. He did explain what a supply vessel did vis a vis a MSV. He told me then that I should make a choice whether I would like to drive a Mercedes or an Ambassador car. I chose the former and joined MSV Samudra Sevak as a Master. Except for a few sailors, fitters and engineering staff, all others were expats on board. Since it was an Indian ship an Indian Master was required to take Command.

Here I saw what professionalism and commitment to work meant. We had various nationalities on board ie Brits, Germans, Australians, New Zealanders, Americans, Norwegians and Dutch, to name a few. What a great bonding we developed working round the clock together. All of them were very highly qualified in their fields.

I got the opportunity of working with very experienced officers who had spent a lot of time working at sea and in the oilfields.

Peter, a Dynamic Positioning Officer and an experienced sailor, who was much senior in age and a Scotsman, would come up with all kinds of jokes and polished abuses. But when it came to work and duty, he was an absolute committed professional, like many on board the ship. To ask Peter to perform any duty, he would do it with lightning speed, even when it was a few decks below the bridge. He would give a gentle salute and with the words, "Captain, here I go."

Andy Grey was one of the most amazing Operations Masters. He had started his career as a diver and subsequently moved to the deck side. He was always very calm and understood the requirements of divers on board.

Since these were ships with a different role, even if someone had any experience sailing on the merchant ships, one had to start from the lower most operational role of a trainee dynamic positioning operator (DPO), a specialist post. DPO is a primary watch keeper at the DP control desk, operating and monitoring the DP system and monitoring other operations around the vessel.

The normal duty of Deck Officers is for a period of twelve hours. It would be in two shifts. The first shift being from 0700 hrs to 1700 hrs during the day and the other shift from 1900 hrs to 0700 hrs during the night. Although I was designated as Master, but the operational role was the duty of a Chief Officer. This was quite nice. After a few sailings I had to switch over to the Night Masters operational role. For some reason I had never been used to sleeping during the day. I thought in case I continued doing this for a month I would probably collapse. To my surprise after finishing my duty at 0700 hrs in the morning and having breakfast, I had a comfortable eight-hour sleep.

Since it was a Multipurpose Support Vessel, it was designed with flexibility and versatility in mind. These vessels are capable of performing a range of activities including supply duties, lifting operations, ROV and survey activities, platform and SPM maintenance, diving, light well intervention and accommodation support. With a helicopter deck on board, we could transfer and receive items and personnel at ease.

As it was a Dynamic Positioning Ship, it was very helpful in monitoring the natural occurrences that take place offshore and helps a ship to maintain its position in the deep sea. Dynamic positioning (DP) is a computer-controlled system to automatically maintain a vessel's position and heading by using its own propellers and thrusters, position reference sensors, combined with wind sensors, motion sensors and gyrocompasses.

Because of DP we could work very close to oil rigs, platforms and oil wells, maintain the position in the open sea to repair pipe lines and carry out other jobs which required us to be in one position. The job of the DPO is very important and he has to be observant with even the minutest problem taking place with any of the sensors that help maintain the position and effect of wind, waves and current. DPOs keep monitoring the position of the ship and have to be very attentive, especially in inclement weather. When the sea is very rough, it can be difficult to maintain position and the operations would be called off. The safety of divers and the ship is always paramount. In these rough weather conditions with strong winds blowing, waves of upto 4 metres and the ship pitching and rolling, helicopters also would not land on board. We always prayed that rough weather should not happen on a crew change day as some of us would be looking forward to signing off and going home.

Apart from the other crew on board, divers play an important role. Divers are a hard working lot, work under water with great risk often carrying out dives to depths of upto 80 to 100 metres.

A typical support team for a single diver comprises of a back-up safety diver, a dive supervisor, a life support technician and a backup safety diver tender. Along with the above requirements, what keeps the divers safe are specialized equipment that includes a diving bell, a decompression chamber, and life support equipment.

It is not an easy task staying in a decompression chamber for four weeks, eating, sleeping and going in the diving bell to work under water in hazardous conditions. It affects the body and mind tremendously. I remember once when diver Jay Thapa came out of saturation dive, I asked him his phone number; he could not remember that. His father was a doctor in the Indian Navy, a qualified diver and a pilot.

While working on deck one of the divers lost his finger and we had to ask for a helicopter in an emergency. Another diver was to accompany him. He put the finger in an icebox even as he boarded the helicopter. A few months later the diver was back on board with his finger very much in place. This would not have happened but for his colleague accompanying him and showing great presence of mind.

Divers have a great sense of humour and at the same time are very hard working. There is an old saying that goes that if you give a diver three balls he will lose one, break one and steal one.

Everyone on board was very co-operative and would undertake all kinds of tasks with total responsibility.

On Multipurpose support vessels in particular safety is very important as we would undertake hazardous tasks. A major incident I recall was when there was a blowout on an oil rig. A blowout is the uncontrolled release of crude oil and/or natural gas from an oil well or gas well after pressure control systems have failed. Modern wells have blowout preventers intended to prevent such an occurrence. An accidental spark during a blowout can lead to a catastrophic oil or gas fire.

We immediately moved to the location to rescue persons who were there, though by then some had already been rescued by a supply vessel. I remember the tool pusher in the boat with bare feet, one steward who had jumped into the water could not be located, and some geologists who were trapped in their place of work and could not be rescued. We were continuously spraying water on the oil rig to douse the fire. At the same time work never stops on these ships, crew change was also taking place by helicopter simultaneously. But for the geologists and the steward everyone else was rescued.

At one stage our ship was on top of a blowout preventer where a leak was reported. It is almost like sitting on a bomb with lots of explosives. Here again divers were taking a great risk, trying to check the leak. Ultimately a Red Adair team was brought to repair this. Red Adair was an American and a daring firefighter, who showed remarkable creativity in fighting oil blowouts and fires. He took his first job in the oil industry in 1938 and served during World War II with the 139th Bomb Disposal Squad in Japan. Red Adair battled almost 2000 oil well fires. Adair was at every major hot spot, from the "Devil's Cigarette Lighter" in the Sahara Desert in 1962, to the deadly Piper Alpha platform in the North Sea in the 1988, to the intentionally torched oil fields of post-Gulf-War Kuwait. John Wayne played him in a movie the "*Hellfighter*".

Once there was a fire on board Samudra Sevak, when my relief, Capt Oberoi was on board. My senior from the Navy by almost 20 years, he had already spent eighteen years in the Merchant Navy. On hearing the fire alarm, he rushed out of his cabin in his night suit and was on the deck helping with hoses trying to douse the fire. During this operation he had burns on his body. He was rushed ashore immediately by helicopter to the hospital, but the infection of burns was so serious that he lost his life. Most had already gone to the emergency stations to evacuate the ship, but this brave sailor gave his life.

As Multi-purpose Support Vessels are specialized ships operating in the oil fields. We had expats on board who trained Indian officers from deck side and engineers. After being trained gradually Indian Officers started replacing expats on board. Even if one had been sailing at sea for many years, one had to start as a Trainee Dynamic Position Officer and slowly move up the ladder, this was for Deck Officers. There was a slight change of working. Indian Officers would demarcate every job that was to be undertaken. Do remember of an incident; once a Helicopter came with a small packet, requested RP Singh with me in on duty to collect it from the Pilot. He immediately told me, "why don't you page for the Bosun to collect it?" Bosun was working a few decks below walking to the helicopter was only a few metres away from the bridge. With expats on board there were no such issues, even if it was the Operations Master, he would go unhesitantly and collect the packet. Bridge of course cannot be left unmanned and one qualified DPO has to be there. For me it was the greatest experience to work with expats, who would undertake jobs looking at convenience and ease with no ego involved.

Samudra Sevak was privileged to be a part of Review of the Fleet by the President of India. This is an exercise carried out for warships but a few auxillaries or merchant ships are also given an opportunity to take part. We got white tunics and trousers made for the complete crew with peak caps and black shoes. It was nice to see everyone on board smartly dressed in whites. When I went for a meeting with the Naval authorities, they complimented us for the fine uniforms and the drill carried out by the crew. On these ships we have no proper uniforms and the crew can be seen wearing all kinds of clothes, depending on the work they are doing.

A month before our daughter Arooshi was born in March 1994, I decided to give a final farewell to sailing. In the heart of hearts I knew that it would be a loss of something very close to me and at the same time miss numerous friends that I had made, spending days together on board. We would all discuss that this was the last trip one was sailing and should do something ashore. Some already had options with them and would take up various tasks; there were some who had farms, running guest houses, properties on rent. There was a master who would undertake plumbing jobs. Munde a colleague of mine from the Navy was running a flourishing business in Mumbai; a diver by profession he would come on short trips when the ship needed any help. Then there were those who had projects to make millions that never took off and others who had various ideas. There were friends like Peter who spent most of their time in pubs and others who just took a break. It was mainly the expat crew who kept themselves busy during the off time. I was probably midway. It was time for me to do something that was close to my heart ie to run the travel business and spend time with the family. It needed full commitment and time to run the business; I realized that either I had to be in it whole heartedly or not at all. It was a great innings to have worked in the oil fields.

Chapter 4

Entrepreneurship Bug - I venture into travel business

In 1987, I wanted to leave the Navy though I was not sure about my plans. I left a fascinating service, without the fear of unknown. When you venture out, quite often things do not fall in place automatically. I got operated for hernia, the main reason being my need to continue riding and playing polo. One of the first things I did was to take a trip abroad and visited Thailand and Singapore; the major part of my savings were spent on this trip. But this was the first exposure of going abroad by air. I had been to a few countries on naval ships.

Initially, I did go for some interviews for a job. Some of the jobs being offered were not something I really wanted to do or were at places I didn't care for much.

My classmate from King George's School, Daulat Chowgule, from a reputed business family from Goa came to know that I had left the Navy. He asked his local representative in Delhi, one Mr Puri to meet me for visiting Goa. He did look after me for the short trip that I was there and gave a proposal for me to develop 500 acres of land near Ponda for farming. Goa at that time did not grow any vegetables and these were brought from outside. He assured that all assistance would be given to me to start this project. There would be good accommodation for me at the farm and in Goa, and since he knew that I was a keen rider, he even assured that there would be some horses kept at the farm for me to ride. The proposal looked good. But at this stage, I was not able to take this offer; so I called him and told him the same. May be staying and working at the farm was not for me at that stage.

Since they were already in shipping and mining, they wanted to start lighters and boats in the rivers for transportation in Northern India. The idea was shelved mainly due to safety and security reasons in certain areas through which the river was flowing.

We were always in touch. I did meet him a few years later, when he told me: "CP, you did not listen to me then, go and look at how successful the project is now in Ponda!"

At the same time I did not want to visit Government offices for work. As I was not doing anything in particular, my Aunt's friend had a contract for running the canteen for Indian Newspaper Society in New Delhi. As she was not able to devote time, she asked me to run it and I could take over the contract subsequently. This was my first venture. Probably I did the job quite well for soon the Secretary called me and said that everyone was so happy and he asked me if I would like to take over running the canteen myself and sign a contract. The Committee would like to meet me and take a final decision. I was called during a board meeting being held under the presidentship of Mr Cama of *Bombay Samachar*. They asked me certain questions regarding running of canteen, my background etc and I was given a contract for three years though normally it was given for a lesser duration.

To my bad luck, the Secretary changed. The new Secretary for some reason tried to make things difficult for me. I wrote a letter to the President stating facts and my grievances. Mr Cama said that he would like to meet me when he was in Delhi next. He said: "You need not have written a letter; making a call would have been good enough." Gist of the matter is that I realized that Mr Cama had enough things to worry about and running the Canteen would not be a part of the Charter and specially when he was in Bombay. He also advised that the new Secretary would make things difficult. I took his hint and gave up the contract. This was my first experience of starting a business, with minor compromises. I could have made this venture successful. It was a great learning experience.

The next venture I tried was that I got a Mother Dairy booth allotted in New Rajendra Nagar. Mother Dairy wanted to expand and have more booths in Delhi. There were a few booths in Delhi at that time. It was an interesting experience.

Fruits and vegetables would arrive at odd times, early in the morning in winters and one had to be there to receive them. Interestingly, the local vegetable vendors would come to help me out and put the stuff inside.

I built such a good rapport with the vegetable sellers that they would advise me regarding the fruits and vegetables that I should order to avoid any wastage. Residents of the locality were very happy; the opening time of the booth was eight in the morning and they would line up even before that. Business started doing well. But the situation soon changed. Chopra, an Inspector from Mother Dairy one day came and checked me out for opening the booth late by a few minutes. I told him that it was being opened on time always but may have been delayed a little due to special reasons. May be Chopra needed to assert his position. Hurt that probably some customers were complaining behind my back, I spoke with the Manager Mr Gupta and told him that I was not keen on running the booth. He was taken aback and told me that he was extremely happy since he was getting good feedback about the booth. I insisted that someone else should take over immediately. He requested me to continue for a month, till the time they found someone to run the booth. I accepted his request. This was another learning experience.

Thereafter I took an agency of Unit Trust of India and Oriental Insurance Company. For the latter, I found it a herculean task as the development officer I was assigned to, was very polite but took a long time for issuing a policy. In case I sent one of my assistants it would take much longer. It did not take me long to realize that he was dissuading me from doing anything. Good sense prevailed and I gave up the idea altogether. Interestingly, after I gave up the agency, he would call me up and send reminders for renewal of my existing policies. I gave up these projects also soon realizing that this was something that I was not keen on.

All these were great learning experiences and I slowly came to understand how people run businesses and challenges faced by them.

Now that I had experienced doing certain things on my own, I finally thought about what I liked most; well it was travelling. I then decided to start a Travel Agency, without realizing as to what I was getting into. A bit before starting the Agency I completed IATA basic courses as a Passenger Agent and a Cargo Agent. I did quite well there. With both options open to me I chose to be a Passenger Agent.

I had no idea as to how to start a company. I walked into the office of Registrar of companies, met Mr Suraj Prakash, who was then the Registrar of Companies. He was kind enough to see me and explained in brief what a proprietorship, partnership and private limited company were. A few days later I met a senior Chartered Accountant friend of mine from school and told him that I had met the Registrar of Companies. He was astonished and asked me how I had managed to meet him. I told him that I just walked in after meeting his Secretary. He said that he had not met him, inspite of his numerous visits on work there. He was far too senior.

Though having no clue of travel business or experience of the private sector, one fine morning I started Neptune Travels as a proprietorship company. My brother, who was running a chemist shop, gave me some place where I could put a table and chair and do my work and use his telephone.

There was only one person I knew in the travel business and that was Cdr Pujji; as and when I was stuck somewhere, I would call him and ask for help or the silliest of questions. He would always say that "he was learning something". Apart from him, I knew no one in the travel business, hotels or any airline.

I would visit various offices, both private and government. I got a mixed response from people, but generally they seemed to be helpful. I had not lived in Delhi before and literally knew no one here, but for relatives; they had also been on jobs with no clue of business. Stumbling along I slowly built up a clientele. I started as one man army; I would take a booking, carry money, get a ticket issued, pay the Agent, pick up the ticket, deliver it and collect the payment. I had limited capital for circulation. I do remember Surya my brother telling me that in case I sold two tickets in a day, I would go dancing on the main road.

It was after a few months of having been in business, that I visited the Vayudoot office. At that time there were only three Airlines in India operating on domestic routes ie Air India, Indian Airlines and Vayudoot. Vayodoot was a Regional Airline, a joint venture between state owned carriers Air India and Indian Airlines. Vayudoot was conceptualised to initially serve the North Eastern Region of India; the airline built up operations close to destinations in the challenging areas. Many of the destinations saw the resumption of civil flights and fixed wing aircraft after many years.

I called up to meet the Mr Harsh Vardhan, the Managing Director of Vayudoot, and gave him a brief introduction about myself. He told me it would be great in case I met him two days later in his office. Two days later I was off to meet him. Those days to get a Agency of an Airline, one had to be very influential. It was a brief meeting and he asked me a few questions. I told him that I had been in business a few months and gave some details on the business I was doing. He liked what I said and promised to arrange an inspection. In a few days, it was all done. This was my first experience, where I realized that there were some people, who took independent decisions and were ready to help without compromising on the requirements. Necessary formalities were completed quickly.

The story did not end here. I had to give a Bank guarantee of Rupees fifty thousand. There was no way that I could have mustered this amount. I went to my Indian Bank Branch and met the Manager Mr Swamy, a very fine gentleman, and gave him my requirement. He showed his concern and looked very supportive; since it was not in his powers, he took me to the Regional Manager of Indian Bank, putting up my case before him. He briefed him about my background and the circumstances for this requirement. The Regional Manager said there was no option and, I should give a deposit of Rupees fifty thousand. Mr Swamy told me that I should see him with all that I could muster for this guarantee. After mustering my savings, bank deposits and shares, I could come with Rupees thirty thousand and was still short of Rs 20,000. There was no way that I would give up this opportunity. Mr Swamy asked me to give him some time and that I should meet him the following day; to my surprise, paper work was completed and the bank guarantee was ready for being given to Vayudoot. Mr Swamy had put a deposit of Rupees twenty thousand from his savings. It was a godsend. There was no reason for him to do that; I have yet to come across a good Samaritan like him and that too a banker. Slowly business started picking up and the first thing I did was to return Mr Swamy's amount.

Soon we had the ticket stock of Vayudoot and at times we were also the top performing agents. The staff at Vayudoot was always very supportive, most unlike any public sector organization; the culture was very different.

Unfortunately, a few years later Vayudoot had to close down as it suffered from low occupancy. The Government did consider closure or privatization. For me, it was very touching loss of a wonderful and memorable association. But like anything else, life has to move on.

We went on a holiday with the family to Yol (Young Officers Living) located in Himachal Pradesh; it was established by the British in 1849. Yol Cantonment was built in 1942. From here we travelled around to Dharamshala and Palampur. I was fascinated by Palampur, a hill station surrounded by tea gardens, pine forests and covered with the Dhauladhar ranges. Our son who was nine years then suddenly turned religious and would be praying at every temple that we visited; he had to be pulled up every time. Finally, I asked him what he was praying for. He said, "Dad I have been praying that I would like to see snow." To fulfill his wish we visited Udechee, located above Dharamshala, where it had snowed a day before. One morning he came and woke me up to say that he could hear the water flowing; there was a spring flowing next to our room.

During this short stay, we fell in love with this place. On coming back to Delhi, we took a decision to close the business and move to Palampur and set up a small hotel. We started telling our clientele regarding our plans to close the business and moving to Palampur. Most of them had got used to us and were not very happy with our idea. Then a close friend who had been in business for a long time told me that I had built a reputation of sorts in what I was doing which had taken a lot of effort and time. Any new venture would take time to establish and I would have to start from scratch. Good sense prevailed and we decided to continue with the travel business.

Now that I was in business, friends from the travel trade, came to my rescue. They were always willing to help unlike the initial days. There was always guidance and other support at hand whether it be getting the tickets, any advice on tours out of India or incoming, or conferences etc. It was very good for me, since I had not worked in any Travel Agency, it was literally a hands down experience. Over a period the list of friends and supporters increased and I could say with pride that I had plenty of well wishers.

The Passport Office started recognizing ex-Servicemen for assistance in issuing of passports.

For this, I met Maj Gen Limaye, the then Director General Resettlement and advised him regarding the criteria. It was big news in the papers a few days later. Many retired officers got the Agency including those who had served in the second world war. There was an Inspector, who had to give the report about my office; he would make sure that he came for inspection when I was not in the office. This he was doing on purpose for various reasons. I went and met the concerned Deputy Commissioner of Police and lo! inspection was completed the same day! My application, however, remained pending, a few years had elapsed by then. I did not give up and met the concerned Deputy Secretary. He got the file and said that since my agency was well established, the file was pending and they did not find it necessary to move further with my application. He opened the file and showed me the letter head on which I had applied for recognition by passport office. I had to tell him that the telephone number, Telex and fax numbers all belonged to some one else and that I was only using their facility. By then a lot of time had passed, the criteria again was changed, any authorized Agent could apply for passports for their clients. We got our application approved in the normal category.

Having been in business for some time, I was moving cautiously and trying to get the necessary recognitions. Anyone I approached in the Corporate sector, would ask, if it was an IATA accredited Agency or had any other recognitions. It did not make any difference even after we had various recognitions. In 1994 we applied for IATA accreditation. There again, my business was still in infancy; IATA required a Bank Guarantee of Rupees ten lakhs, apart from meeting other criteria, which we did. It was again impossible for me to muster the necessary amount/assets for this bank guarantee. My brother, VP, who had always been a well wisher and a great support at all times came to my rescue. He repaid his home loan and hypothecated the house to Indian Bank to raise funds. We could thus meet the bank guarantee requirement, and with this the company was in main frame of business.

My wife Neeru has been the backbone of the company and supported in establishing the business. In the early years she would come to office with Arooshi, who was just a month old. Everyone knew her from the Airlines or hotels and not to forget our esteemed clients. When Arooshi was growing and needed her more she would come for half a day and spend some time with her. There were times when our clients called and she was not in the office; rarely calls would be forwarded to me. That is the time I realized that not many people knew me. A lady who had been travelling with us for many years, wanted to talk to her, but since she was not there, her call was connected to me. She had some requests and I was trying to explain to her as to what was possible and what could not be done. She told me that "I do not know who you are. I have been travelling with your company for many years. Neeru never takes more than a few minutes to help out and meet all requests."

Neeru in the absence of staff would handle the counter, accounts and co-ordination of field staff to deliver documents to clients. In those days there were documents, tickets and vouchers to be delivered, and cheques and documents to be collected. Later, thanks to technology most of these jobs were being done electronically.

Gradually the scenario changed. Indian Airlines, the only domestic carrier opened up giving tickets stocks. It was not easy but we managed to get the ticket stock and gave the necessary guarantee.

We started covering all aspects of travel be it ticketing, tours, passports, visas, travel insurance, foreign exchange, conferences and incentives. Horse riding and polo was something that I was passionate about. With this passion in mind started horse safaris in different places in India, mainly covering Shekhwati, Jodhpur and Udaipur. I would make it a point to go with the riders as much as I could. I would visit these places beforehand and check out the horses and facilities personally. We assisted Swedish television to make a film on Elephant Polo. Now Elephant Polo has been stopped. We have organized a number of polo events that have received a wide coverage both in the electronic and print media.

After IATA accreditation, we became members of various trade organizations like PATA (Pacific Asia Travel Asociation), TAAI (Travel Agents Association of India), IATO (Indian Association of Tour Operators) and were recognized by the Ministry of Tourism, Government of India. This gave us an opportunity for meeting colleagues from hotels, airlines and travel companies.

I was privileged to have served as Treasurer and Secretary of Travel Agents Association of India in the Northern Region from 1998 to 2004 ; then as Member of the National Committee of Tourism of Confederation of Indian Industry in 2016 and 2017 and Executive Committee of Pacific Asia Travel Association from 2011 to 2015.

Over the years travel business has been changing phenomenally. In earlier days we had to call the Airline to make bookings, do manual fare calculations and write the tickets. It was not before long in 2004, we moved from manual tickets to electronic tickets.

We used to deal with American Express for getting foreign exchange for our clients. I do remember one day Khandelwal who was looking after our organization for sales, telling me that time was not far that you would be using a mobile phone and making a booking on the computer. This became a reality too soon.

Then came Global Distribution System (GDS), where we could make bookings of flights, hotels and other travel related services across the world from one centre. Indian Airlines was not on GDS for many years. We had a data circuit from Safdarjung Airport to our office, passing through four telephone exchanges. It was like a hot line for making a booking. With a fault in anyone line, data circuit would not be working. There were only a few agents who had this facility in Delhi. Before the advent of GDS, it was only airlines that had computers for making the booking. I do remember walking into the Air India office and on one of the computers, it was written: *"Do you know what does the computer do? In a fraction of a second, it tells you that there is no seat available!"*

Gradually with Open Sky Policy by the government, more airlines started coming into the field though some disappeared as quickly as they came. Low cost carriers changed the aviation scene totally, making travel affordable for many.

The impact of technology on travel agents, including the availability of personal computers, cell phones and the internet, has been significant. We have tried to keep pace with technology and always added various products and services to our portfolio to service our clients.

Meanwhile, in 2006 we started Neptune Foundation, a CSR initiative to give back to society. Foundation's initiative is focused on caring for the girl child and elderly as also to saving the dying art forms in villages. It is a totally self sustained initiative with support of certain well wishers.

The biggest take of being an entrepreneur apart from taking risks, challenges, innovation, providing employment and doing what I really wanted to, was being my own boss.

Advising and making arrangements for people to see places in this beautiful world, have memorable experiences and the tourists come back to tell us of the good time they had, has been a most satisfying experience. In the bargain, I did manage to travel to over 70 countries and visit numerous places and make good friends all over the world.

We have been moving ahead and progressing with the good wishes of our clients, friends and well wishers. I cannot forget the marvellous team and the family support without whom nothing would have been possible. A major lesson that I have learnt over the years is that when you are passionate and honest in whatever you do success will follow. Because of this I have had a smooth transition from government, to public sector to private sector. As Walt Disney once said, "All our dreams can come true, if we have the courage to pursue them."

Author Show jumping at National Defence Academy

Author as a cadet(Photo in the background) and at Reunion in
National Defence Academy

Author and Neeru at Sudan Block, National Defence Academy

Author, Neeru and Arooshi at Hut of Remembrance,
National Defence Academy

Author astride Beauty, Roop Niwas, Nawalgarh, Shekhawati

Frescoes behind Penny extreme right, Neeru with Arooshi in lap -
Shekhawati (Rajasthan)

Punakha Dzong(Bhutan)

Judges from left Ved, Shobha, Neeru, Alpana and Sarita, selecting
winners of Painting Competition organized by Neptune Foundation

Winners displaying their work, Annual Painting Competition at Arya Kanya, Gurukul, New Rajendra Nagar by Neptune Foundation in Association with Rotary Club of New Delhi

Neptune Foundation Charity Polo Match at Jaipur Polo Grounds, New Delhi

Neptune Foundation Charity Polo Match-Teams with Neptune Cup
(Author is second from left)

His Master's Voice music store, Oxford Street, London

Entrance to The Famous Grouse Experience at the Glenturret Distillery, Crieff(Scotland)

Author in Capri

Amalfi Coast, Italy

Author with late Dr Thawan Duchanee, Thai cotemporary painter, architect and sculptor in Chiang Rai

Chapter 5

Of Havelis and Horses and an Ancient City

Over the years I have travelled the length and breadth of India including the famous touristic spots but after decades have passed, only some places have left an indelible mark on my memory for different reasons. Some of the most memorable visits were unplanned and in some cases some strange power drew me there. I do not wish to torment the reader with details of my experiences. My main focus would be to take the reader to some special places both in and around the country that left a deep impact and especially some exotic places abroad some of which are paths less travelled.

Around September 1994, we decided to explore Shekhawati in the state of Rajasthan. The main attraction for me was the stories of horses I had heard. This was a time when there was no google and one took help of road maps and friends. Amit, a friend and Rajasthan expert, guided me to go to Dundlod via Neem Ka Thana. One fine morning I picked up our car and with some references of places started our journey to this magnificent place. There were shorter ways, which we discovered later; but on this trip it was a longer route, aiming for Dundlod as the destination. I stopped the car at various places asking for directions and was shown the way to go forward, till the time we asked for directions from an elderly gentleman at Neem Ka Thana. He said, "In case you keep pronouncing the way you are doing, it would be impossible to reach Dundlod." After the guidance given by the gentleman, it was a smooth sailing till we reached Dundlod. In those days the roads were in poor shape and it did take us a long time. My daughter, Arooshi, complained that my driving was bad and the car made lots of noise. Little could I tell her that these were not the roads of Delhi. Subsequently we visited Shekhawati several times.

Shekhawati, as the name suggests is the land of Shekhawat Rajputs. The term Shekhawati directly relates to its founding father Maha Rao Shekha Ji, the literal meaning of word *Shekha+wati* in local language means the garden of Maha Rao Shekha; descendants of Shekha Ji are called Shekhawat Rajputs. The Shekhawat Rajputs ruled this area for more than 500 years. Other than the Rajput community, *Marwaris* (the business class) and agrarian communities like *Jats* and *Malis* have played an important role in the growth and prosperity of Shekhawati region.

Around 1352, another region of Shekhawati was witnessing the rule of a new clan, the Kaimkhanis. Kaimkhanis are Muslim Rajputs. This clan was founded by Nawab Qaim Khan, who was born Karamchand, a Rajput, in the Churu district of Rajasthan. He was converted to Muslim religion by Firoz Shah Tuglaq. Kaimkhanis established and developed the town of Jhunjhunu and Fatehpur. The hold of the Kaimkhanis on the region was broken in 1730 when Shardul Singh of the Shekhawati clan took over Jhunjhunu. The Kaimkhanis were recognized as a martial race by British. Even today the horse mounted cavalry of Indian Army has many Kaimkhani recruits.

The realm of lovely havelis, harking back to the yesteryears, epitomizes the beauty of Shekhawati, a region that comprises of Sikar, Jhunjhunu and Churu. It is a major landmark and tourist destination of colourful Rajasthan. The land is laced with innumerable beautiful havelis or grand mansions that are guaranteed to capture one's imagination. It is a haven for a true connoisseur of art and architecture. A riot of colours encapsulates the spirit of this vibrant landscape.

Dundlod was our first stop; it lies in the heart of Shekhawati. The family of Dundlod are the descendants of Kesari Singh, the fifth son of Shardul Singh. Dundlod fort was built by him in 1750 AD. After having travelled through sandy tracks of Shekhawati, we entered Dundlod to see the magnificent sight of the beautifully painted havelis of the Goenkas and the towering fort which stands in the middle.

As we entered the imposing Suraj Pole gateway of the fort, we felt we had stepped into a bygone era. We then proceeded to the Bichla Darwaza and turned into the main courtyard of the fort from the Uttar Pole to face the steps which led us to the majestic Diwan Khana.

The Diwan Khana was built in Mughal architecture and was furnished with Louis the XIV furniture. It had a magnificent library, with a very rich collection of rare books on Indian History. We also saw the family portraits which reminded us of the times gone by in history. Above this lies the Duchatta, from where the ladies watched the court ceremonies in purdah.

We were honoured to meet Col Raghuvir Singh, popularly known as 'Rags' and his son Raghvendra Singh. Colonel Rags was an old timer who had served in the Cavalry Regiment of the Indian Army. He had lots of stories to tell and was an accomplished rider and a polo player.

The following day we visited Mandawa; it is one of the most happening towns of the Shekhawati region. Thakur Nawal Singh built the fort at Mandawa in 1755 AD. Mandawa houses a legacy full of heritage and Rajput art. Any trip to Shekhawati region is incomplete without a visit to Mandawa. The interiors of Mandawa Fort are influenced from Sheesh Mahal of Amber Fort, with lots of mirror work in the walls and the ceiling. The Durbar Hall is a grand portion of the fort. The other buildings of the town were built by the wealthy merchants Marwaris.

Mandawa Fort has been converted into a luxurious heritage hotel known as Castle Mandawa; infact they are pioneers to start heritage hotels in Rajasthan. It is probably one of the best places to discover the legacy of Shekhawati through the redefined history and luxury of Castle Mandawa. It has medieval turreted towers, and palanquin-roofed balconies that blend with modern comforts in old-world rooms. Family portraits, antique cannons and arms add to the charm of this family-run hotel where tradition still runs strong. Even time is measured by a different clock, a huge brass gong struck by the resident timekeepers at the fort every hour.

We spent a few days in Nawalgarh, which is located almost in the centre of Shekhawati. The town was founded in 1737 by Nawal Singh, one of the five sons of the Rajput ruler Shardul Singh. The arrival of merchants from Jaipur increased the town's prosperity and some of India's most successful merchants were from here. The town is quite compact and we could reach most of the *havelis* on foot.

In 1928, Rawal Madan Singh the scion of the erstwhile estate of Nawalgarh, Rajasthan gave a complete makeover to Roop Niwas converting his country house and stables into his permanent home. Later, in 1981, he opened his doors to guests so they could enjoy the hospitality of the family managed Roop Niwas.

Rawal Devendra Singh and his family are wonderful hosts. They continue the old tradition and welcome guests with the same warm hospitality as did their ancestors.

Nawalgarh is famous for frescoes, like most of Shekhawati. Podar Haveli is one of the well preserved havelis in Nawalgarh, which has been converted to a museum. It was built in the year 1902 by Anandilal Podar. The Haveli has excellent frescoes exceeding 750 in number; all are more than a century old.

The Haveli was converted to a Heritage Haveli Museum by Kantikumar R. Podar, grandson of Anandilal B, Podar, with the aim to build up a cultural centre to exhibit the Rajasthani heritage for the promotion of tourism in the Shekhawati region.

The Haveli Museum truly represents all the characteristics of the haveli, a two storied building, with open big platform outside the entrance gate, main gate with wooden carving, two open courtyards with open Nohra (open land surrounded by wall) and big living rooms with windows for proper light and air.

The frescoes in this Museum along with its pillars, arches and the artistic carved wooden gate are the best-preserved items. The gate between the outer courtyard and the inner courtyard is unique by itself and has been hailed as amongst the 10 best gates in India.

The frescoes involve a wide range of subjects. They depict not only Indian gods and goddesses or scenes from Indian mythology but also cultural and social life of rural India prevalent at that time. Some frescoes also depict the modern trend that had set in India such as trains, changes in dress code, etc.

However, with the passage of time, these frescoes were damaged or faded. Kantikumar R. Podar decided to restore all the frescoes in the Podar Haveli. The work was undertaken in 1992 under the supervision of the specialists in the field.

The other haveli was the Morarka Haveli, which definitely needed restoration.

Rawal Devendra Singh was passionate about horses and there were a large number of horses kept in his stables in Roop Niwas. He took personal care, which made every ride an enjoyable one; most rides are personally conduced by him. He has all three predominant breed of Indian horses in his stables, namely the Marwari, Kathiawari and Sindhi. The most popular and indigenous Indian breed of horses in the state of Rajasthan are the Marwari which originate from the Marwar region. Marwari horses are known for their hardiness and are quite similar to the Kathiawari horses.

The Marwari is thought to have been bred around the 12th century AD where it quickly became a favourite of the martial clan, the Rathores. The Rathores ruled the Marwar region from their capital city of Jodhpur, to the immediate west of Jaipur. Used throughout history as a cavalry horse by the people of the Marwar region, the Marwari was noted for its loyalty and bravery in battle.

The breed, with its distinguishing marks is well represented across early historical periods of painting, especially miniature painting, albeit in a secondary role to elephants.

During British Rule, Indians were heavily discouraged and often forbidden from riding Marwaris. The British favoured their own Arab bred horses and associated the Marwari with the Hindu caste system. The number of Marwari horses declined significantly during the British rule, a trend that continued after Independence. By the early 1990s a government survey estimated that only 500 to 600 specimens remained, revealing the Marwari to be on the verge of extinction. This low point triggered a remarkable 'call to arms' to save the Marwari, as an 'Indigenous Indian horse breed' with a proud and noble history. Organizations were formed to save the Marwari from extinction with breeding, research and education programmes, including with both government and private sector support.

Stocks of Marwari were on the rise again with a focus on the historically admired attributes of speed, stamina and suitability for arid conditions. The breed was trained to behave with great bravery in battle conditions and its handsome bearing are as highly valued today, as they were historically.

The standout physical characteristic of the Marwari is distinctive inward curving ears, seemingly almost meeting at the tips. The origin of this striking appearance is unknown but can be seen in examples of early Mughal miniature paintings. The breed is also prized for its striking presence and 'doe-eyed' beauty in females. This is accentuated by the Marwari being a naturally gaited horse with a four-beat lateral gait. This gait is smoother in appearance and substantially more comfortable for a rider and horse in trying conditions such as long-distance desert travel.

The beautiful terrain of Shekhawati and the sand dunes made it a wonderful area for horseback riding. We would go for rides in the morning and evening. During the ride, breakfast would be served en route nicely laid out on top of a sand dune or at a farm in the outskirts of Nawalgarh, with the Bhopa singing and playing mesmerising music.

A ride in Rajasthan can be of varied durations. It is a great experience when the complete camp moves for a duration, with stoppages en route. There are jeeps, camel carts accompanying the riders.

Thakur Durga Singh, would brief us before and during the rides. His knowledge is vast as a keen observer of history, culture, religion, farming, current affairs and horses. The inquisitive can have endless conversations with him on a number of subjects like agriculture, rainwater harvesting, solar heating and healthy cooking. He would be always ready to share his experiences.

On one of the rides in Nawalgarh, a hoof of one of the front legs of my horse went into a hole; it stumbled and I came off the horse. It was not the first time I had taken a toss and I managed to break the impact of my fall. Devendra Singh of Roop Niwas Palace in Nawalgarh and others galloped full speed to get the horse back, which had sped off after dropping me. I was very impressed with their concern. Nancy, a doctor, who was riding with us, got off the horse to check that all was well with me and nothing untoward had happened. I complimented them for the quick action in getting the horse back for me. Promptly came the reply from Devendra Singh, "Since it was a new horse, we were worried that it might get lost and hence we chased it!"

Having ridden for a long time and happy with the experience, we were all walking our horses towards Roop Niwas, when suddenly horse " Beauty" took off, like a pigeon out of the hat. There was no way I could stop it; it ran through the desert. I could see the road, tractors and other vehicles plying, the flag of Roop Niwas Palace. Finally, the horse stopped at the stables. To my amazement on reaching the stables I was told, "Sir, this is the fastest horse in Shekhawati !" I said with some feeling, "Thanks for letting me know that!" I wondered what could happen if a novice tried to ride that horse, but then they carefully check out the experience of the rider before giving a horse.

Making horses gallop in sand can be fun; perhaps it gives the rider some sense of security of riding on soft ground and horses also have to use more energy when their hooves sink in sand than moving on a firm surface. During one of the rides, Phil Salt, a co-rider was galloping on a long stretch of a big sand dune. Although he had started to ride a bit late in life, he was always full of energy and enthusiasm. I was under the impression that the horse had taken off with him. Concerned and worried, I managed to go near his horse and to slow him down and asked him if all was well with him. He said, "It was great and I was enjoying it!" I admit I felt a bit foolish then.

After a long ride and the muscles stretched a bit, Gadu Ram, the barber, would be waiting to give a massage; when he was not doing that , he would be making magnificent designs on camels, cutting camel hair with scissors.

It was an experience to ride in the desert on a moonlit night. After a long ride we would take a break for dinner at the ancestral farm belonging to Thakur Durga Singh. A memorable way to spend an evening with exquisite Rajasthani cuisine, drinks flowing and local folk singing and dancing to keep us entertained. Riding back to the stables at midnight was something that we would always remember.

Music and folk dances are an integral part of Rajasthani culture.

Bhopa Ram Lal and Bhopi Tapashi his wife, kept us entertained throughout our stay. During their performance the Bhopas sing and play the Ravanhattha, a bowed stringed instrument with a resonator formed from a coconut-shell covered with raw hide provides accompaniment to vocal singing. The Bhopas are the priest singers of the folk deities in Rajasthan. They perform in front of a scroll, known as *phad* or *par* in Rajasthani that depicts the episodes of the narrative of the folk deity and functions as a portable temple. The Bhopas carry this phad traditionally and are invited by villagers to perform in their localities during times of sickness and misfortune. Traditionally, the phads are kept rolled in transit. After reaching a village or town, the Bhopas erect the phads between two poles in a suitable public place shortly after nightfall. The performance goes on throughout the night and terminates only in early morning. The Bhopa sings various episodes from the narrative of Pabuji and his wife known as Bhopi holds an oil lamp near the visual being described. The Bhopi also sings some parts of the episodes.

They would be all over, be it before starting a ride, stopping en route and of course welcoming us back on completion of the ride. One morning Penny, a friend, during breakfast told me; "The Bhopas do sing well and the music was good but please tell them that not to wake me up early morning singing outside my room !"

Kiki, a diplomat at the US Embassy would come regularly for horse riding trips to Nawalgarh with us. She was so impressed with the Bhopas that she got a CD recorded of their songs and music. A performance of theirs was also arranged by her in Delhi. She did it all to help out Bhopa and family to raise some additional resources for them to enable them to buy a piece of land. They had never travelled out of Nawalgarh before.

A short drive away from Nawalgarh is Sikar. The fresco paintings on the ancient havelis, temples and forts captivate people from across the globe. Sikar was the dynasty of royal Shekhawat kings. There are many royal Shekhawati families residing in Sikar. Three most prominent business families of India, Bajajs, Birlas and Goenkas all traditionally belong to this area.

We spent a few memorable days in the vibrant land of Shekhawats seeing colourful havelis and having a fascinating time riding in beautiful region on local breed of horses.

Varanasi — The Ancient City

I had never visited Varanasi though I had arranged for lot of guests to visit Varanasi on their request. I got a bit curious about this city, especially when I heard that it was supposed to be about 5000 years old. My friend Nicola, head of German Press in India had visited Varanasi a number of times. For all her guests and friends visiting India, she ensured that Varanasi was on top of their itinerary. One day I could not resist and asked her what was so special about Varanasi. She told me then: "Go and see it for yourself."

So in the beginning of 2003, I made a plan to visit Varanasi, also known as Benares or Kashi. It is one of the most visited cities and on the wish list of travellers and photographers who want to capture the myriad colours of life and perhaps in this case death. I realized later that a visit to Varanasi at least once, is a must. It helps one come to terms with one's mortality.

In the morning my wife and I were picked up from the hotel by our guide Gyanendra Tripathy a scholar of history. We had to walk through the streets of Varanasi which were remarkable with the traffic, the bazaars, the temples and holy shrines which were found everywhere and of course, the maddening crowds.

Gyanendra told us that there were an estimated 23,000 temples in Varanasi and some of the important ones that we would be visiting were Kashi Vishwanath Temple of Shiva, the Sankat Mochan Hanuman Temple and the Durga Temple.

There was a lot of rush at Kashi Vishwanath Temple. Gyanendra had organized with a priest for us to visit the temple; we ducked under the doors and were in front of the deity to offer our prayers. He explained that Kashi Vishvanath Temple was one of the most famous Hindu temples dedicated to Lord Shiva. The temple stood on the western bank of the holy river Ganga and was one of the twelve Jyotirlingas, the holiest of Shiva temples.

My brother-in- law R.K. Sundd, who was associated with the water works in Varanasi, on retirement joined Sankat Mochan Hanuman Temple as a volunteer and also Sankat Mochan Foundation. This temple is believed to have been built on the very spot where Tulsidas had a vision of Hanuman. Sankat Mochan Temple was founded by Tulsidas who was the author of the *Ramacharitaamanas,* being the greatest version of Lord Ram's story written in Awadhi. There is a place, where he is supposed to have sat and written the great epic.

I had the honour to meet and be blessed by Veer Bhadra Mishra, the Mahant (high priest) of the temple, who had been working for cleaning and protecting the Ganga river. Its projects were funded in part by aid from the United States and Swedish governments. Mishra was the former Head of the Civil Engineering Department at the Indian Institute of Technology (Banaras Hindu University) Varanasi and was awarded United Nations Environment Programme's (UNEP) "Global 500 Roll of Honour" in 1992 and later the *TIME* magazine's "Hero of the Planet" award in 1999. Sankat Mochan is the only organization that runs Swatch Ganga Research Laboratory and gives regular Ganga water quality updates. Since I knew His Excellency Johan Nordenfelt the Ambassador of Sweden in India, on meeting him I mentioned about the great work being done by Sankat Mochan for cleaning up the Ganga. He was very pleased and said that it was always nice to get a good update from a third person and it was an endorsement that the Swedish Government had been putting money in good hands.

Dom Raja is the one who has control of all cremations on the Ghats in Varanasi. Gyanendra later during the day took us to cremation ghats ie Manikarnika ghat and Harishchandra ghats and told us that for the Hindus, Varanasi is an auspicious place to die and be cremated by the river as dying there released one from the cycle of death and rebirth (moksha).

The *doms* (who actually handle the corpses in the cremation ghats) begin their funeral duties by offering a prayer to Kallu dom. The doms build up the funeral pyre methodically. To make sure the body keeps burning they poke it with long poles from time to time. Dom Raja is the offical keeper of Varanasi's sacred flame. About 35 families from the community live around the town's main "burning ghats". These ghats cover an area of about seven square kilometres each, lining the banks of the river. He told us that the doms collect money for lighting the pyre, depending on the dead person's status. The ghats are serene and peaceful.

Next morning we took a boat ride at dawn in the river. Gyanendra told us that Varanasi presented a unique combination of physical, metaphysical and supernatural elements. According to the Hindu mythology, Varanasi liberates soul from human body to the Ultimate. It is the Ganga Ghats of Varanasi that complement the concept of divinity. The Ganga Ghats were full of pilgrims who flocked to the sacred river to take a dip in the holy Ganges, which is believed to absolve one from all sins. Watching people come down to the river early in the morning, taking a bath in the river, performing rituals, and worshipping the Sun was a unique and almost divine experience.

There are a number of temples on the banks of the river. The old buildings, ashrams and palaces along the river side look as colourful as a rainbow when the sunlight hits them. It is at the Banaras Ghat where we could see life and death together. There are a number of Ghats alongside the river. Some of the prominent and popular Ghats in Varanasi are the Dasaswamedh Ghat, Manikarnika Ghat, Harischandra Ghat, Assi Ghat, Shivala Ghat, Man Mandir Ghat, Darbhanga Ghat, Ahilyabai Ghat and the Kedar Ghat. After the boat ride, we walked in to the oldest part of Varanasi through its famous narrow streets. Gyanendra stopped at one of the shops and asked us whether we would like to have a traditional Banaras breakfast; we were quite delighted. Breakfast consisted of a plate of kachori sabzi with some gulab jamuns and jalebis on the side. There were a number of people lining up for breakfast. It was a relishing meal.

Street food has been an essential part of the Indian culture and cuisine. There are a number of street foods from across the country that are famous, but nothing can beat the hot and crispy *kachoris* and *samosas* from Varanasi. To top it we had the famous Banarasi paan; it is almost same as other paans of any other part of India. But the process of making it, way of service and giving it different sizes and shapes is remarkable and has made Banarasi paan distinct from other paans. Banaras has had a long tradition of paan being served and prepared in each and every corner of street. There is no street in Varanasi where one could not find a paan shop. Serving of paan and offerings have great a tradition from ancient times.

One cannot do without shopping in Varanasi. Silk weaving, perhaps the most popular art of Varanasi and especially Banarasi silk sarees form an indispensable part of an Indian bride's trousseau. The art of making the world-famous gold and silver brocades and richly worked saris have been known to have passed from generation to generation much like family jewels without losing their charm. Besides Banarasi saris and brocades, one can look for wonderful pieces of brassware, copperware, wooden and clay toys and antique designs of heavy gold jewellery.

After Varanasi, we visited Sarnath situated 13 kilometres north-east of Varanasi. Perhaps this visit occurred because there was a bit of the Buddhist in me; whatever be the case, Sarnath touched a chord within my core.

Sarnath is a destination for many faiths and cultures like the Hindus, Budddhists and Jains. It is the place where Gautama Buddha first taught the Dharma; then Buddhist Sangha had originated here and came into existence because of the enlightenment of Kondanna. One kilometre away from Sarnath is the village Singhpur where Shreyansanath was born. He was known as the eleventh Tirthankara of Jainism. This is why Sarnath has also been an important pilgrimage site for Jains.

After Gautama Buddha attained enlightenment at Bodh Gaya, Bihar, he came to Sarnath. At Sarnath, he preached his first discourse in the deer park. And with that discourse he set in motion the "Wheel of the Dharma."

We visited the Archaeological Museum at Sarnath which was built for placing and protecting the historical artifacts, located near the archaeological ruins across the road. It has various ancient objects from the Buddhist arts, images of Hindu Gods etc and consists of five galleries and two verandahs.

Emperor Ashoka visited Sarnath around 234 BC and erected a stupa here. Several Buddhist structures were raised at Sarnath between the 3rd century BC and the 11th century AD. This place was later raided by the Turks and most of the stupas were demolished or left in ruins.

Apart from the Buddhist importance that this place holds, Sarnath has also been famous for housing the Lion Capital or the Ashoka Pillar from which the Governemnt of India adopted the Emblem of India on 26 January 1950. Emperor Ashoka the Great, guided by his first wife, Vidisha Devi erected the Lion capital to mark the spot where Buddha first taught the Dharma. Forming an integral part of the emblem is the motto inscribed below the abacus *"Satyamev Jayate"* meaning "Truth Alone Triumphs."

The emblem has four Asiatic lions standing back to back—symbolizing power, courage, pride, and confidence—mounted on a circular base. At the bottom it has one horse and a bull. At its centre it has a beautiful wheel (Dharma chakra). The abacus girded with a frieze of sculptures in high relief of an elephant (of the east), a bull (of the west), a horse (of the south), and a lion (of the north). This emblem is preserved in Sarnath Museum.

Sarnath made me feel relaxed and I felt overwhelmed by a feeling of peace from within. It left a deep impact on me.

Chapter 6

A Feel of Central Asia - Uzbekistan, then and now

Around November 2003, we got an opportunity to organize an international conference at Tashkent, the capital city of Uzbekistan. But before going further I would like to give some background of the region and the people who live there.

In the middle Paleoloithic period from 100000 to 35000 years ago people in Central Asia were isolated from Europe and elsewhere by ice sheets, seas and swamps. The Homo Sapiens neandertalensis remains found at Aman Kutan cave near Samarkand date roughly 100000 to 40000 years ago and are the earliest known human remains in Central Asia.

Central Asia's recorded history begins in 6th century BC, when the large Achemenid Empire of Iran held satrapies beyond the Amu-Darya river ie Sogdiana, Khorezm and Saka.

In 330 BC, Alexander the Great defeated the last Achemenid Darius III. In 329 BC he crossed Amu-Darya and occupied Central Asia.

In 138 BC, Chinese general Chang Chien came to Farghana desiring to purchase famous Farghana Heavenly horses, which as per legend sweated blood. He noticed that the local merchants showed a great deal of interest in his dress made of silk. Parthia was the most voracious foreign consumer of Chinese silk at the close of 2nd century BC. After this Parthia silk was going to Rome. In about 105 BC, Parthia and China set up embassies and started official bilateral trade along the caravan route that lay between them. With this the famous Silk route was born.

In the 1st Century BC, the Kushans, descendents of Chinese Yue Zhin tribe controlled northern India. Afghanistan and Sogdiana formed its core in

Ghandara region. At the height in the first centuries after Christ it was one of the four great powers of the world along with China and Parthia. For a thousand years after that Central Asia was the scene of pendulum like shifts of power between the nomadic hordes of the heartland (South Siberia) and the sedentary civilizations of Eurasia's periphery. Both sought to profit from Central Asia's long distance trade routes. Meanwhile, the Turks appeared on the scene at this time. In 3rd century AD Sogdiana was occupied by Sussanids of Iran. They lost their possessions in the 4th century to the Huns. The Huns were followed by the Turks of Turk Khanate in 6th century. In the 8th century the Arabs came to Central Asia and converted people to Islam. By the 9th century Central Asia had given rise to peaceful and affluent Sumanid Dynasty. By early 10th century, internal strife at court had weakened the Samanid Dynasty and opened the door for two Turkic tribes to divide the empire, the Ghaznevids in Khorasan south of Amu Darya and the Qarakhanids in Transoxiana and the steppe region beyond Syra-Darya. In 1219 Genghis Khan brought his two hundred thousand army and conquered whole of Central Asia. After his death in 1227 his empire was divided into three parts. Central Asia went mostly to Chagatay, the second son of Genghis Khan.

The fracturing of the Mongol empire immediately led to resurgence of the Turkic people. From one of the minor tribes near Samarkand rose the tyrant Timur also known as Tamerlane.

After assembling an army and wresting Transoxiana from Chagatay rule, Timur went on a nine year rampage which ended in 1395 with modern day Iran, Iraq, Syria, Turkey and Caucasus all victims of his blood lust. He also despoiled Northern India. The founder of India's Moghul Dynasty was Babur, his grandson. From 1409 to 1449, Samarkand was governed by the conqueror's mild, scholarly grandson, Ulugbek. In 1500, Muhammad Sheybani brought the Uzbeks to Central Asia. He defeated the last Timurids and established control over most territory of Central Asia. After them in mid 18th century three Uzbek dynasties divided empire into three parts, the Kungrats established Khiva Khanate, the Mangits controlled Bukhara Emirates and the Mings had Kokand Khanate. Meanwhile, on the northern territories there was the Great Horde of the nomad Kazaks.

In 1864, Kokand was occupied by the Russians, a people who had Nordic and Slav ancestry; in 1865 Tashkent also fell. In 1868, Bukhara was made a protectorate. Khiva Khanate fell in 1873. The battle of Geok Tepe in 1881 was the main event in the 1880-81 Russian campaign to conquer the Tekke Turkomans. Its effect was to give the Russian Empire control over most of what is now Turkmenistan, thereby nearly completing the Russian conquest of Central Asia.

After the great October Revolution, also called Bolshevik Revolution in 1917, the second and last major phase of the Russian Revolution, the Bolshevik Party seized power in Russia, inaugurating the Soviet regime. On the territory of Central Asia five Soviet Republics appeared: the Uzbek and the Turkmen SSR in 1924, the Tajik SSR in 1929, the Kyrgyz and Kazak SSR in 1936. But in 1991 all Central Asia countries proclaimed their independence. By end of the year Soviet Union collapsed. On 25 December 1991, the hammer and sickle flag of the Soviet era was lowered for the last time at the Kremlin.

Visit to Tashkent, Bukhara and Samarkand

I embarked on a day flight from Delhi for Tashkent. We were to be a part of a major International Conference we were organizing there. We had a separate immigration clearance at the Airport, since these were all VIPs and we were out of the airport in no time.

It was a time when not many people from India were visiting Uzbekistan. Apart from the action packed time in Tashkent during the Conference we did manage to find some time to explore Tashkent. Converting a few hundred dollars you got a big bundle of Soms. While changing money in the hotel, we would not even count it and make payment where required.

My wife, Neeru had to join me a day before the conference to assist in the arrangements. I told the main organizer, Mansur that my wife would be coming the following day and he knew that I would not be able to make it to the airport. He said: "CP do not worry, the actual VIP is coming. She would be well received." Her name was announced in the aircraft to come forward and there was a car waiting for her at the tarmac. She was taken in the car and was out of immigration in no time and driven straight to the hotel.

Tashkent the capital of Uzbekistan is the biggest, modern and most cosmopolitan city of Central Asia. Since 2500 years people have been living here where the western tip of Tien Shan pans out into the Kizul Kum. After independence in 1991, the city made a rapid progress in economical and industrial field; however the glimpses of the ancient history, traditions and culture exist till today. There has been a settlement on the Chirchik river since the 1st century AD though it was called Chach or Shash until 8th century. Later it was called Binkath in 8th and 9th centuries and Tashkent (city of stone) in the 11th century. Historically, it was a strategically important, well-defended crossroad on the Silk Road and it is the most likely location of a stone tower marking the midpoint between Europe and China that was mentioned in Ptolemy's Geography.

We started our tour visiting Monument of Courage. Tashkent was the fourth largest city in the Soviet Union but it changed forever in 1966 when a catastrophic earthquake struck. The city had to be almost completely rebuilt and has a curious blend of Islamic and Soviet influences. The monument was erected in 1976 and was dedicated to the 10th anniversary of the devastating earthquake. It is located at the probable epicentre of the earthquake and shows that it was right at the centre of the city and that it caused significant damage. It shows parents with a baby in nightgowns and a clock that indicates 5:24 AM. Around 100 people lost their lives and around 300,000 people were left homeless after the earthquake. Since Uzbekistan was part of the Soviet Union at that time, the government involved all 15 Soviet republics to rebuild the city. The monument became a symbol of courage for the people; even a terrible earthquake could not wipe out the city. It is a memorial to the fighting spirit of simple people who would support each other in the hardest of times and no one would be left alone.

A visit to Tashkent would be incomplete without a visit to the Chorsu Bazaar. It is very interesting to walk around the market and get a feel of local life. On counters of the Bazaar you will find fresh fruits, dried fruits, spices, vegetables, bread (*lepeshka*) and horse meat. Also are available here traditional souvenirs like *kurpacha* (colourful sitting mattresses), skullcaps, *chapan* (traditional quilted cloaks) and ceramics. There are bakeries that make *lepeksha*. Shopkeepers are friendly to visitors and make the experience even more memorable.

The large blue dome is the central part of the bazaar and was built in the traditional style with blue glazed tiles in 1970s.

Amir Timur square is the centre of Tashkent. There are four major roads from this point leading to different parts of the city. The square was established in 1882 by the order of Russian military general Mikhail Chernyaev. In the centre of the square is the monument dedicated to Amir Temur or Tamerlane, the great ruler and conqueror. The square is a good representation of new and old buildings from the Tsarist, Soviet and modern eras, in combination with the historical figure of Amir Temur.

Tashkent has a good choice of museums to visit. One of the most remarkable ones is the Applied Arts State Museum. It was a house built in 1898 in traditional style by artisans from Tashkent, Samarkand, Bukhara and Ferghana for Alexander Polovstev, a wealthy tsarist diplomat. It has a beautiful collection of suzanis or traditional embroideries, displays masterpieces of handicrafts, ceramics, jewellery and musical instruments. The museum is compact and does not require much time, but to see more of applied arts and paintings, it is better to head to the State Art Museum of Uzbekistan. Museum of History has more than 200,000 artifacts, including a Buddha statue from the 1st century BC.

We had heard a lot about the Tashkent metro. We took a ride in the metro mainly to experience it. It was started in 1977. These metro stations are supposed to be most beautiful in the world. Every station shows a part of Uzbekistan's history and depict stories through portraits, plaques or architectural features.

Donkey carts seemed to be quite a common mode of transportation. Donkeys are tiny and also have a saddle on top of them, where at times the cart driver could be seen sitting and driving the cart. Whilst we were walking on the road, the driver of a donkey cart stopped me; started calling me "Jimmy, Jimmy!" and was dancing. Later, I found out that he was talking about Mithun Chakraborty, an Indian actor, who had become a cult figure thereafter the popularity of his movie *Disco Dancer*. "Jimmy Jimmy Jimmy Aaja" was a song in the movie.

One evening we went to a local restaurant for dinner. We ordered some vegetarian plov and vegetable. Suddenly Joshi, a colleague who was also there and on his first visit abroad, whispered in my ear "Be careful, they also serve and eat horse meat." On the next table there was an Uzbek family; their child of about five years came upto me and would not go back to them; may be because I was wearing my mink Russian cap.

A cultural evening was organized by the Indian Embassy for us. The General Manager of the hotel was an admirer of India. He took personal care and ensured a delicious Indian buffet for dinner. A team of Uzbek artists had specially come from Bukhara; they were playing Indian musical instruments such as harmonium and mridangam. I got to know they had learnt by watching video cassettes, with no formal training from a music teacher. Zubanesa was singing Hindi songs; dressed in a saree, she looked very much an Indian. When I met her after the programme, she could not speak Hindi at all, but sang well. She had also learnt to sing by rehearsing listening to Hindi songs. Dancers from Bukhara gave a spectacular performance with energy and passion. The traditionally graceful, swaying movements and slow rotations were mesmerizing.

After the conference we had some time in hand. We took a flight from Tashkent for Bukhara. It was a short flight in an old plane of the Russian era and quite noisy. The pilot was highly qualified and the landing was absolutely smooth, much better than the landings of modern jet aircrafts.

Our driver Mohammed was there to receive us with Zubanesa, the girl whom we had met singing during the cultural programme in Tashkent. She had decided to show us the city. We paid a short visit to her place; they offered us black tea (*kora-choy*) in beautifully hand crafted tea cups. It was like a dream come true and memories of the silk route flashed back and it was live revision of what one had learnt in school.

Bukhara is an ancient oasis city along the fabled Silk Road and it is said that the sun shines up from the city for it is so noble. The name comes from the Sanskrit word *Vihara* meaning monastery. For centuries it was a centre of trade and Islam, earning the title Bukhoro-i-Sharif. The city itself boasts of impressive architecture and history. It is one of the few places in Central Asia where one can feel the heartbeat of ancient Central Asia.

The city was founded in the 1st century AD. By the time of its capture by Arabs in the early 8th century, Bukhara had become an important trade and cultural centre. It was a leading centre of Islamic learning under the Arabs and the Persian Samanid dynasty, which held the city in the 9th and 10th centuries. It later was captured successively by the Qarakhanids and Tatars and in 1555 it became the capital of an Uzbek emirate. The emirate was conquered in 1866 by Russia, which held it as a protectorate from 1868 to 1920. Then the emir was removed and the city was made the capital of the Bukhara People's Soviet Republic. From 1924 to 1991 the city was incorporated into the Uzbek Soviet Socialist Republic till the time Uzbekistan became an independent republic in 1991.

The best part about Bukhara is that many of the historical sites are within walking distance.

Our first stop was Kalyan Minaret also known as the Tower of Death; the 48 metre, baked brick tower was constructed in 1127. With an ornate gallery at its top and glazed designs etched into the exterior, the tower was known for its impressive dimensions and its artistry. When Genghis Khan arrived around 100 years after the minaret's construction, local legend has it that the Khan looked from the base of the spire to the top and the steep angle caused his hat to fall off. Admiring the audacity of the tower, although known to be ruthless, he spared this tower. The tower has been used as an observatory and during times of war, it served as a lookout to watch for invading armies. The tower was used for carrying out executions of criminals, the last known execution took place during the last stages of the Russian Revolution in 1920.

The Ark fortress is the most ancient archaeological monument in Bukhara. The legendary Siyavush, whom Firdousi glorified in his famous epic Shahname, is supposed to have constructed the fortress. The Ark was an ancient government seat. In front of the fortress there is a square named Registan.

Bolo Hauz Mosque is a beautiful mosque. It was built in 1721 with money donated by rich Bukhara residents. The mosque looks elegant and splendid, since it was built for the ruler's visits. It features 20 pillars that hold up its ceiling. The pillars are wooden and are all over covered with artful carvings.

Chor Minor meaning four minarets also known as the Madrasah of Khalif Niyaz-kul, is a historic mosque. It is located in a lane northeast of the Lyab-i Hauz complex. It is protected as a cultural heritage monument and also it is a part of the World Heritage Site Historic Centre of Bukhara. Right across are some small shops from where I bought a mink cap from a young girl, who spoke fluent English. When I asked her how was it that she knew the language so well prompt came the reply, " I learnt it from tourists."

As regards the towers of Chor Minor, three of them were used for storage and one has a staircase leading to the top floor. All of them are topped by domes covered by blue ceramic tiles. Each of the four towers has different ornamental motifs. Some say that elements of decoration reflect the four religions known to Central Asians. One can find elements reminiscent of a cross, a Christian fish motif and a Buddhist prayer wheel, in addition to Zoroastrian and Islamic motifs.

Lyabi-Khauz Ensemble is a beautiful pond area, is the popular name given to one of the peculiar architectural ensembles in Bukhara which is also the city's main attraction. In ancient Bukhara the "khauz" meaning pond was the main source of water supply and each residential district had its own khauz. The biggest and the most important khauz - Lyabi Khauz, was built in 1620 next to the Shakhrud canal on the instructions of Nadir Devanbeghi, a courtier. It is located in the centre of historical district with lot of shops and cafes.

Next morning after a five hour drive we reached Samarkand. En route we stopped at a tea stall; we needed sugar tried to explain to the stall owner using all kinds of words to explain him to get sugar but nothing worked. We asked our driver to come to our rescue. He asked him to get *"shakkar"*, a word commonly used for sugar in India!

Upon capturing Samarkand in 329 BC, Alexander the Great reportedly exclaimed, "Everything I have heard about the beauty of Samarkand is true except it is even more beautiful than I could have imagined." Soon afterwards he declared himself a god.

Samarkand, being kind of an old greybeard among other cities of the world, embodies the stories of countries and nations and shows how time influences generations of people. Just like the locations of the first civilizations – Rome, Athens, Babylon, Alexandria, Byzantium, and Memphis – Samarkand's fate was to go through dangerous upheavals that would test its strength and the resilience of its citizens.

Because of geographic location, some cities along the Silk Road were convenient resting stops and transfer points of goods from one caravan to another. Samarkand was one such city and so it was attractive to rulers throughout Central and West Asia who wished to control the lucrative trade.

The city of Samarkand has been at the crossroads of world cultures for over two and a half millennia and is one of the most important sites on the Silk Route traversing Central Asia. Located in the Zerafshan River valley, in north-eastern Uzbekistan, the city enjoys the benefits of abundant natural resources and settlements in the region can be traced back to 1500 BC.

The city was later ruled by Central Asian Turks in 6th century, the Arabs in 8th century, the Samanids of Iran in 9th and 10th century and various Turkic peoples between 11th and 13th century before it was annexed by the Khwarezm Shah dynasty in the early 13th century. It was later destroyed by the Mongol conqueror Genghis Khan in 1220. After it revolted against its Mongol rulers in 1365, Samarkand became the capital of the empire of Timur (Tamerlane), who made the city the most important economic and cultural centre in Central Asia. Samarkand was conquered by Uzbeks in 1500 and became part of the Khanate of Bukhara. By the 18th century, it had declined and from the 1720s to the 1770s, it was uninhabited. Only after it became a provincial capital of the Russian Empire in 1887, and with the arrival of the railway in 1888, Samarkand became an important centre for the export of wine, dried and fresh fruits, cotton, rice, silk, leather and it recovered economically. It was also the capital of the Uzbek Soviet Socialist Republic between 1924 and 1936. Samarkand consists of an old city from medieval times and a new area built after the Russian conquest of the area in the 19th century.

Since then the city has been part of the Persian, Seleucid, Greco-Bactrian, Kushan and Hun Empires. The people who have lived there and the religions they have followed are no less comprehensive. In the pre-Islamic era one would have found evidence of Zoroastrianism, Buddhism, Hinduism, Judaism and Nestorian Christians. It was declared a world heritage site by UNESCO in 2001.

We went to Registan Square; it became the new centre of Samarkand after Afrosiab was destroyed by the invading Mongols. Since then it has been Samarkand's central square. It was a place where important announcements were made and even executions were carried out here. It is a place for celebrations and tourists come here to see the numerous important buildings.

Ulugbek Madrasa on the west side is the oldest, finished in 1420 under Ulugbek. Beneath the little corner domes were lecture halls and at the rear a large mosque. About 100 students lived in two storeys of dormitory cells, which were in good condition. The other buildings were imitations by the Shaybanid Emir Yalangtush. The entrance portal of Sher Dor Madrasa opposite Ulugbek's and finished in 1636 is decorated with roaring tigers. In between is the Tilla Kari Madrasa, completed in 1660, with a pleasant garden like mosque courtyard.

Shahi Zinda translates as living king; this site is a fitting memorial place for the nobility of Samarkand. It is one of the oldest and longest-running examples of a continually constructed historic site in the world. The site was used for burials from the 12th to the 19th centuries with most of its mausoleums built between the 14th and 15th centuries. Various temples, mausoleums and buildings were continually added throughout the ensuing centuries from approximately the 11th century to the 19th. The result is a fascinating cross-reference of various architectural styles, methods, and decorative craftsmanship as they have changed throughout a millennium of work. The *Living King* to which the name refers was the cousin of the Prophet of Islam named Kusam ibn Abbas, who is said to have brought Islam to this area. It is also an important place for pilgrimage. Except for a few early tombs the rest belong to Timur's and Ulugbek's family and personal favourites.

The gigantic congregational Bibi Khanum Mosque in the north east of Registan Square, is the largest of its kind in central Asia, measuring 109 x 167 metres and capable of hosting nearly 10,000 worshippers. Even in ruins, it was easily the tallest building in Samarkand until the late 20th century. Intended as the congregational (Friday) mosque of Timur's beloved Samarkand, it never truly fulfilled its promise as it was beset from the beginning by structural flaws that became apparent almost as soon as it was constructed. It was built under the orders of Tamerlane, who was very demanding and ordered it to be torn down several times before he was satisfied with the result. Almost a hundred elephants were brought to Samarkand from India, on one of Tamerlane's conquests to help with the heavy lifting. It is said that when Timur looked upon the completed entrance (*iwan*) he was dissatisfied with the height and ordered it to be brought down, executing the amirs responsible for the construction.

One of the enduring legends about the place suggests that it was actually Tamerlane's wife who wanted to surprise the ruler with a magnificent mosque. She ordered the best architect to work on the project, but he fell in love with beautiful Bibi Khanum and refused to complete it without a kiss as a reward. As her answer she brought forty painted eggs and pointed out that they all looked different but inside they were the same. She offered other girls but he turned them down, saying that if he had forty buckets filled with water and one with wine, only one could turn his head. Beaten, she agreed to a kiss on the cheek. Right before he reached her she put a pillow in between them, but his kiss was so passionate that it still left a mark on her cheek. Ashamed of the mark, the queen ordered all women to cover their faces. When Tamerlane found out about the kiss, he ordered both of them to be thrown from the minaret. Wings appeared upon the shoulders of the architect as he stood on top of the minaret and he flew away. The Queen asked for permission to wear all her silk dresses at once. Thus, when she jumped they cushioned her fall or maybe even served as a parachute. It is one of the jewels of Taimur's empire. It collapsed in an earthquake in 1897 and was restored after Uzbekistan's independence.

Guri Amir is a mausoleum of Amir Timur, his two sons and two grandsons, including Ulugbek. It occupies an important place in the history of Turko-Persian architecture as the precursor and model for later great Mughal architecture tombs, including Humayun's Tomb in Delhi and the Taj Mahal in Agra, built by Timur's Persianized descendants, the ruling Mughal dynasty of North India. It has been heavily restored. Amir Timur wanted to be buried in a simple tomb in his home town of Shakhrisabz, where he was born. When he died on his way to China in 1405, he was buried here, because the passes to Shakrisabz were snowed and the passage inaccessible.

Ulugbek Observatory is one of the important observatories in the world of the middle ages, built by Ulugbek in 1420s. There was a marble sextant here. The device which was under the ground is well preserved. The arc of the instrument is made of marble with two barriers. Ulugbek the grandson of Amir Timur, was less interested in conquering the earth than gazing at stars and he became more famous as an astronomer than a ruler. In Ulugbek Observatory worked such outstanding astronomers as Al Kashi and Ali Qushji. Despite being a brilliant astronomer Ulugbek was beheaded in 1449 and the observatory was destroyed. It was rediscovered in 1908.

A short walk to the north of Registan Square and next to the monumental remains of the Bibi Khanum Mosque, one reaches Siyob Bazaar, Samarkand's most important and largest market. Part covered and part open-air, the bazaar is largely modern in appearance but in many ways provides a direct link to the city's ancient trading heritage. Covering a vast area, this is a true marketplace of the eastern tradition selling everything from fruit, vegetables, herbs and spices to dried fruits, sweets, local breads and nuts. Those travelling the Silk Road brought handicrafts as well as fresh produce, such as peaches and melons from the nearby Zarafshan Valley. Many of these same goods can be found at the bazaar today.

By the time we finished our exploration, a full moon was up and Registan Square was bathed in soft moon light.

After a little over a four hour drive from Samarkand we reached Tashkent International Airport. When we came from Delhi it was an Air Bus we had travelled in. When we reached the Airport, it was J.N. Dixit, who was a down-to-earth person and a former Ambassador, helping me to collect the passports during immigration. Later he became the National Security Advisor, Government of India.

We boarded an Ilyushin aircraft. These aircrafts were also used by the Soviet Military for delivering heavy machinery to remote areas, aerial refueling and as a command centre. Experience was so different from our last flight: the seats were not so comfortable for a passenger aircraft and it did give a feeling of flying in a military aircraft. While the aircraft was getting ready to taxi, I was looking for a place to put my cabin baggage. There was an Israeli gentleman sitting next to me. Probably a regular on these flights, he put my bag on a vacant seat. The air hostess had no objection to that. It was a different but enjoyable flight experience.

Chapter 7

A Peerless Island and Majestic Mountains: Mauritius and Bhutan

The visit to Mauritius was not planned. One day Rajiv Bajaj, my friend with Air Mauritius, asked me if I would like to visit Mauritius. At times things not planned work out better much to our pleasant surprise. And that is how it was in July 2005. For Indians visa is given on arrival; there was no reason for delay and so I along with a couple of friends shortly embarked on a flight for Port Louis, the capital of Mauritius.

Mauritius, an Indian Ocean island nation, is known for its beaches, lagoons and reefs.

A large community in Mauritius is of people of Indian origin. People from British India, during the beginning, first arrived in Mauritius to work as indentured labourers, commonly referred to as coolies, who mainly worked in sugarcane fields. Mauritius took about 450,000 such labourers making it the greatest British colony recipient of indentured migrants.

We checked in at Hotel Maritim, a resort type property. In the evening we were at the beach for dinner, with nicely laid out tables. When we sat down to eat the manager announced that the Chef was on leave and we would have to cook dinner ourselves. We were taken by surprise.

All raw materials were ready, with cooking pans and aprons for us to wear. Someone like me who has never cooked was in a bit of a fix; the best I had done was to make tea and perhaps salad once in a way. One of the chefs came to my rescue and helped me make some dishes. It was a great experience. We all enjoyed this.

Next morning we went to Il Aux Cerfs by speedboat from the jetty; it is a lagoon on the eastern coast. It is a place for all kinds of adventure on surface and underwater. We took part in para-sailing, snorkeling, skiing and undersea walk. Undersea walk was a great underwater experience; we literally walked on the ocean's floor while admiring the sensational marine life adding colour to the environment. We were taken under water by experienced guides and were wearing oxygenated 'helmets.' On completion of this exhilarating experience we were given certificates for doing the undersea walk.

In the evening we were having our dinner. During the course of conversation, Rahman our host remembered that I was a keen rider and had also played polo. I was aware that the resort had horses. Much after midnight he looked me up and asked if I would like to go for a ride in the morning. Since it was late at night I hesitantly nodded my head. I had not slept for too long when I was woken up by an early morning call; "Sir, Good morning, wake up call for you for riding." A car picked me up and I was there at the stables. The resort had an excellent facility for riding and well bred horses.

The Manager of horses, Nath, had been a jockey at the Champ de Mars race course, a thoroughbred horse race track in Port Louis. It was founded in 1812, making it the oldest race track in the southern hemisphere, and one of the oldest in the world. Nath was delighted to welcome me. I did tell him that I had been riding for quite some time. Soon he gave me a black stallion to ride, which had retired from racing.

Slowly we moved on the beach. Started walking the horse, trot, then broke into a canter. Nath felt comfortable and was convinced that I could ride well and soon we were galloping on the beach. It was a dream come true, something I had always wanted to do; gallop on the beach with waves passing by.

Later we went outside the resort for a long ride and Nath told me a lot of stories about the horses and people of the island. We were walking back and Rahman was quite amused to see me riding. He met us during breakfast and announced that "CP was riding and no one was holding the horse!!"

Our guide for rest of the trip was a young lady named Rita who came and picked us up from the hotel. She started the tour giving us a brief description of Mauritius and background of people on the island and her ancestors. We started the North Island tour with a visit to the Botanical Garden which is a home to a large variety of tropical plants. It has over 650 varieties of plants. Next stop was Sugar Estate and Museum; here one could listen to the stories on importance of sugar in Mauritius.

Port Louis, apart from being the capital of Mauritius is the largest city. We saw beautiful French colonial buildings the notable being the Government House and the Municipal Theatre. The busy Port Louis Waterfront offers exciting shopping and entertainment venues as also world class hotels and restaurants.

The craft market and Port Louis central market are great places to visit and pick up local products. We took a leisurely walk and saw the Anglican and Catholic cathedrals, the main city Mosque, Chinatown, the Supreme Court house, the 18th century Barracks and the Natural History Museum are all in close vicinity.

We went up Fort Adelaide also known as La Citadelle. It offers a panaromic view of Port Louis and its harbour.

The following day we toured South of Mauritius. It is famous for its many nature reserves, breathtaking scenery, nature, mountains, parks and plenty of attractions.

The Crocodile & Giant Tortoises Park is set in a beautiful rain forested valley with natural fresh water springs. It is home to various species of animals, reptiles and plants. There are thousands of Nile crocodiles in the park. A unique experience was an encounter with the giant tortoises and turtles. We got a chance to feed and play with them. The park also has a rare collection of butterflies.

The village of Gris Gris is located on the southern tip of Mauritius. This place is probably named after a puppy of a French cartographer Abbott de la Caille, who surveyed the island in the middle of the 18th century. This part of the island is not surrounded by coral reefs and this is why thick waves crash directly on the cliffs. It has spectacular cliffs that drop abruptly amid beautiful beaches and strong winds blowing from the Indian Ocean.

Bois Cheri is the first tea plantation in Mauritius that dates back to 1892 and is the biggest tea producer in Mauritius. We were taken on a guided tour of the factory and the tea plantation. It was a great opportunity to discover the history, stories of Boi Cheri and the importance of tea production in Mauritius. Tea production museum gives in detail the history of tea in Mauritius. It offers a panoramic view of the southern part of the island.

Saint Aubin House is an elegant plantation house that was built in 1819. It was built from wood of dismantled ships; the plantation is an homage to a life in Mauritius that no longer exists. The estate no longer produces sugar, but in the gardens of the house there is a traditional rum distillery. We got a chance to discover the vanilla plantation of the estate and the interesting transformation process of vanilla orchid from flower to the aromatic pod.

Grand Bassin also known as Ganga Talao is located in the mountainous southwest region of Savanne in Mauritius. It sits approximately 550 metres above sea level and is said to have a depth of 18 metres, its waters teeming with an abundance of fish and eels. However fishing is strictly prohibited given the spiritual significance of the site.

It is a sacred lake, which according to legend, is connected to the holy river Ganges in India. Ganga Talao is a place for Hindus to meditate, chant, make offerings and pray and it serves as an important pilgrim site during Maha Shivaratri. Beside the lake there is a temple dedicated to Lord Shiva and other Gods including Hanuman, Lakshmi, and others.

The last day I was lucky enough to have an opportunity to experience swimming with the dolphins!

Having spent enough time working at sea had been seeing dolphins all the time and being an underwater specialist I knew dolphins as highly intelligent and active mammals. They utilize sonar to their advantage when navigating through the ocean. Sonar is also referred to as echolocation and it provides dolphins with an advantage of hearing and detecting things with precision. Apart from detecting objects in the water, dolphins also depend on sonar to communicate with one another, including their young. Sonar not only helps dolphins to hear, but it gives them a clearer picture of objects underwater.

Very early the next morning we were in the car leaving for Grand Baie. After a short drive, the sun started to show itself as we headed South through Port Louis. It was a pleasant drive and on the way we passed through small villages and we could see locals starting their day, with some small tea shops opening and fishing boats sailing into the sea for their morning catch. We arrived at the meeting point, in the little town of Riviere Noire (Black River) by about 7 AM. On arriving we met the representative from the boat company and soon we were on our way to Tamarin Bay to see the dolphins.

The boat captain and the crew were an interesting lot. They briefed us in general, about safety measures in the boat and about sustainable dolphin watching. The Bottlenose Dolphin and the Spinner Dolphin have made the West Coast of Mauritius a place for them to rest and sleep before going to the deep sea for their fishing.

One would imagine that swimming with the dolphins would be being with tamed mammals; well here it is an experience to swim with wild dolphins. They practically swim all over you, communicating with each other.

There were many boats around us but I was the only one who jumped in the water wearing a mask and flippers. There were two trained divers in the water as a safety measure. It was one of the finest experiences and I was literally swimming with them. Divers sense the movement of dolphins underwater, with a hawk eye and guide you to see them. I had the feeling as if they were playing with me and were whizzing past, some of them coming as close as three to four metres. You could see a number of them in the vicinity.

There was another consequence of my jumping and swimming in water. Devesh, a friend of mine was so impressed and motivated that when I met him a few months later, he told me that he had started learning swimming. It was not bad for a person to do so in his forties.

All said and done, it was truly a sublime experience and a fitting way to end the visit to the beautiful Mauritius Islands.

Giving Back to Society

Much before my trip to Mauritius, there were many things running in my mind. There was a strong urge building up in me to do something for the less fortunate in our society. As I would often tell my friends when we are surrounded by millions of poor and people struggling to make ends meet, how can we close our eyes to this stark reality?

I have always told my family and friends that we have to count one's blessings. However, I could actually concretize my inner desire to give back to society after many years and after some exposure to institutional charity work. This happened towards the end of 2006 making the year a milestone year in my life.

I had become a Rotarian in 1999 on the behest of Mr Sudarshan Agarwal, who retired as the Governor of Uttarakhand and Sikkim. I met him a few times at a common friend's place. One evening Mr Agarwal handed me a form to become a member of Rotary Club of Delhi. He proposed my name for membership and soon my application was approved. At this stage, I had no idea what Rotary was all about. After becoming a member of Rotary Club of Delhi, I was initiated in Rotary projects and activities. After spending a few years in this club, I decided to resign as I felt I was not contributing anything worthwhile. Almost after a year a friend and a well wisher, Pulin Trivedi asked me to join Rotary Club of New Delhi of which he was a member. There has been no looking back after switching over to Rotary Club of New Delhi. It gave me an opportunity to meet professionals with diverse backgrounds, exchange ideas and make lifelong friends. Most importantly, it gave me an insight into what it was like to serve and to give back to society.

Rotary started with the vision of one man, Paul Harris, a Chicago Attorney on 23rd February 1905. Rotary is an organization of business and professional leaders who provide humanitarian service, encourage high ethical standards and help build goodwill and peace in the world. There are more than 34,000 clubs in 200 countries and over 1.2 million members worldwide. Rotary has definitely played a great role in my life to appreciate what charity was all about and helping people in need.

Rotary Club of New Delhi is a dynamic and vibrant club with friendly members. Our club has been undertaking various projects like supporting schools, carrying out health camps, water harvesting, installing computer labs, blood donation camps, starting a major skill development centre, student exchange programmes and helping many needy individuals. Rotary has been one of the main organizations involved in eradicating polio from India and many other parts of the world. Our club has had a regular involvement in this project.

The Birth of Neptune Foundation

One afternoon I was taking a flight and my son Dhruv had volunteered to drop me to the Airport; he was studying in first year of college. We got into a discussion and I asked him what we could do to help people in need. Dhruv said that we should start an NGO (Non-governmental organization) to look after girls from poor backgrounds and their education in particular. With this thought and idea from Dhruv, Neptune Foundation was founded in 2006.

Neptune Foundation is an endeavour at making a difference, an effort at bridging the gap and awakening the sensibilities of today's materialistic individual. It is an initiative to make this world a better place where basic dignity is not the privilege of a blessed few. Meant to aid those less fortunate, Neptune Foundation's mandate is now broader including caring for the girl child and the aged, and to save the dying art forms in villages.

Just a few days after we had started Neptune Foundation, I happened to meet Professor Ranbir Singh teaching in a college run by a big business house. During our brief conversation we discussed how his college was being supported by the NGO of a business house. I was inspired by the mission of education for all and had started an NGO on my own. We had just started small and were supporting the education of two girls. He was very happy to hear that and told me in case every person in India who could afford it would take on the education of one child there would be no uneducated children in India. His words were a great encouragement.

It has been quite some time that Neptune Foundation has been in existence. We have been doing regular programmes focused on girls, such as on hygiene, AIDS awareness, medical camps, scholarships for the needy and meritorious, awards for the best student in an academic year, and finally vocational training. We have been organizing educational tours, painting competitions, and stationery and books for school.

Regular Charity polo matches are organized by us, which has become an annual event, probably the only polo event for the girl child in India, which has been a great success, giving publicity to our NGO and focussing attention on our cause. The event is attended by celebrities, corporate leaders, defence personnel, bureaucrats, royalty, political leaders, and diplomats, to promote and be a part of Neptune Foundation's cause. One TV Channel reporter during an interview did ask me why I was organizing a charity polo match and was it not elitist. She did not respond when I reminded her that Prince Charles also played polo matches for charity.

My son Dhruv plays an important role in running Neptune Foundation and also takes part in the charity polo matches.

Mahatma Gandhi's granddaughter Tara Gandhi Bhattacharjee on one occasion came to watch one of our charity polo matches. She had been decorated with one of France's top honours the Order of Arts and Letters for her contribution in promoting peace, solidarity, culture, education, and development. She had been working for the Kasturba Gandhi National Memorial Trust, founded by Mahatma Gandhi in memory of his wife to serve needy women and children of rural India. It was such a pleasure talking to her. During the conversation I told her we were focusing on the girl child and their education, apart from other initiatives that we were taking. Her response still rings in my ears when she said that boys needed to be educated more than girls. This indeed is very true, when we read and hear about many atrocities being committed by men on women.

The following day I received a mail from her, thanking me for inviting her to attend the polo match along with her assistant as she was in frail health. In fact it was an honour for us to have the presence of such a renowned personality to grace the occasion and learn from her vast experience in the field of social work.

From our resources, well wishers and needless to mention Rotary Club of New Delhi, of which I am a member we have been able to set up a library, sewing centre and an open gymnasium at Arya Kanya Gurukul located in Rajendra Nagar. We have facilitated complete kitting of the girls newly designed school uniforms. Since it is a residential school, we have tried to increase facilities inside the school, as it is not possible for the girls to go out of the school premises.

In Arya Kanya Gurukul, a trophy has been instituted in the name of my father Capt Faqir Chand for the best all round student in the school; it also carries a cash award. An annual painting competition has become a regular feature and all children and staff eagerly await this event to take place.

We give scholarships to girls from the weaker section of society for education. It is just the beginning; we will endeavour to add more children, and also the aged and others under various programmes that we would undertake in future for the needy. Over 2000 children have benefited till now from our projects and programmes.

Mountains and Happiness: Trip to Bhutan

Bhutan is a land where history and mystery permeates its past. I had read and heard so much about Bhutan and its global standing as one of the happiest places in the world.

It was a pleasant morning in November 2006 when I and a group of friends took off from Delhi by Druk Air, the only airline that was operating to Bhutan those days. We were flying high and enjoying the Bhutanese hospitality on board. After some time the entire Himalayan ranges were in sight from the window. The pilot made an announcement that as the sky was clear we would see Mt Everest, the highest peak in the world, 29028 feet above sea level. It was an amazing sight to see Mt Everest in all its radiant glory. It is a dream of every mountaineer or a traveller to climb or see the magnificent mountain. I was reminded of the book "*Nothing Venture, Nothing Win*" written by Sir Edmund Hillary, a remarkable life story of one of the greatest adventurers of our times. On 29 May 1953, Hillary and Tenzing Norgay became the first climbers to have reached the summit of Mount Everest. They were part of the ninth British expedition to the Everest led by John Hunt.

After some time the aircraft started a steep descent and landed smoothly while we took in the breathtaking view in the narrow valley of Paro.

Some years ago the monarch of Bhutan had explicitly laid down that the country would not follow the typical path of modern economic development which would be secondary to the pursuit of happiness and contentment in the true Buddhist tradition. Even now within the democratic set up, the country follows what it calls gross happiness product ie GHP and not the concept of gross domestic product or GDP commonly seen across the world. The uniqueness of this philosophy was recognized by the UN sometime back and a World Happiness Day was instituted. The Bhutanese government holds a periodic survey among the people to measure the level of "happiness" based on many parameters. Many countries have started their own happiness index but in the western world the parameters still measure material well-being to a large extent unlike the Bhutanese. However, as many journalists have recorded, in recent years external cultural influences have started to impact Bhutanese society specially the youth. But in general the Bhutanese fiercely preserve their traditional culture as far as possible.

Bhutan's first gift to us as we disembarked from the aircraft was cool, clean fresh mountain air. We were received at the airport by our guide Norbu Wangmo. We commenced our drive to Thimpu, covering a distance of 50 kilometres, drove following Pachu river, passing through suburbs and villages of Thimpu. This is probably the only capital in the world with no traffic lights. From the time we landed, we experienced genuine hospitality and politeness of people. Everyone was neatly dressed, looking relaxed and happy.

Coming to Bhutan for Indians is convenient, a voter ID or passport is good enough to enter. The two countries are interwoven and share a lot of common culture and habits. One can pay in Indian Rupees at all places in Bhutan.

We stayed at a traditional hotel. I wanted to make a call to Delhi from the hotel. I asked the receptionist in case I could do so. He said "Sir, the telephone line is disconnected, as the owner has not paid the bill and is travelling to India." It surprised me but typically showed the honesty and simplicity of the local people.

We took a short tour of the city visiting Tashichho Dzong, Thimpu Chorten, Royal Textile Academy of Bhutan, amongst other places. Thimpu Chorten is one of the important landmarks and it welcomed us with traders selling souvenirs, incense and other items for tourists. Royal Textile Academy trains and educates youths on Bhutanese textiles. Importance of textiles can be seen with dress code enforced across Bhutan, men wear a Gho, a knee-length robe tied at the waist and women a Kira, an ankle-length sari-like garment accompanied by a light jacket known as a Tego.

On the following morning we drove to Punakha/Wangduephodrang across Dochu La. Located at a height 10,130 ft, Dochula is a scenic location with chorten and prayer flags which decorate this highest point on the road. Since the sky was clear we saw various beautiful lofty mountains and peaks.

We reached early to visit Punakha Dzong or (Palace of Great Happiness). Our guide, Norbu told us that we would not be able to go inside due to certain time restrictions of entry. I thought we should make an attempt and spoke with the security person at the gate. I requested him to make an exception for us and gave him my military background. He immediately obliged. Norbu was astonished and said that my charm worked. Punakha Dzong was built in 1637 by Shabdrung Ngawang Namgyal; it is located at the junction of the Phochu and Mochu rivers. This majestic dzong served as both the religious and the administrative centre of Bhutan in the past. It has a six-storey, gold-domed tower. We visited the courtyards that hint at the depth of history. It was a fascinating sight to see the monks praying, an embodiment of spiritual tradition that is inherent here.

Later in the afternoon after a short drive through Lobesa we reached Soposkha village. From there walking through the terraced fields we reached Chimi Lhakhang also known as the "Temple of Fertility", situated on a hillock in the centre of the valley. As the name suggests childless couples desirous of having a baby visit this Buddhist shrine to seek blessings. After praying and getting the blessings, it is widely believed that they would be blessed with a child soon. Walking through Soposkha village gave us a rare glimpse of the daily life of the villagers. There were lots of handicraft shops selling thangka paintings and other curios on the way to Chimi Lhakhang.

Chimi Lakhang was built in 1499 by the 14th Drukpa hierarch, Ngawang Choegyel and the site was blessed by the "Divine Madman", Lama Drukpa Kunley, an enlightened Buddhist master who practised the Vajrayana form of Buddhism. He followed a non conventional and outrageous style of teaching. Drukpa Kunley roamed around the countryside and indulged in song and dance, alcohol and women. In short, he meant to go beyond the norms and conventions set by the society.

What immediately captured our attention were murals and graffiti on the walls with giant phalluses. Kids were playing and life seemed to go on in the most normal manner possible. For a moment it felt awkward, but because such murals were almost on every wall it became fun to look at. There were doors with phalluses on both sides and then there were shops with wooden imitations of the male sexual organ.

Among Lama Drukpa Kunley's most important achievements is taming the fierce demon of Dochu La pass. He imprisoned her and buried her in the main chorten where Chimi Lhakhang was built.

The following day after breakfast we drove back to Paro descending back down from Dochu La, following the way back up the dramatic Wang Chhu and Paro Chhu river valleys, before crossing through Paro town towards the north end of the valley.

En route we visited Simtokha Dzong, one of the oldest fortresses of the country and known as the place of profound tantric teaching. It was built in 1629 by Zhabdrung Ngawang Namgyal. This Dzong is said to guard a demon that had vanished into the rock nearby, hence the name Simtokha, from *simmo* (demoness) and *do* (stone). It now houses a school for the study of the Dzongkha language. This was the first structure to incorporate both monastic and administrative facilities and is the oldest dzong to have survived as a complete structure.

After resting for a while in the hotel, later in the day we visited Ta Dzong. Bhutan was threatened with numerous attacks from Tibet in the mid-17th century and the temporal ruler at the time built the Paro Ta Dzong (watch tower) to protect the Paro Rimpung Dzong against these invaders. The watch tower is built above the Paro Dzong. According to history the Dzong's fourth floor was used as a prison cell in the past. A removable bridge connected the prison cell with the third floor and the fifth floor isolating the fourth floor. This strategic design was used to successfully confine the prisoners. An underground passage is said to have existed connecting the Dzong to the Pa Chu River. The secret tunnel was used to fetch water during times of war.

Unlike other Dzongs in the country, the Ta Dzong has a circular shape built with two and a half metre thick wall adorned with traditional windows spread sporadically. The structure is completely built of stones and wood, without the use of nails. After remaining uninhabited for a long time, upon the command of the third King of Bhutan, Jigme Dorji Wangchuck, the Dzong was renovated and inaugurated as Textile Museum in 1968.

The National Museum is a major tourist attraction today. It houses many antiques and precious objects ranging from ancient and modern scroll paintings (Thangkas), earthen, copper and bronze pots dating back to 17th century and variety of swords. There are also exhibits of objects and artifacts relating to insects and animals of Bhutan, ancient arms, weapons and farming tools.

Some of the highlights of the museum's collection include an egg laid by a mule, a horse horn, original iron links used to build the Tamchog suspension bridge and stone axe (Namchag) which was used during warfare and hunting.

From Ta Dzong we took a leisurely walk down the trail to Rinpung Dzong, meaning "fortress of the heap of jewels" which has a long and fascinating history. Along the wooden galleries lining the inner courtyard are fine wall paintings illustrating Buddhist lore such as four friends, the old man of long life, the wheel of life, scenes from the life of Milarepa, Mount Sumeru and other cosmic Mandala. We walked back to the hotel through narrow paths.

On the penultimate day of our stay in Bhutan we made it for a hike to Taktshang Monastery. It is one of the most famous of Bhutan's monasteries and landmark in Bhutan, perched on the side of a cliff 900 metres above the Paro valley floor. It is said that Guru Rinpoche arrived here on the back of a tigress and meditated at this monastery and hence it is called "Tiger's Nest." This site has been recognized as a most sacred place and was visited by Shabdrung Ngawang Namgyal in 1646 and is now visited by all Bhutanese at least once in their lifetime. Having heard various tales from others regarding the hike being easy we went ahead. But it was not as easy as I thought.

We left the hotel early with our guide Norbu. We started our hike; the scenery en route was breath taking. There were a number of people ascending to the Tiger's nest of all ages from the young to the elderly doing the climb at their own pace.

It took us close to three hours to reach the Tiger's Nest; we spent some time looking around and enjoying the magnificent view. Most appreciable part of coming here was the remoteness of this site. After some time, we started on our way down. One would normally imagine coming down would be faster but it took us almost as much time to come down as we had taken to go up. Interestingly, guides and tourists alike would exchange pleasantries and ask how much time they had taken to reach the top. We could hear various durations mentioned by different people. It was a great opportunity and learning experience to undertake this wonderful hike.

In the afternoon we drove to the basc of Drukgyel Dzong, a ruined fortress where Bhutanese warriors fought Tibetan invaders many centuries ago. The snowy dome of sacred Chomolhari, "mountain of goddess" can be seen in all her glory from the approach road to the Dzong. Later we visited the 7th century Kyichu Lhakhang, one of the 108 temples built in the Himalayas by Tibetan King, Songtsen Gampo. The building of this temple marks the introduction of Buddhism in Bhutan.

In the evening we explored the local market and the main street. It is lined with colourfully painted wooden shop fronts and restaurants. Paro is the best Bhutanese town to explore on foot and it is worth strolling and we picked up souvenirs from local shops.

Having waited for many years to visit Bhutan the experience was exhilarating. The Dzongs, the flags flapping, the breathtaking nature and innate friendliness and honesty of Bhutanese; these memories would remain embedded in my mind for a long time. And though not a researcher I was sure I had met the most contented and happiest people in my life.

Chapter 8

Fast Track Europe: Brussels, Luxembourg and Amsterdam

Belgium is located at the western end of the northern European plain, covering an area of 30,510 square kilometres; the neighbouring countries are France, Luxembourg, Germany and the Netherlands.

Belgium is one of the most urbanized and densely inhabited countries in the world with about 97 percent of the 10 million inhabitants living in cities. Brussels the capital has approximately 1 million residents. Interestingly the political symbolism differs with the region and the socio-political environment. The strongest national symbols are the Monarchy and the national soccer team.

In the year 2007, I decided to visit Brussels and a few other nearby towns. I stayed at a hotel centrally located in Brussels knowing that one could easily walk around to see the most touristic places which are located close to the city centre. My guide Oliver was ready to take me around the beautiful city in the morning. To start off he gave some facts a good overview of Belgium and Brussels.

The main languages of Belgium are Dutch and French; they are also the joint official languages. Although German is also recognized as the third national language, it is not used frequently in the national administration.

Belgium is heavily dependent on foreign trade. Belgium is considered to be the world's diamond capital. As per Antwerp World Diamond Centre in 2015 USD 48.3 billion worth diamonds were imported and exported from Antwerp. Belgium is also an important producer of several industrial minerals, including limestone, dolomite, sodium sulphate, silica sand and marble. Livestock raising is the most important single sector of Belgian agriculture accounting for over 60 percent of agricultural production.

Belgian farmers breed some of the finest draft horses in the world including the famous Percherons.

The city of Brussels is the largest municipality of the Brussels-Capital Region and the de jure capital of Belgium. The city of Brussels covers most of the region's centre as well as northern outskirts where it borders municipalities in Flanders.

We started our walking tour at the heart of the upscale Sablon neighbourhood that lies in the Grand Sablon and Petit Sablon squares, neatly divided by the 15th-century Église Notre-Dame. While the big square boasts quality antiquarians and chocolatiers, the smaller version makes for an especially lovely garden.

From Petit Sablon we walked towards the Place Royale, a historic neoclassical square in the Royal Quarter of Brussels. It was built between 1775 and 1782 as part of an urban project including Brussel's Park. It is rectangular and symmetrical in shape and is flanked by some of the main museums in the city including the Magritte Museum which is one of the constituent museums of the Royal Museums of Fine Arts, Art Nouveau, Musical Instruments Museum and Art Deco precursor Bozar.

From Brussel's Park we walked across to the Royal Palace which represents part of Belgium's constitutional monarchy. The Royal Palace of Brussels serves as the official palace where the king welcomes foreign heads of states and conducts events. At the request of Queen Mother Paola, acclaimed conceptual artist Jan Fabre plastered the ceiling and chandelier of the palace's Hall of Mirrors with 1.6 million scarab shields. The intriguing mosaic is titled Heaven of Delight, though Fabre claims to have hidden skull figures in the work as a reference to Belgium's not too gentle colonial past in Congo. It is built on the ruins of Coudenberg Palace, a very old palatial complex dating back to the 11th century.

From the Royal Palace we went to Mont des Arts garden. Oliver explained the Mont des Arts has had quite an eventful history. The park created by Jules Vacherot at the request of Leopold II in the run-up to the Expo of 1910, disappeared under the project of René Pechère as Expo 58 drew near. Oliver suggested that we should stop at TonTon Garby's restaurant which is famous for sandwiches. It was amazing; the owner treated us like old acquaintances. He asked for our preferences of fillings and cheese for sandwiches. It was one of the most delicious sandwiches I had ever had.

After grabbing our sandwiches as we were walking across to Manneken Pis. Some children who were passing by guessed that I was a tourist and asked full of mirth: "You want to see the peeing boy?" Then they gave directions. We both had a laugh. Manneken Pis is Brussel's pride and joy, a small statue of a rebellious boy peeing into a water fountain. The name Manneken Pis was first mentioned in archives dating back to 1452. Before that he was named Petit Julien and was a part of a public fountain on the same street corner. The stone statue was replaced by a bronze sculpture made by Hiëronymus Duquesnoy the Elder in 1619.

A few minutes from Manneken Pis we stopped at Moeder Lambic supposedly the mother of all beer bars. One cannot stay in Brussels without trying some of the famous Belgian beer. This bar has a great collection of awesome Belgian and foreign beers. We ordered a Belgian beer. The atmosphere was great with sweet sounding music playing in the background.

From there we wandered towards Grand Place which is the central square of Brussels. There were a lot of people here. Grand Place is known for its decorative and aesthetic wealth. It is surrounded by the guild houses, the City Hall and the Maison du Roi. It is considered as one of the most beautiful places of the world. The Grand Place of Brussels was registered on the World Heritage list of UNESCO in 1998.

We ended the tour at the Bourse, which is Belgium's 1873 stock-exchange building. It is closed to visitors but one can still enjoy its grandiose neoclassical facade, which is brilliantly festooned with friezes and sculptures, reclining nudes, lunging horses and a multitude of allegorical figures. Some of the work is by Rodin, then a young apprentice sculptor. I bid goodbye to my superb guide Oliver for making my day experiential and a memorable one.

The following morning I took a train to Luxembourg.

Luxembourg: Birth place of Schengen

Luxembourg is the world's last grand duchy since 15 March 1815, a territory whose head of state is a grand duke or grand duchess. The Grand Duke of Luxembourg, His Royal Highness Henri is the monarchial head of state of Luxembourg. Luxembourg is the world's only sovereign grand duchy and since 1815 there have been nine monarchs.

Luxembourg is one of the smallest countries in the world about 2586 square kilometres in area, located between Belgium, Germany and France and is the birthplace of the idea of a unified Europe. The Schengen Agreement is the treaty which led to the creation of Europe's Schengen Area within which internal border checks have largely been abolished. The Schengen Agreement was signed on 14 June 1985 near the town of Schengen in Luxembourg.

Luxembourg's financial sector is the largest contributor to the domestic economy. There are 144 banks in Luxembourg with more than 120 branches and subsidiaries of foreign banks. Since its banks have a high level of liquidity this happens to be the main reason why Luxembourg is Europe's main banking and financial centre. It is the second richest country in the world with GDP per capita of $ 116786 in 2018 as per World Bank. It also has a very liberal tax regime which attracts many top artists, sports people and others to invest or take up residence here.

I had a beautiful train ride from Brussels. I got down at the train station Gare de Luxembourg which is built in Moselle Baroque Revival style and is a marvel in itself. From the Gare de Luxembourg I walked over to the Grand Hotel Cravat. The hotel is a mix of old world charm and modernity. The signature style of the hotel with its marble, period tiling and olive, ochre and gold colour scheme creates a unique atmosphere. Some floors by contrast are modern and high-tech.

I checked in at the hotel and put my bags in the room. With time in hand and being at leisure, I wanted to explore the beautiful city on my own and went on a stroll. While walking I met one gentlemen named Khalid. I approached him wanting to get some directions mainly to the Chocolate house. He asked me where I was from. I told him that I was from India and in response, he told me that he was from Morocco. We were friendly very soon and we sat down at a café for a cup of coffee. It was an interesting conversation that we had for more than an hour. He only spoke French and obviously, his English was not that good. On the contrary, I knew a bit of French but then that was as bad as his English. I had studied French as one of the subjects in the Academy. Although it was quite an effort on my part to converse with him, with some effort I was able to recollect a lot of words of French and that helped the conversation to go on. Khalid talked a lot about Morocco and how he had come here a few years back and what it was like to be staying here. He had moved here alone initially leaving his family behind and then started working in a restaurant. He had now comfortably settled with his family, and his children were going to school.

Interestingly, he was fond of Hindi movies and knew much more than me about the movies and Indian actors. Then we got up and after a short walk we reached the Chocolate House.

We had our lunch at the The Chocolate House of Luxembourg located directly opposite the Grand Ducal Palace in a classic medieval building dating back to the mid 15th century. It is known for it's chocolate of course, but there were cakes and sweets and one could also enjoy savoury pies and salads. When the terrace is full, like it was on that sunny day, one has no option but to sit inside. Sitting inside had its own charm as we had a nice view of the Grand Ducal Palace through the windows.

After a delicious lunch, we took a walking tour of the historic old quarter of the city; it was a good way to familiarize oneself with the city. The tour guide was Francois, who was fantastic and spoke fluent English. I was intrigued by this place, since the beginning. The historic old quarter is one of the World Heritage sites — it includes the beautiful Notre Dame Cathedral, Grand Ducal Palace, Corniche, Monument of Remembrance and Constitution Square. It was an overwhelming experience to actually see what one had read about so much.

The city is so small that one can cover most of the central places by a leisurely walk; there is no requirement for any mode of transport.

The following day, I visited Kirchberg, the financial centre crossing over the Grande-Duchesse Charlotte bridge commonly known as the "red bridge". As Luxembourg is home to one of the key infrastructures of the European capital market, it connects international investors to Europe and European investors to the rest of the world. The financial centre helps the European finance industry to access international capital markets. With an investment fund distribution market covering over 70 countries worldwide, the Grand Duchy also plays a crucial role by attracting big international investors to Europe.

The Grand Duke Museum of Modern Art is the foremost museum dedicated to contemporary art. Famous Sino-American architect Leoh Ming Pei chose the historic site of the Fort Thungen for the construction of the museum. It is ideally located between the Place de l'Europe and the Old Town. I also visited the glass cathedral erected on an ancient Vauban fort and decorated with stained glass by artist Wim Delvoye. A few metres further on one finds the Philharmonie with its more than 800 vertical columns and fitted out with world class acoustics.

Major European institutions can be found aplenty in Kirchberg and they make Luxembourg the third capital of the European Union. Heading downhill along sneaky and narrow road behind the museum, I arrived at the Drai Eechelen fortress, one of the few remaining fortresses that used to ring the city. From this vantage point I could see the historic old city of Luxembourg perching on a plateau across a green gorge.

Late afternoon I met Wolfgang Hochgatterer, my friend from India who had worked in Delhi for VAI, an engineering and plant building company for the iron and steel industry. He took me to the Grund Area, a calm place with a feel of a small village.

With its quiet and relaxing atmosphere the Grund district is a great place to wander around, enjoy the beautiful landscapes surrounded by trees, and the stone buildings and ancient bridges. From here we could enjoy a magnificent view of the green heights of the centre of the city and the historic buildings.

Located in a basin, we had to go down the small winding cobbled streets and along the water points to be able to walk in the Grund. This place was historically the most populated area in the seventeenth century. The Grund is a district with less than 1,000 inhabitants and is preserved from traffic. The Grund today is a charming and trendy place located close to the city centre which beautifully combines its architectural heritage, culture and has plenty of charming "British" style places to go for a drink in the evening when the neighbourhood comes to life.

Wolfgang was nostalgic about the wonderful time that he had spent in India. After a few drinks and dinner in a restaurant we walked back to the hotel.

The national motto of Luxembourg, *"Mir wëlle bleiwe, war mir sin"* (We want to remain what we are), captures the two dominant goals of contemporary society; protection from linguistic or other imperialism on the part of its more powerful French and German neighbours and protection from economic and political instability. Luxembourg's contributions to the arts are not largely known outside its borders; it has a rich cultural history, especially in music, painting and photography. Its evolving museums, concert halls, theatres and galleries testify to its citizens' growing appreciation of culture. The great majority of Luxembourg's native citizens are Roman Catholic, but there is also a small number of Protestants, Jews, and Muslims. There is a fundamental social division between native Luxembourgers and foreign-born residents. Portuguese immigrants are likely to hold lower-status jobs such as street cleaning, bus driving and as waiters in restaurants. Luxembourgers speak, read, and write in French, German, and Luxembourgish; most can switch between them effortlessly. Luxembourgish is the national language, while German and French are both languages of administration. The major newspaper publishes most international news in German, cultural features in French and classified advertisements in Luxembourgish. Their languages reflect the grand duchy's common interests and close historical relations with its neighbours. Luxembourg's climate is temperate and mild. Summers are generally cool, with a mean temperature of about 17° C; winters are cold but seldom severe, average temperature being about 1° C.

After spending two wonderful and memorable days in Luxembourg, truly a picture postcard place, I took the train to my next destination, Amsterdam.

On to Amsterdam

After a wonderful scenic train journey from Luxembourg I reached Amsterdam. After getting off the train I asked one gentleman the way to the tourist office. I had put my brief case on the floor while talking to him. He advised me to keep it in my hand. "It is a busy station and before you know some one will walk away with your brief case". It was a good advice to be cautious. On reaching the Tourist Office I asked the girl for booking a hotel. She asked me whether I would prefer to stay in the red light district or any other place. My immediate question to her was whether the red light district was safe. She replied it was as safe as any other place. Anyway, I booked a place outside the red light district.

Amsterdam from its humble beginnings as 13th century fishing village on a river bed today is a major hub for business, tourism and culture. It is a city of 1500 bridges, 50 kilometres of canals and boasts of more bicycles than people, apart from numerous beautiful tourist attractions.

In the afternoon I decided to take a canal boat cruise of the UNESCO World Heritage-listed canals which lasted for about an hour. It was a nice way to see Amsterdam's canal front sights. The boat cruised past some top attractions such as the Anne Frank House, City Hall, Westerkerk the church where Rembrandt is buried, and many 17th century gabled houses and bridges.

Next morning I started my visit from Dam Square. It is the most important square of Amsterdam. Originally it was a 13th century dam on the river

Amstel and was used as a fish market where ships could dock and unload goods.

Dam Square has a number of important buildings like Royal Palace, NieuweKerk (New Church), Madame Tussaud's wax museum, Beurs van Berlage an old stock exchange building now used as a concert hall and an exhibition area.

From Dam Square I walked across to De Wallen. There are three red light districts in Amsterdam. The biggest and most famous is De Wallen. This area is one of the safest in the city in spite of its reputation as it is heavily policed. The majority of venues here are windows, but these are interspersed with sex shops, sex theatres, peep shows and erotic museums.

Anne Frank House is one of the most important and popular museums in Amsterdam. The house is located on the Prinsengracht canal in the centre of Amsterdam. It contains the secret annexe where the young girl Anne Frank and seven others hid from German occupation during World War II. It was here that she wrote her now world famous diary published as *The Diary of Anne Frank.*

Anne Frank was born in 1929 in Frankfurt. The Frank family moved to Amsterdam in 1933. Hostilities broke out in 1939 and within a year the Netherlands found itself under Nazi occupation with the Jewish population experiencing increasing persecution.

In July 1942 the Frank family went into hiding in concealed rooms in the secret annexe at Prinsengrach 263, the building where her father Otto Frank worked. It was here that Anne just 13 years old started to write her diary giving a unique and touching perspective of wartime Amsterdam through the eyes of a teenage girl.

After two years the family was betrayed and the secret annexe was discovered by the Germans. In September 1944 Anne and her sister Margot were taken to Auschwitz-Birkenau and then a few weeks later they were relocated to the Bergen-Belsen concentration camp. They died there of typhus in March 1945 as per official records.

Three major museums are located in Museum Square, the Rijksmuseum, the Van Gogh Museum and the Stedelijk museum. Later, I visited Vondelpark which is the largest city park in Amsterdam and located near these museums. Vondelpark was full of people enjoying their day, dog walking, jogging, roller skating, listening to music or just lazing around.

The Heineken Experience is a must do in Amsterdam. Heineken has always been one of the most popular, the biggest name and one of the most traditional Amsterdam beers. After Heineken constructed a larger and more modern brewery on the outskirts of Amsterdam, they converted their former home into a museum that opened in 1991. Here one learnt the history of Heineken beer family and the complete brewing process. It offers four floors of multimedia exhibits, historical brewing artefacts and a tasting bar.

From Amsterdam, after a brief but very exhilarating trip, I finally prepared to take the journey back home.

Chapter 9

United Kingdom: A Walk with tradition and modernity

The United Kingdom (or UK) is an island country located off the northwestern coast of mainland Europe. The United Kingdom comprises the whole of the island of Great Britain, which contains England, Wales, and Scotland, as well as the northern portion of the island of Ireland. The name Great Britain is sometimes used to refer to the United Kingdom as a whole.

At one time the British Empire was so huge that it was referred to as "the empire on which the sun never sets." British started to establish overseas colonies in the Americas in sixteenth century. The expansionist activities of the British empire gathered momentum in the eighteenth century.

British expansion, particularly in Asia, was facilitated by the construction of trading posts set up by the East India Company. It evolved from a small enterprise run by a group of London based merchants, which in 1600 had been granted a royal charter conferring the monopoly of English trade in the whole of Asia and the Pacific.

The East India Company developed beyond a purely commercial enterprise when war between Britain and France spread to India in the mid-1740s. The Company established military supremacy over rival European trading companies from France and Portugal and subjugated local rulers, culminating in 1757 in the seizure of the province of Bengal.

In 1765, the Mughal Emperor granted the Company the *Diwani* (the right to harvest the revenues of Bengal, Bihar and Orissa) which provided funds to bolster the Company's military presence in the sub-continent. Further territorial acquisitions in India during the late eighteenth and early nineteenth centuries cemented the change in the Company's role from mere trader to a hybrid sovereign power.

Faced with this transformation and with growing concerns about mismanagement and corruption, the East India Company was finally dissolved on 1 June 1874.

From India further expansion was undertaken through Asia and by 1913 the British Empire was the largest to have ever existed.

It covered around 25% of the world's land surface, 23% of the world's population including large swathes of North America, Australia, Africa and Asia, while other areas especially in South America were closely linked to the empire by trade.

The United Kingdom has made significant contributions to the world economy, especially in technology and industry. But perhaps the biggest contribution to the world has been the English Language, which is spoken and understood all over the world except for a few places.

London is United Kingdom's largest metropolis and also one of the world's oldest cities. It was founded by the Romans and their rule extended from 43 AD to the fifth century AD, when the Empire fell. It covers an area 1579 square kilometers; the river Thames divides London in Northern and Southern halves. It has a population of 7.75 million.

It is an international financial centre for Europe and is one of three world financial cities alongside New York and Tokyo.

London is a very well connected city, especially with the underground rail network. The most popular places to be visited are in close proximity and can be explored at ease. With my friend Col H.P. Singh popularly known as Horsei we started our visit to the UK in July 2008 with the iconic Tower of London. We put Tower of London as the first place to be visited in the morning since we were told by friends that it gets quite busy during the day. Immediately on entering we headed straight for the crown jewels which happens to be the most visited and the busiest place. Having reached early we had easy access to the crown jewels which have been stored here for over six centuries. There are more that 23,500 jewels here and their total value is said to exceed GBP 20 billion. The Crown of Queen Elizabeth is also on display here; it is set with 2,800 diamonds and holds the most famous diamond in the Royal Regalia, the *Koh-i-Noor*. It was once the largest known diamond which originated from India. Visitors from around the world come to see this diamond. A mint was installed in the Tower to make coins and it was treated as a high security zone. Anyone caught tampering with the coins would be given a horrific punishment. It was a place for execution and was used as a prison and the Tower has held custody of Scottish Kings, French Dukes, other Royalty, thieves, religious conspirators and politicians. It was often used as a military store and barrack when need arose. No visit to the Tower of London would be complete without seeing a "Beefeater", officially known as a Yeoman Warder of Her Majesty's Royal Palace and Fortress of the Tower of London. They are ceremonial guardians of the Tower of London. Just seeing the Yeomen Warders can be exciting enough. It was interesting to join a Beefeater on a tour of the Tower of London since nobody knows more about the Tower than the Yeoman Warders; he took us on an impressive tour of the tower and kept us engaged with thrilling stories.

The London Tower Bridge is located close to the Tower of London. It is a suspension bridge on river Thames. The bridge was commissioned on 30 June 1894. Victorian Gothic style is used to esthetically integrate Tower Bridge with the Tower of London. It is a functional bridge and bascules are raised three times a day for boats and ships to pass.

The exhibition shows photos and other displays and films to tell the story of Tower Bridge and is housed in bridge's towers, walkways of the bridge and in Victorian engine rooms. The Glass Floor across the high level walkways is a permanent feature and provides a spectacular bird's eye view of London life from 42 metres above the river Thames.

A short walk from Tower bridge HMS Belfast, a Town-class light cruiser, is permanently moored as a museum ship on the Thames. She is now a part of the Imperial War Museum. She was launched by Anne Chamberlain wife of the then Prime Minister Neville Chamberlain on St Patrick's Day in 1938 and was commissioned into the Royal Navy on 5 August 1939.

HMS Belfast saw action escorting Arctic convoys to the Soviet Union during 1943 and in December 1943 it played an important role in the Battle of North Cape assisting in the sinking of the German battle cruiser Scharnhorst. It also played an active role in the Korean war from 1950-52.

The cruiser was used for peace time duties till time came for her de-commissioning in 1963. She Was to be scrapped but saved by HMS Belfast Trust. HMS Belfast Trust was formed in 1971 to lobby for preservation of the ship as a museum. Eventually the government agreed and handed the ship over to the trust. But six years later the financial position of the trust was not in good shape and the trust merged with the Imperial War Museum.

After a lovely walk along beautiful river Thames we reached Big Ben which is one of iconic land marks of London. Big Ben is the name given to the massive bell which weighs more than 13 tons and is lodged inside the clock tower.

The clock tower is just beside the Palace of Westminster (Houses of Parliament). The history of the British Parliament spans over 900 years from the time of Anglo-Saxons to the present. It is the home to House of Lords and House of Commons.

The location of Westminster Abbey has long been the site of important places of worship through London's history. Archaeological excavations and research have revealed that there has been a Christian church here since at least 960 AD when the Saxon King Edgar ordered the construction of the first abbey.

William the Conqueror was the first monarch to be crowned in the abbey when he held his coronation here in 1066. In all 39 monarchs have been crowned in the church. Little of these old religious sites remain however, as in the 13th century a new abbey was built in the Gothic style.

The church has more than 600 wall tablets and monuments and more than 3,000 people have been buried in the grounds here. Westminster Abbey is not just the resting place of monarchs, because as early as the 1400s poets and writers began to be given lasting memorials in the church and many were buried here in recognition of their work.

There is also the Grave to the Unknown Soldier. This tomb contains the body of an unidentified soldier who lost his life in World War I and was laid to rest in 1920. In Britain the Grave of the Unknown Soldier remains a symbol honouring those who sacrificed their lives for the country but were never identified.

Cabinet War Rooms are a group of basement offices in Whitehall which served as offices during World War II. These were occupied by Prime Minister Winston Churchill and other ministers and are located near the Parliament.

The War Rooms were made of reinforced concrete slab up to three metres thick installed above the rooms. The Cabinet War Rooms became fully operational on 27 August 1939, a week before Britain declared war on Germany and were in use until 16 August 1945.

The Cabinet War Rooms now houses the Churchill Museum, a biographical museum exploring the life of Winston Churchill.

After seeing Cabinet war rooms, we strolled through St James Park to Trafalgar Square. It is the largest square in London. It is a popular meeting place and considered to be the heart of the city. In the middle of the square stands a tall column honouring Admiral Nelson. The name of the square commemorates the victory of Admiral Horatio Lord Nelson over the French fleet at the Battle of Trafalgar, a naval battle that took place on the 21 October 1805 near Cape Trafalgar, just off the Spanish coast.

We started the day with watching of the spectacular ceremony of changing of guards at Buckingham Palace. Suddenly a big crowd gathered and we had to look for a vantage point. The Queen's Guard hands over responsibility for protecting Buckingham Palace and St James's Palace to the New Guard. It is a ceremony carried out with precision with bands, pipes and drums playing.

Queen Elizabeth II lives at Buckingham Palace, with her husband, Prince Philip. Buckingham Palace is the London residence and administrative headquarters of the monarchy, where all major official ceremonies and events take place.

Kensington Palace is a working Royal Residence. It has been the residence of successive Kings and Queens till 1760. It was the birth place of Queen Victoria; she was born here in 1819. She moved to Buckingham Palace after ascending the throne in 1837. The palace has been home to Diana, Princess of Wales, Princess Margaret and The Duke and Duchess of Sussex. It is also the London home of The Duke and Duchess of Cambridge and their children.

The Palace State Apartments are opulent and sparse. These were used for audiences and meetings. These rooms do contain sculptures and works of art. It covers the complete story about Queen Victoria from her childhood.

After visiting Kensington Palace we walked through Kensington Gardens to Royal Albert Hall. It is London's most popular venue, where grand performances take place.

The foundation stone of the Royal Albert Hall was laid in 1867. It was named in memory of Queen Victoria's husband Prince Albert who had died six years earlier. It was officially opened on 29 March 1871 by the Prince of Wales on behalf of his mother.

The glass dome that covers Royal Albert Hall is the largest unsupported glass dome in the world covering an area 20000 square feet. During the First and Second World Wars, the Hall's roof was used as a navigation point by pilots on the London skyline. It is home to almost 400 events held every year. The world's greatest musicians, artists, dancers, sportsmen and statesmen have appeared at the Royal Albert Hall.

Later we visited Harrods at Knightsbridge. Harrods was founded in 1849 by Charles Henry Harrod. Originally a single room mainly selling groceries, it had expanded into a department store by 1880. It has 330 departments, offers over 5000 brands covering an area of 1.1 million square feet and is the largest department store in Europe. The store's motto "All Things For All People" has historically meant you could buy anything at Harrods.

I do remember a gentleman with a lady at Harrods, presumably his wife. Obviously she was on a shopping spree. She was only picking up the most expensive things; even when she touched anything he would quietly pull a calculator from his pocket. Probably he was converting it to the currency from where he came for his convenience! I did pick up some knick-knacks to say that I had shopped at Harrods. The best part was that I had a burberry coat with me which was brought for me by an Admiral from London. It had been kept in a cupboard for many years. Looking at the cost in Harrods, the first thing that I did on my return to India was to get it dry cleaned. I have now used it for many years and on all my trips to cold places.

Our day ended with a visit to the Hyde Park; it is one of the largest parks in central London and one of the Royal Parks. It is famous for Speakers' Corner which is located in the North East corner. It is the oldest living free speech platform in the world. It is also a traditional place for rallies, protests, and a place to assemble or terminate marches. Everyone is welcome to join in the discussions and anybody can turn up and talk on any subject they like as long as it is lawful.

Historic figures such as Karl Marx, William Morris and Vladimir Lenin were all frequent orators at Speaker's Corner, and George Orwell described it as "one of the minor wonders of the world."

In London, I would stay with my friends in Berkshire which is a county in South East England and is home to one of the oldest and largest Royal Residences in the World the Windsor Castle. It was built by William the

Conqueror in 1070. It is the official residence of Queen Elizabeth II and is the largest inhabited castle in the world. The royal court usually stays in the castle from April to June, but more permanent residents, in what resembles more a fortified village than a castle, include the constable, governor, the knights of Windsor and their families and a Household Regiment battalion of the Guards. Windsor is also home to a huge art collection and the Royal Library.

I was asked by Brigadier V.P. Singh, a renowned polo player of India to get pick up sticks for polo balls to be used during polo matches. I had been his cadet in the National Defence Academy; he was then a Major and the Equitation Officer. Any request from him was a task that I had to accomplish. We used to have pickup sticks with nets to pick up the ball which was a bit cumbersome. Not knowing much of the area around and not having much time in hand, I requested a family friend Nina to help me out. We drove from one tack shop to another and different polo facilities in Berkshire. None of them had them, till the time we reached one polo club which had these pick up sticks with them. The girl at the club told me that she had only two pick up sticks left and were to be exported to Dubai. I requested her to ask her boss in case the shipment could be delayed and these could be given to me as I was here on a short trip. He did oblige and I could bring them along.

Although I did have some idea of equestrian activity here, but looking for polo pick up sticks was quite an exercise. In the bargain we saw plenty of riding stables which cater from beginners to professional riders. Later Nina told me that the trip with me around helped and her children had taken up riding. Also most prestigious polo clubs are located here one of most famous being the Guards Polo Club. Ascot Racecourse and Royal Windsor Racecourse are two famous Racecourses in Berkshire. Ascot Racecourse was founded by Queen Anne in 1711. Both the destinations are famous for racing and events, memorable places to spend summer evenings.

Horsei and I decided to visit the Guard's Polo Club, being polo players. Horsei had known Major Ronald Ferguson and played Polo with him. Major Ferguson was a polo manager initially to the Duke of Edinburgh and later, for many years to the Prince of Wales. His daughter Sarah is the former wife of Prince Andrew, Duke of York. In his normal style Horsei wanted to impress me with his connections whether women or famous personalities. We stopped our car and Horsei asked one of the Wardens outside Windsor Castle, "Where does Sarah Ferguson stay ?" Prompt came the reply: "She does not stay here anymore." My friend did not know that Sarah Ferguson was divorced in 1996 and Major Ferguson had passed away in 2003.

Later, Horsei and I visited Eton a small historical town on the opposite bank of the River Thames from Windsor Castle connected by Windsor bridge. It is a quiet and peaceful place. It was a nice walk all the way to Eton College which was founded in 1440 by King Henry VI. Eton is one of the UK's most exclusive boarding schools. The list of alumni includes people like Karl Marx, Antony Armstrong-Jones, 1st Earl of Snowdon, George Orwell, Boris Johnson and Christopher Lee to name a few.

Pub culture is an integral part of British life. Pubs are a place to go to socialise, relax and have a drink. It is something you should experience if you want to learn about Brits and their culture, even if you don't drink alcohol. Going to pubs is fun and a great experience.

The Romans were the first to introduce pubs 2000 years ago known as Tabernae's. It was around 700 AD Ale houses opened and became popular amongst poor classes. A few centuries later these became more popular with affluent class.

By 1830 beer was seen as medicinal and not bad for the health especially as alcohol at this time was healthier than water. Gradually this became popular that is to have a drink and have good time. Due to anti-social behavior and the Government to keep things in control started issuing pub licences. Due to prosperity in the coming years by 1870 there was one pub for 116 persons.

The golden period for pubs did not last long as both the World Wars destroyed many pubs. With depression setting in not many could afford to visit pubs. With tough competition being faced by pubs, gradually the number of pubs have reduced. In spite of the number of pubs reducing they are still an important part of British life.

When staying with friends in Berkshire we would meet on Friday evenings at the Jolly Gardeners pub located in the heart of the village of old Windsor. The staff is friendly and pub has a great ambience. My friends would be more than happy to meet here during my visits since I cannot drink more that a pint and they could polish off a few of them.

On to Scotland

After spending a few days in and around London I flew down to Edinburgh. Some facts about Scotland need mention. The recorded History of Scotland begins with the arrival of the Roman Empire in the 1st century, forcing the Picts and Gaels to cease their historic hostility to each other and to unite in the 9th century, forming the Kingdom of Scotland. Scotland was once an independent country and had its own monarch but is now in a union with England, Wales and Northern Ireland and is now in the United Kingdom.

Scotland has a population of around 5.2 million mainly spread across seven cities namely Glasgow, Edinburgh, Inverness, Aberdeen, Perth, Dundee and Stirling. The main language spoken in Scotland is English, while Scots and Scottish Gaelic are minority languages.

Major industries include banking and financial services, construction, education, entertainment, biotechnology, transport equipment, oil and gas, whisky, and tourism. The economy of Scotland is closely linked with the rest of Europe and is essentially a mixed economy.

Edinburgh has been Scotland's inspiring capital since 1437 when it replaced Scone. It is a world class city in an unforgettable setting where centuries of history meet. It lies on the east coast of Scotland on the south bank of the Firth of Forth the estuary that opens into the North Sea.

The name Edinburgh is rumoured to originate from the old English of "Edwin's fort", referring to the 7th century King Edwin of Northumbria. The city is also affectionately called by the Scots as "Auld Reekie" referring to the pollution from coal and wood fires that left dark smoky trails from chimneys through the skies. It has also been named the Athens of the North due to its topography; the Old Town plays a role similar to that of the Athenian Acropolis. The history of Edinburgh has survived for centuries and guaranteed Edinburgh a title as a UNESCO World Heritage Site in 1995. The Scottish Parliament resides here.

I started my tour by visiting the splendid Edinburgh Castle. It is one of the oldest fortified places in Europe, with a long rich history as a royal residence, military garrison, prison and fortress.

Mons Meg, is one of the greatest medieval cannons ever made. It has barrel diameter of 51 centimetres making it one of the largest cannons in the world by calibre, barrel length of 280 centimetres and length of 406 centimetres. It has stood here for centuries. This was given to King James II in 1457. The Half Moon Battery built in the aftermath of the Lang Siege (The Scots word for long) of 1573 was armed for 200 years by bronze guns known as the Seven Sisters.

Crown Square is in the heart of the castle; it joins the Great Hall, the Royal Palace, the National War Memorial and the Prisons of War.

It has several museums such as the National War Museum, Scottish National War Memorial, Royal Scots Museum, and Royal Scots Dragoon Guards Museum. These give in depth insight into military history.

The Royal Palace has been the residence of Royals. Some major events that took place were Queen Mary of Guise died in the palace in 1560. Her daughter, Mary Queen of Scots gave birth to James VI here in 1566. James VI was crowned king of Scotland when he was just 13 months old. In 1603 he was the first monarch of both Scotland and England. King Charles I was the last monarch to stay at the palace.

The 'Honours' of Scotland are the oldest Royal Regalia in Britain and are kept in the castle, which includes the crown. Also displayed with the Crown Jewels is the Stone of Destiny, the symbol of Scotland's nationhood and the Sword of State which was presented to James IV in 1507 by Pope Julius II and has a blade a metre long. The Sceptre is surmounted with three figures supporting a crystal globe, a cut and polished rock crystal with a Scottish pearl on top. A gift from the Pope possibly given by Innocent VIII to James IV in 1494 was remodelled by James V who even added his initials to the sceptre.

Prisons of War held hundreds of prisoners including Caribbean pirates. The first official prisoners of war were the crew of the French privateer the Chevalier Barte. Sir Thomas Grey an English knight was imprisoned here. It was during imprisonment he started writing the Scalacronica, a chronicle documenting the history of Britain.

Prisoners of war came from France, America, Spain, the Netherlands, Ireland, Italy, Denmark and Poland. Most were sailors, many of them Americans fighting in the War of Independence. The vaults have been recreated as the vaults would have looked in 1800s and showing the life prisoners would have led.

After the tour of Edinburgh Castle I started walking down the Royal Mile which is the most famous street connecting Edinburgh Castle with the Palace of Holyrood house.

Castlehill and Castle Esplanade are located closest to Edinburgh Castle. Castlehill is the impressive volcanic hill located right in the centre of Edinburgh and is one of the Masterpieces of the Old Town Castle Esplanade;

the large flat area in front of the castle's Gate House was built in 1753 as a parade ground for resident troops. This is the oldest part of Royal Mile.

It is in Castle Esplanade that The Royal Edinburgh Military Tatoo takes place during the summers. It is an annual event where military tattoos are performed by British Armed Forces, Commonwealth and international military bands. It has also played host to many concerts and famous artists have performed here.

From Castle Hill I walked down to the Lawnmarket, the name is derived from land market where produce from surrounding countryside was sold. It is a place to pick up souvenirs. In 1477 a cloth market was established here. Trade continued here till late 1700s. The market boasts of some of the best preserved examples of courtyards and land developments in the city.

High street has a lot of shops, pubs and restaurants. As I started walking down there was the statue of one of the world's greatest philosophers, David Hume. He is credited to influencing famous German philosopher Immanuel Kant.

St Giles Cathedral is an ornate piece of 14th century architecture. The Cathedral is dedicated to Saint Giles, the patron saint of cripples, lepers and nursing mothers. He is also the patron saint of Edinburgh.

The Canongate lies towards the bottom of the Royal Mile on the tail of the Castle rock. Until 1856 Canongate was an independent burgh separated from the city and outside the walls. The wall that divided the burghs was located on Jeffrey Street between Edinburgh and Canongate.

Less than 100 metres long, Abbey Strand lies at the bottom of the Royal Mile which connects the end of Canongate to the Palace of Holyroodhouse.

The Palace of Holyroodhouse is the Queen's official residence in Scotland set against the backdrop of Arthur's Seat at the foot of Royal Mile. The Palace was started in 1501 and completed by Charles II.

Another major attraction I went to was the underground city. Having moved around in Edinburgh, it is difficult to imagine that there was an underground city here. Hidden beneath the city is a tangle of streets, tunnels and vaults. This was the underground city on which more structures and buildings were built. These ghost towns were forgotten for centuries. Middens were found containing toys, medicine bottles, plates, and other signs of human habitation. It is in this fascinating underground city that people lived in misery.

In the underground city vaults on the North Side of the Cowgate arch form a series of tunnels and vaults and are mainly used for ghost tours. The vaults on the South side of the Cowgate arch form a venue called The Caves and The Rowantree which hosts private events, weddings, private dining, live music and the occasional club night. For around 30 years the vaults were used to house taverns, workshops for cobblers and other tradesmen as well as storage space for merchants. The city's poorest residents lived in these claustrophobic, dark and dingy vaults.

I took a Ghost Tour with a group of visitors to discover the darker side of the city. Our guide Victoria was unique; she explained all about the underground city, telling us many stories often with a dramatic flourish. We walked through lot of dark areas with narrow lanes and rooms of varied sizes. Our concentration was with her all the time who kept telling us tales about history and scary things that happened here. I was busy listening to one of her spine chilling ghost and witch stories. Suddenly, someone grabbed me in the dark dressed like a witch! I felt trapped in a haunted house. It was part of the show but I almost jumped out of my skin! When you come out, it is difficult to imagine that under a bustling area there is a ghost town.

Later, I visited The Royal Yacht Britannia which is one of the best visitor attractions of Scotland. She was home to Her Majesty the Queen and the Royal Family for over 40 years and sailed over 1.1 million miles around the world. Britannia was the first Royal Yacht to be built with complete ocean-going capacity and designed as a Royal residence to travel around the world and double as a hospital ship in time of war. After glorious service she was decommissioned in 1997 which marked the end of a long tradition of British Royal Yachts dating back to 1660 and the reign of Charles II.

The Yacht had a capacity of 250 guests and carried a platoon of Royal Marines and 21 officers with 250 Royal yachtsmen while carrying the Queen or the royal guests. Apart from hosting state functions she was an ambassador for British business promoting trade and industry around the globe. Four Royal honeymoons were enjoyed on board Princess Margaret and Anthony Armstrong-Jones being the first in 1960. She has entertained kings and queens, world leaders and celebrities such as Winston Churchill, Nelson Mandela, Bill Clinton, Elizabeth Taylor and Frank Sinatra. The tour for the group of visitors started after a formal welcome at the Visitor Centre located in Ocean Terminal. The terminal is the gateway and boarding point for the ship which is the entrance to Royal Yacht Britannia Museum. It has a replica Lego model of Britannia on display. We viewed the historical royal photographs in the gallery and learnt about the history of Royal Yachts before getting on board the ship.

Tour of the ship starts from the Bridge to the State Apartments, Royal Family's living quarters, Crew's Quarters and finishes at the gleaming Engine Room. To the forward is the functional part of the vessel, where crew and operational equipment is located in a cramped condition. The five decks on board are open for public viewing.

The next day after an hour's drive from Edinburgh I reached Glasgow. Glasgow is a port city on the River Clyde. It is Scotland's largest city, and it forms an independent council area that lies entirely within the historic county of Lanarkshire. It covers an area of 175 square kilometres and has a population of 584000.

Glasgow was created as a royal burgh in 1450 and its university was founded in 1451. Glasgow prospered as a market centre because it's strategic location between Highland and Lowland Scotland. After the union of Scottish and English crowns in 1603 Glasgow grew significantly.

Glasgow's economy includes traditional heavy engineering, advanced engineering and manufacturing, aerospace technology and development, notably the production of satellites, information and communication technology, software engineering, renewable energy and low-carbon innovations. The city's BioCorridor has assisted in the research, development, and production of pharmaceuticals, bioinformatics and medical technology. Glasgow also has a huge retail sector, which is a centre of film and television production and is an important global financial and business services hub. Tourism has also been increasing over the years.

Glasgow boasts of a couple of museums. Our first visit was to Kelvingrove Art Gallery and Museum located in a red sandstone building. It opened in 1901.

The museum has 22 themed galleries and on display are an astonishing 8000 objects. The museum is divided in two parts, *Life* and *Expression*. The Life galleries represent natural history, human history and prehistory. The Expression galleries include the fine art collections. A significant part of the paintings collection comes from the bequest of Archibald McLellan. The important collection of French 19th century paintings includes works by Monet, Gauguin and Renoir. Further highlights are Rembrandt's 'Man in Armour, 'Christ and the Adulteress' by Titian and Salvador Dali's 'Christ of St John of the Cross.'

It has one of the finest collection of arms and armour and Egyptian artifacts. Also on display is a giant elephant, World War II Spitfire and dinosaur eggs. This collection is of international significance including the R. L. Scott's bequest which had been one of the finest private collections of European arms and armour in the world.

After visiting Kelvingrove Art Gallery and Museum I walked across through the park to the University of Glasgow. It was founded by Papal Bull in 1451 and is one of the ancient universities of Glasgow. The university was situated in the High Street for 400 years before moving to its present site on Gilmorehill in 1870. The main building was designed by Sir George Gilbert Scott in Gothic style and the campus has more than 100 listed buildings.

Alumni or former staff of the university include James Wilson, a founding father of the United States, philosopher Francis Hutcheson, engineer James Watt, philosopher and economist Adam Smith, physicist Lord Kelvin, surgeon Joseph Lister, and seven Nobel laureates and three British Prime Ministers.

After visiting the University we went to Byres Road, one of the most vibrant streets. It is full of restaurants, bars and shops. Restaurants serve fine food and wines. We had a quick glass of wine and snacks to move to our next place. Although one could have spent a lot of time here, we had to rush to squeeze in rest of our afternoon programme. Byres Road was formed from a small village called the Byres of Partick, occasionally called the Bishop's Byres. Byres Road was to be renamed Victoria Road many years ago but obviously that was never achieved may be due to proud nature and opposition of the local residents.

In the afternoon we went to Loch Lomond with some friends which is a short drive from Glasgow. Loch Lomond is located in the Trossachs National Park. It is a big and beautiful lake. It is a nice place to spend a pleasant afternoon, with plenty of water activities like spending time on a boat, kayaking, canoeing or wind surfing. There were plenty of keen anglers around trying to catch fish. We decided to hire canoes. It was Nirmal, my friend from Glasgow with me in the canoe, a qualified engineer by profession. So were other friends in canoes; none of them had probably been in a canoe before. Before getting in the canoe, we were advised to put our mobile phones, keys and other valuables in a bag. Probably the company hiring the boat must have done this from experience. We got into the canoes. Slowly we moved into the lake paddling. Till then Nirmal was following my instructions sincerely. His confidence grew as he knew that he was in canoe at the helm of which was a seasoned master mariner and a yachtsman. In the excitement he got up to wave to other friends. Before I knew, the canoe had toppled and we were both in the water. The other canoe followed in our footsteps and they were also soon swimming in water.

It was reasonably cold and I was recovering from flu. Obviously we were drenched in water and there was no time to dry our clothes. Since all our clothes were drenched I being their guest and not having been too well, I was given a jacket to cover myself. Luckily this was left in the bag with other items before we got into the canoe. We got into the fancy cars wearing wet vests and underwear and only I had a jacket on. Sheepishly we entered the house. No one wanted to tell the families as to what had happened.

In the evening we went for a meal at famous Mr Singh's India Restaurant. It was a week day and the restaurant was absolutely full, with mainly Europeans. We were just a few with local Asian friends. The restaurant is very popular with Glasgow locals. It's through this continual support that Mister Singh's has had the opportunity to evolve from a single restaurant into a fully fledged brand and has a chain of restaurants. Ambience was great and the food was absolutely authentic North Indian.

The following day I reached Gleneagles from Glasgow in about an hour. Gleneagles first opened its doors to outsiders in 1924 at the height of roaring 20s. This magnificent countryside estate in the heart of Scotland was described as a "riviera in the Highlands". It is a glorious playground of country pursuits. The hotel is an epitome of luxury. The service is par excellence here; it can be felt from the time one is welcomed on the steps of the hotel.

I had to rush from my room after checking in and changing for a meeting. I had left my stuff and dresses thrown all over. When I came back to my room after the meeting I could not see any of my stuff around. I thought probably I had entered the wrong room by chance. Everything was meticulously placed in the almirahs!

The 850 acre Gleneagles estate offers an array of attractions with world class golf courses and an equestrian school. It is also famous for hosting the G8 summit of world leaders in 2005.

The Equestrian School at Gleneagles is one of the finest in Scotland. It provides all Equestrian activities with beginners' lessons, dressage, show jumping, cross country, trail rides and polo lessons. It has plenty of natural surroundings for a relaxing trail ride in Perthshire country side. One evening were sitting for a formal dinner, the Master of ceremonies requested us to walk out with our glasses. We did not know what was the objective. It was drizzling and we could hear the music of bagpipes; we could not see anything but slowly the music became louder. It was a most memorable and spectacular sight to see the smartly dressed pipers in traditional Scottish outfits suddenly appearing from dark and marching towards the hotel. No wonder the music of pipes during war spurred the troops to courageous action. It is also said that traditionally one of the purposes of the bagpipe was to provide music for dancing.

Also, there was a performance of Highland dancing. Interestingly, we had Highland dancing in King George's School. I felt quite at home and joined them in dancing. It is part of the Scottish culture and the dance has spread in various countries across the world.

According to tradition, the old kings and clan chiefs used the Highland Games as a means to select their best men at arms and the discipline required to perform the Highland dances allowed men to demonstrate their strength, stamina and agility. The first documented evidence of intricate war dances being performed to "the wailing music of bagpipes" was at the second marriage of Alexander III to his French bride Yolande de Dreux at Jedburgh in 1285.

Over the years Highland dancing has moved from being an exclusively male pursuit, to one that today includes more than 95% of female dancers. There are various legends associated with Highland dancing.

I went for the Famous Grouse experience organized with a group which is a must at the Glenturret Distillery. It is Scotland's oldest distillery set on the banks of the River Turret in the beautiful town of Crieff in Perthshire. Glenturret is the malt whisky produced here using the traditional methods and equipment while the Famous Grouse is the blended whisky that is based upon the Glenturret Malt. It has the distinction of being the most visited distillery in Scotland.

In the Famous Grouse Experience tour they explained the process of making whisky and creating a blend (Famous Grouse). Novices and whisky enthusiasts alike enjoyed this distillery tour. Having been a teetotaler for a long time and off late graduated to having a glass of wine or beer once in a few months it was a wonderful tour giving exposure and knowledge about whiskies. It was a guided tour where we saw the milling, mashing, fermenting and distilling process. We were shown a video show and also given an opportunity to blend one's own whisky, where the ability to detect different aromas is tested. They told us about the traditional production of the Glenturret Highland single malt and we learnt the art of blending at the spiritual home of The Famous Grouse. We were also made to classify the whisky based on aroma. Glenturret is the only remaining distillery in Scotland able to demonstrate the traditional hand-made whisky making experience.

I was curious to see the warehouse which houses the maturing casks of Glenturret whisky. There is a sample room within the warehouse where one can taste whisky taken out of small casks. I wanted to be there to see how the casks are stored and was offered some whisky to taste. The guide was a bit disappointed when I told him that I do not drink whisky. I asked him what I should do with the whisky that was given for tasting. He asked me to throw it as it was not allowed to take whisky out as it was a bonded warehouse. Legally, once taken out duty should be paid.

Before leaving the hotel there was a pleasant surprise of gift of a bottle of The Famous Grouse Whisky; on it was inscribed, *"The famous CP"*. My initials were printed on the bottle! It is kept safely in my bar at home to remind me of this great experience.

Chapter 10

Italy: My Second Home!

Italy and the spring and first love all together should make the gloomiest person happy

- Bertrand Russell

I have visited Italy a number of times and have fallen in love with this country. My first major trip to Italy was in 2009. It is a charming country that has slowly started growing on me after my first sojourn there.

Italy is a fascinating place; the visit can be packed with interesting things to do and see without ever running out of activities be it visiting amazing historic places, food, wines, sea, lakes and fashion. Italy has the largest number of artistic and documentary properties declared World Heritage sites by UNESCO. Rome, Florence, Assisi, Venice, Siena, Pisa or Naples are only a few of the most famous art cities in the country and there are lovely old world towns and villages to be found everywhere.

Italy has spawned intellectual giants in the fields of literature, art and science. Homer, Virgil, Dante, Columbus, Michelangelo, Vivaldi among others have straddled the international stage and held the world in thrall for centuries and continue to do so even today.

Italian cuisine is food typical of Italy. It has developed through centuries of social and economic changes with roots stretching to antiquity. Italy has been synonymous with good eating. There are incredible variety of different dishes and recipes in every municipality, province and region. The journey through Italian gastronomic culture is something not to be missed.

The ancient Greeks called Italy "Enotria", or land of wine because even in those days the peninsula was known for its exceptional wines. There is nothing like the pleasure of tasting wines, surrounded by its natural setting, a glass of Chianti or Brunello di Montalcino in Tuscany, of Barbera or Barolo in Piedmont or of Prosecco di Valdobbiadene in Veneto or of Lambrusco in Emilia Romagna. Then there are the Sicilian wines and the white wines of Friuli and Trentino-Alto Adige, the great red wines of Valtellina, just to mention a few famous examples. Italian wines are a world of flavours to try for pleasure of the palate, the eyes and the heart.

Every visit to Italy has given me a new experience and every time there has been so much more to learn and explore. My friends and family think that it is my second home and for me it actually is. All visits have been unforgettable and special. No wonder over 50 million visitors cross the borders of Italy every year.

I am not certain which book had more influence on me about Italy; *"Under the Tuscan Sun"* a memoir by Francis Mayes or *"Eat Prey Love"* by Elizabeth Gilbert. To me Italy was similar to what was written in their books but perhaps much more beautiful and fascinating.

During my numerous visits to Italy, I learnt to speak Italian which makes me feel at home among friends and locals. I have visited practically every nook and corner of Italy: Rome, the home to the Vatican as well as landmark art and ancient ruins, Florence with its Renaissance masterpieces such as Michelangelo's "David" and Brunelleschi's Duomo, Venice the city of canals and Milan, Italy's fashion capital and many smaller places. There was so much to enjoy in the islands of Sicily, Sardinia, Capri and Ischia.

It is difficult to choose as to what places I have liked in Italy. On one of my first trips, I visited Naples; it is famous for it's history, culture and pizzas we are all familiar with. There's a saying that Rome is the heart of Italy but Naples is its soul. The city is chaotic yet beautiful at the same time.

In May 2009, I arrived in Naples. I made friends during the flight with Dieter who was a co-passenger sitting next to me. Dieter had been a regular visitor to Italy and during conversation we realized that by chance we were staying in the same area in Naples. We hired a taxi from the Airport. The taxi drivers at the airport and specially in Italy can be quite charming. At the same time with their smooth talk you could land up over paying. Dieter's experience came in handy; he knew exactly what was to be done and fixed the fare. Dieter gave me a brief as to how laid back the Italians were and especially those in Southern Italy. Whilst we were on our way to the hotel he started a conversation with Ricardo the taxi driver and told him that drivers in Italy do not follow traffic rules and drive rashly. Ricardo said "True we do not and at the same time we keep two licenses, one for the police and the other for driving. So it is not easy to be fined by police!!" Anyway I was a mute listener to their conversation. Ricardo spoke about his visit to Mumbai where he had been a few years back. Soon we were at Dieter's hotel where he got off. My hotel was only a few minutes away. On the way to my hotel, I asked Ricardo why was it that my friend was quite critical of Italy and the drivers here. He said: "Well Sir, I was only having fun, he is a German. I drive all over Europe and very little in Italy. We know how to drive well !"

When I arrived at the hotel my suitcase lock for some reason was badly damaged; it looked like some one did try to open it. Anyway, the hotel staff helped me open it by breaking the lock. It just might be worthwhile to listen when people tell you to be careful in Italy.

In the evening, I went to one of the oldest pizzerias in Naples, L'Antica Pizzeria da Michele. Naples is also known as the home of pizza. This pizzeria was founded by Salavatore Condurro in 1870. The Condurro's pizza making origins go even further back as the grandfather was a pizza maker at the court of the Bourbons. In 1844, the grandfather made a pizza for the Russian Czar Nicholas II and his wife Alessandrina Feodorwna who had come to visit King Ferdinand II. For this occasion he made a special pizza just for them the *cosacca*. The legend says that they enjoyed the pizzas so much that they gave the Neapolitan king a present of two bronze statues now in the gardens of the Royal Palace in Piazza Plebiscito. The rest is history. The choice here is simple; the Condurro family have only made two types of pizzas ie Marinara with tomato, garlic, oil and oregano and Margherita with mozzarella cheese, tomato, oil and basil the pizza reputedly created in honour of Queen Margherita when she visited Naples in 1889 . I ordered Margherita.

Next day in the morning during breakfast (*colazione*) I had porridge, cornetto (croissant), crostata(pie) and a hot cup of Capuccino. My guide Valentina (feminine name from the Roman name Valetinus meaning healthy and strong) took me around Naples, which is studded with numerous attractions. She started with a brief on the language spoken here ie Neapolitan, a Romance language spoken by about seven or eight million people in southern Italy especially in the city of Naples and in Campania and southern Lazio. Neapolitan is part of a continuum of dialects spoken in most of southern Italy though many would use the term "Neapolitan" only to refer to the dialects spoken in and around Naples. It is primarily a spoken language. Naple's location near Pompeii, Mt Vesuvius, Capri, and Sorrento also makes it a good starting point for exploring Southern Italy.

I told Valentina that I had heard Naples was not a safe city. She said that it was better to avoid going out alone at night and it was a good idea to take precautions that any visitor should do going to a new place. She added that Camorra, a mafia type crime, does operate in Naples and had been operating since 17th century . But usually they did not bother the common tourist but were involved in bigger crime rackets.

We first visited Villa Floridana which is situated in the middle of the Vomero hill; this villa was the summerhouse of the duchess of Floridia, Lucia Migliaccio, wife of King Ferdinand of Bourbon of the kingdom of the two Sicilies. It was built in 1816 as a gift from King Ferdinand to his wife. It has beautifully manicured gardens, an expansive view over Naples Bay and an ornate fountain filled with turtles. It also houses the National Museum of Ceramics.

We wandered through Castel Nuovo (New Castle) which is the large medieval castle that stands out along the coastline. It is an authentic symbol of the royal dynasties of the Kingdom of Naples. The art museum houses a gallery of 17th to 19th century Italian paintings including works from Luigi Crisconio and Carlo Vanvitelli.

Later, we went to Museo Nazionale di Capodimonte (National Museum of Capodimonte); this is the Napolitan National Gallery a museum featuring work by Baroque and Renaissance artists. Some of the big names here include Giordano, Caravaggio, Bellini, and Titian.

We stopped by Piazza del Mercato (Market Square) this market has been Naples' main market square since the 13th century. It sells everything from household goods to fresh produce and handmade souvenirs. It is a lively and busy place ideal for shoppers and is the market area of small artisan shops.

In the Angevin period death sentences were carried out in the square. It is an important square for the Neapolitan people; here the revolt of Masaniello (known as Tommaso Aiello) was born. He lived in one of the alleys adjacent to the square. A characteristic of the square is its irregular shape and it is set between four churches.

In the evening we went to market place close to the hotel with Arturo a Mexican whom I had met in the hotel over a drink in the bar. There were some shops and there was one person selling laptops, which were kept in the boot of the car and there was one on display on top of his car. This person gave a proper demonstration and a couple of people were watching it. Arturo enquired about the cost of the laptop which was given as 250 Euros. The cost did sound too good to be true and he found this as an attractive offer. He paid him the amount. Laptop was packed in a bag and given to him. He was quite excited to have got a nice bargain. We reached the lobby of the hotel and he announced to some of his friends about the purchase. Everyone wanted to have a look at the laptop. Arturo opened the beautiful laptop bag he found some salt bags in shape of the laptop packed inside! With so many people watching him it was surprising as to how the seller brought the laptop from top of his car and gave him another bag instead. We did not venture to go back and catch the cheat who would have left the place by then in any case.

The following day along with guide Valentina, I visited Vesuvius and Pompeii. Vesuvius is the only active volcano in mainland Europe and has produced some of the continent's largest volcanic eruptions. It overlooks the Bay and City of Naples and sits in the crater of the ancient Somma volcano. Vesuvius is most famous for the 79 AD eruption which destroyed the cities of Pompeii and Herculaneum. It has erupted at least three dozen times after that. Though the volcano's last eruption was in 1944, it still represents a great danger to the cities that surround it and especially Naples.

It's absolutely safe to visit Mount Vesuvius; at the same time one should be prepared for any eventuality. Vehicles do not go upto the top. The trail to the top is just under another 200 metres. It is quite convenient to walk up.

There is an interesting fact when Vesuvius erupted in 79 AD. Pliny the Younger son of a Roman diplomat was in Misenum across the Bay of Naples from Vesuvius. He described the eruption in a letter to the Roman historian Tacitus and the letter is recognized as the first detailed account of a volcanic eruption. He described an ash cloud shaped like an umbrella pine that rose high in the sky turning day into night. Today scientists call explosive volcanic eruptions that produce large clouds of rock, ash and gases "Plinian" eruptions.

Later we came down to Pompeii; it is one the most famous Roman sites in the world frozen in time. Pompeii was just another Roman seaside resort until Mount Vesuvius erupted in 79 AD. Just a day later thousands of people died and the whole city was buried under a blanket of volcanic ash 25 metres deep and forgotten until it was unearthed by explorers 1800 years later.

When we arrived at Pompeii the first thing we noticed was its size. Although no one knows for sure it is estimated that 20,000 people lived here and the archaeological site covers over 160 acres. There is a lot to explore here. Valentina made the tour short and sweet covering major aspects and important places.

The layer of ash did an amazing job of preserving the details of the buildings from the colourful frescoes and ornate mosaics to the underground engineering used to heat the baths.

Inside the main city walls we walked through the paved city streets. The layout is just as it would have been before the eruption with private homes mixed in with shops, restaurants, temples and an amphitheatre. The extent of the preservation gives an amazing insight into how the Romans lived here.

In the evening at a get-together with some friends I met Giovanni a businessman from Capri who was on a short visit to Naples. Exchanging pleasantries I mentioned that I would be visiting Capri and spontaneously he extended an invitation for me to meet him there.

The following day, on a bright and sunny morning, I embarked on a high-speed ferry from port of Molo Beverello for Capri. It was a short sailing of forty minutes with the ferry moving swiftly and rapidly leaving behind the gorgeous skyline of Naples .

The ferry secured alongside the jetty in Capri and soon I was in one of the most famous places in the world. Capri is a picturesque, colourful and getaway with crystal clear waters. Carlos a Brazilian driver from the hotel who was smartly uniformed picked us up and in a few minutes we reached the hotel. The hotel had a picturesque view of Capri harbour and the Tyrrhenian Sea.

Captivating Capri

On reaching my room I was drinking a macchiato in the balcony of my room enjoying the beautiful scenery. After some time I asked Roberto the General Manager of the hotel that I would like to meet Giovanni. Roberto knew him and called him and arranged a meeting. I was soon dropped by Carlos at Piazzetta a small square and one of the most fashionable places in Capri. The nickname Piazzetta comes from its rather small size; this rectangle is just a few square meters almost wholly occupied by bright cafe tables. It only took a few minutes of observation over a glass of Capri Rosso to understand why the Piazzetta is often called the drawing room of the world. Everyone from rich to the poor sit here elbow to elbow. Capri Rosso is made predominantly from *Piedirosso,* a red-wine variety almost entirely restricted to Campania.

We thought that it would be a short meeting. After a few glasses of wine we had our lunch. This is how the Italian meal is structured; it started with Antipasti (appetizers) which consisted of oil-cured veggies, followed by Il Primo (first course) of soup, Il Secondo (the main course which consisted of baked vegetable with basil, and then Il Contorno (superb salads or insalata). This was followed by La frutta e l dolci (fruit and desserts) had fresh fruits and lemon gelato followed by an espresso. It was well over two hours that we had spent having our lunch not realizing how time had flown by. Grazie (thanks) to Italian hospitality.

My host had organized a boat tour for me. I was soon in a boat sailing around the magnificent and beautiful island of Capri. There were a couple of tourists in the boat. We sailed around the coastline of Capri on board a traditional gozzo boat; it is the best way to see the beauty of Capri including the Faraglioni, Marina Piccola, the lighthouse, the Blue Grotto and we stopped for a swim in the sea off the coast. Our guide Giuseppe made the tour very exciting, explaining about the places we were seeing en route; he was full of zeal, energy and knowledge.

Grottoes are world famous caves. There are three of them; the Blue Grotto or Grotto Azzurra, the White Grotto or Grotto Bianca and the Green Grotto or Grotta Verde. We went to the Blue Grotto which is a sea cave. We were transferred to the smaller boats, which can pass through the narrow opening of the rocks and once we were inside the view was absolutely amazing. With sunlight passing through an underwater cavity and shining through the seawater it created a blue reflection that illuminated the cavern.

The Green Grotto is absolutely amazing with blue colour reflecting off the walls of the cave resulting in a beautiful emerald tone radiating from the cave. The White Grotto is a bit different and the boat comes close to the sides of the cave to see the stalagmites and stalactites hanging from top. One stalagmite in particular and near the statue of Madonna is a representation of Mary in Catholic and Orthodox churches.

The buildings in Capri white washed or coloured with the bright pastels that are favoured on the island seem to flow into one another as they frame the streets they surround. The streets are suitable only for pedestrians with small and colourful markings on the streets.

The following day we visited Anacapri a comune on the island of Capri. The Ancient Greek prefix ana- means "up" or "above" signifying that Anacapri is located at a higher elevation on the island than Capri. Administratively it has a separate status from the city of Capri. It is a small and quaint town.

We visited Villa San Michele which was the dream home of the Swedish physician Axel Munthe. Munthe first came to Capri in 1885. He built his villa on the ruins of an ancient Chapel dedicated to San Michele. He is supposed to have said "My house must be open to the sun, to the wind and the voice of the sea just like a Greek temple and light, light, light everywhere!" Capri is a great place for shopping with a number of designer shops. Various perfume brands are available here, Carthusia being the original perfume of Capri.

Lemons are the symbol of Capri. Almost every house has lemons in its garden; they appear on street signs, door fronts, on benches and in the shops you can get all kinds of lemon candy and the famous liqueur limoncello. The pasticcerias also sell a local pastry called Delizia al Limone (lemon delight).

A visit to the island is incomplete without having Limoncello di Capri. As far back as the turn of the last century "nonna (grandmother)" Vincenza Canale one of the first hoteliers on the island used to offer a glass of Limoncello to her guests at her famous guest-house the "Mariantonia". Since then people in the island have continued to meet at the end of the day to sample this delicious liqueur.

To this day Limoncello di Capri continues to be made using the same time honoured recipe. A natural liqueur with excellent digestive properties Limoncello di Capri is made by macerating lemon peel taken from lemons grown and picked on the island. It is a simple natural product free of colourants, stabilisers, additives and preservatives, which embodies all the authenticity of the original recipe.

As I wanted to visit the Amalfi Coast I took a ferry from Capri to Marina Piccola (Small Marina) in Sorrento leaving the island with sweet memories and may be another day we could spend longer time to cherish and enjoy the beautiful island. The bewildering landscape of Amalfi Coast covers a distance of 50 kilometres from Sorrento to Salerno.

I decided to cover this distance by road, making stops on the way and enjoying the scenery and the beautiful view of the Tyrrhenian Sea.

I spent some time in Sorrento; it is named after the sirens and the beautiful mermaids a small town overlooking the Bay of Naples. It has a beautiful view of the Bay, Piazza Tasso a cafe-lined square. The historic centre has narrow alleys and is home to the 14th century Church of San Francesco. It is a nice and quiet place, where one can spend some relaxed time.

After a short drive I reached Positano the ancient and the first town of Amalfi Coast. Buildings here are colourful and spectacular. The Ancient Romans built a number of villas on the coast of Positano the ruins of which can be seen in the vicinity of the Church of Santa Maria Assunta; the tiled dome of the church can be seen from every nook and corner. It is believed that the town was founded in 9th century. The church holds an 18th century black Madonna.

The ancient port in a small cove has been used since medieval times and reached its peak in the 16th-17th century. By the 20th century Positano was just a simple fishing village before tourists discovered this hidden corner of paradise in the 1950s and 60s when the rich and famous came here. It was once the favourite place for famous artists like Pablo Picasso, Paul Kee and writer John Steinbeck.

The Positano beach, Marina Grande Beach was full of people swimming in the blue water. Being a sea lover I did not waste any time to change and go for a swim. It is the longest beach on the Amalfi Coast most popular, liveliest and cosmopolitan. The beach lies almost directly opposite the archipelago of Li Galli; there is a string of restaurants and bars and a famous discotheque (Music On the Rocks). It is easy to see why the beach has become the focus of the town's social life where the locals come to mingle with the world's celebrities and tourists. It is from here that excursions along the coast and shuttle boats to the nearby bays depart. There are other small beaches which are not so busy. However each has its own charm.

There is a story from ancient times that goes with the name Positano. A Turkish boat beached just off the shores of what has since come to be known as Positano. Aboard the ship there was a painting of the Virgin Mary. The captain heard the painting whisper "*posa, posa*" ('set me down, set me down') and obediently he threw the image into the sea. Miraculously the ship floated.

The next day I went to the town of Amalfi which was once a formidable maritime super power. It is located between Positano and Salerno centuries before Papal dominance of the Italian peninsula. It was one of the four most powerful maritime republics that included Amalfi, Genoa, Pisa and

Venice. As a result there are a lot of historic sites. It is included in UNESCO world heritage sites. From Amalfi beaches, one sees crystal clear blue water. These are great for all kinds of water activities be it swimming, boating, snorkelling or scuba diving.

With guide Aldo we started our tour from Piazza Flavio Gioia, which is in front of the port and the most central place from where all kinds of transportation takes place be it boats, buses or taxis. There is a statue of Flavio Gioia and the Piazza is named after him; the navigator who perfected the use of the compass between the end of the 12th and the beginning of the 13th century. The Amalfitani were the first in Europe to rely on this property of the magnet.

With a comfortable walk along the sea on the Lungomare through the Piazza and narrow streets we reached Piazza Duomo. It was constructed in 987 AD; it is said at that time there were two churches inside. It had been renovated into one church in the beginning of the 13th century. Saint Andrea the patron of the town is enshrined in this duomo. The Golden facade is neo-gothic style. The central bronze doors were cast in Constantinople and brought to this church in 1065. It was the symbol of wealth and power of the Amalfi Maritime Republic at the time. To visit the Duomo (Cathedral) we entered by beautiful long stairs through the "Chiostro del Paradiso (Corridor of Heaven)."

After passing the corridor we visited Duomo Museum. There is an underground room devoted to St Andrea and main part of Duomo. The marble altar is lavishly decorated. Inside the Duomo is Baroque style architecture rebuilt in the eighteenth century. It is nicely decorated with fine gold and is a functional church used for the Mass.

We walked up the hill from Piazza Duomo and reached Valley of the Mills. We passed some abandoned paper mills and then we were at the Paper Museum, a restored 18th century paper mill in the middle of the village and a library with over 3000 texts on the origins of paper. Amalfi's famous paper was produced by hand with cotton shipped from Egypt making Amalfi one of the earliest locations where paper was produced in Western Europe.

Soon we were at Ravello, looming more than 365 metres above the sea level and is named as the City of Music. It has thousands of years of history, an enchanting mountaintop setting on Italy's most beautiful coastline and views that have captivated countless souls, inspired artists and filled hearts with passion. It was a favourite place for people like Jackie Kennedy.

This place is so beautiful that it has been described as "a natural balcony overhanging Amalfi."

There are two famous gardens here one is 13th century Moorish style Villa Rufolo that became famous because Richard Wagner drew inspiration from the garden for his opera Parsifal. The other place Villa Cimbrone is another famous garden and hotel. It served as a love nest for Greta Garbo and Leopold Stokowski in the 1930s. We bought some souveniers and its famous colourful ceramics.

The Ferrari Experience

In one of the later trips to Italy with Neeru and my daughter Arooshi we visited the Ferrari Museum in Maranello. We decided to take a test drive of Ferrari as there are some companies who organize these and are located just outside the museum. Antonio our guide asked me who would like to drive the Ferrari. I asked Arooshi to get in the driver's seat. She was quite excited and had got her driving license only a few days before. Whilst driving in the excitement she raised her hands taking them off the steering and exclaimed "Oh my God!" Antonio with a smile asked her to take it easy and put her hands back on the steering.

Arooshi is always ready to explore on gastronomy. In Florence our friend Sarah wanted to take us to an Indian Restaurant for dinner and she did give an option to us in case we would prefer to go to an Italian Restaurant. She quietly tapped me and whispered in my ear "Dad, are we crazy that we would like to eat Indian food in Italy?" She had indicated her choice as we have always tried local cuisines and delicacies.

From a very young age my daughter showed potential of becoming a veteran traveller. Once we visited Sikkim and we went to Nathu La Pass, which connects India with China. We were there at a time at the border when some Chinese soldiers came down as Indian soldiers were already there on the Indian side. There is only a wire fence which demarcates the border. They were very happy to see Arooshi, she was only three years old then and they held her in their lap as for them also to see children was not a normal sight and she was also thrilled. After the Chinese soldiers handed her back we told her that she had gone to China with the soldiers, she said "No Papa my foot was on the Indian side !"

I once went on a trip to Ranthambore; Arooshi was all of five years old and I was staying in a Resort. During the day I got busy in a meeting and late in the afternoon I realized that she was all alone in the room and was concerned whether she had her lunch or not. I checked up with the Front Office Manager, regarding her. He came back and told me that she had called up the room service and ordered her lunch and asked them to get some DVDs!

Before turning ten years old somehow she came to know that her United States visa would expire soon. She came up to me and said, "Papa, my visa is expiring, can I visit the US with Mom?" Well off she was on a holiday of a life time with her mother.

Ten days before her twelfth birthday, she accompanied us to Maldives; she had another reason ie that after twelve we would be paying full fare for the flight ticket and that we should take her along.

I was there for a conference on the cruise ship Super Star Libra which was operating from Mumbai and I knew that I would remain quite busy. Arooshi was eleven years old. I decided to take her along to give her an exposure of sailing on a ship. After spending some time on board she was in and out of the cabin and knew all the whereabouts of the ship. Having spent enough time on ships I could tell her a lot about ships and the sea. The ship sailed from Mumbai to Goa and back; we decided to stay on board in Goa once she anchored in Mormugao Harbour.

There is an experience that she remembers even today apart from the fascinating time that she had spent on the cruise ship. On completion of the sailing ship secured alongside a jetty on Ballard Pier. We quickly disembarked from the ship with our bags as we did not have much time in hand to catch our flight to Delhi from Mumbai. Something that came to my advantage was that I knew the Mumbai Port and the city very well.

The fastest way to move from the ship was by the buses being organized by the cruise company as we were one of the first passengers to disembark from the ship and immediately we got in the bus to Green Gate which was the exit point from Ballard Pier.

We took a taxi from Green gate for Mumbai Chhatrapati Shivaji Maharaj Terminus Station. We knew that in case had we decided to go straight to the Airport, we would not make it in time to due to traffic congestion on the roads. All the time I kept telling Arooshi to move fast, she would keep running, dragging her bag, with a smile. From the railway station we got on a sub urban train to Ville Parle. We rushed out of the railway station and took the first available auto rickshaw to Santa Cruz Airport. We reached the Indian Airlines counter and were the last passengers. Before we could say anything the girl at the Indian Airlines counter said "are you two Sharmas? Please rush as we have been waiting for you". In a short duration of less than two hours we had used different modes of transport to catch a flight. We were on a ship, bus, train, car, auto rickshaw and an aircraft.

Over a period she has become a veteran traveller. Even today when we travel together she would make a perfect plan working with the minutest details of things to be done and seen. She is a perfect guide and my best travel companion.

Chapter 11

Sawasdee: Welcome to Thailand

I along with my wife took the trip to Thailand in October 2010 and we arrived at Suvarnabhumi International Airport. The flight was uneventful.

Thailand is one of the few countries where one can see the hospitality, politeness and people being welcomed by locals from the core of their heart. Everyone from locals, to hotel staff and shopkeepers greet tourists with the greeting *Sawasdee ka* (greeting by a female) while *Sawasdee khrup* (is the greeting by a male) meaning Hello or Wai (like *Namaste* in India). There are many beautiful places in the world but it is the local people who make the destination popular and welcome. At the same time one has to be alert as there are many small time gangsters who target innocent tourists to make some easy money.

Bangkok or Krung Thep meaning *"City of Angels"*, is a shortened version of the official Thai name of Krung Thep Maha Nakhon. It is a vibrant and urban city full of life, delicious street food, green and lush parks, a network of rivers, amazing shopping arcades, some of the biggest markets in the world and of course its friendly people.

We started our tour by visiting the Royal Grand Palace. It has been the official residence of the Kings of Siam (and later Thailand) since 1782. The King, his court and his royal government were based on the grounds of the palace until 1925. It is still used for official events; several royal ceremonies and state functions are held within the walls of the palace every year. It is one of the most popular tourist attractions in Thailand.

In the same compound is located Wat Phra Kaew or the Temple of the Emerald Buddha. It is regarded as the most important Buddhist temple in Thailand. It is a highly revered Buddha statue meticulously carved from a single block of jade and is an image in the meditating position in the style of the Lanna school of the north, dating from the 15th century AD. Unlike other temples it does not contain living quarters for monks; rather, it has only elaborately decorated holy buildings, statues, and pagodas. Other attractions in Wat Phra Kaew include a model of Angkor Wat which was built under the order of King Rama IV when Cambodia was under Siamese control. The model was later recreated in plaster at the behest of King Rama V to celebrate the first centenary of the Royal City. The murals inside tell the Ramayana epic in its entirety. On the stone columns of the balcony verses are inscribed that explain the depiction in the murals. Each gate of the balcony is guarded by the five-metre tall *'Yaksa Tavarnbal'* (Gate-keeping giants), the characters taken from the Ramayana.

Wat Pho the temple of the Reclining Buddha is located south of the Grand Palace. It is the oldest and largest temple complex in Bangkok; it houses more than 1,000 Buddha statues which is more than any other Wat in Thailand. Most of the statues were brought over from abandoned temples in places such as Ayutthaya and Sukhothai by order of King Rama I.

After the foundation of Bangkok in the Ko Rattanakosin area in 1782 and the construction of the Grand Palace, King Rama I ordered the construction of the Wat Pho. The temple was built on the site of an older Ayutthaya era temple named Wat Photharam right next to the Grand Palace.

During the reign of King Rama III the temple complex was renovated and enlarged which took over 16 years to complete.

The temple is famous for its enormous gold plated Reclining Buddha statue. The statue named Phra Phuttha Saiyat was built during the reign of King Rama III in 1832 and is 46 metres long and 15 metres high. Although the figure is sometimes referred to as the lying Buddha or the sleeping Buddha, the Reclining Buddha shows the passing of the Buddha into final Nirvana.

The Wat Pho became a centre for knowledge and study of traditional Thai medicine. A massage school was founded here that still exists today; around it you will find stone statues showing various massage techniques. Thai massage, massage courses are given here and are open to anyone.

Since we were keen to know more about Thai boxing we went to a school close by. We were given a demonstration and back ground of the immensely popular sport. Thai boxing is the general western term for this Thai contact sport which is known as 'the art of eight limbs.' The sport gets this name because participants use their shins, elbows, knees and fists during each

Muay Thai match. Originating as part of the training regime of the Thai military, Muay Thai is today an extremely popular sport throughout Thailand. Every town and city has its own stadium for the sport. They made us wear gloves and practice some of the moves. It was thoroughly exhausting.

It was a busy day and at night we came back to the hotel. It was a bit late but I asked Neeru if she would like to go out for a walk. She said she would rather rest and I could go out if I liked to. I came out of the hotel and there were these guys waiting with Tuk Tuks thinking that I was on a loose end. I did not show any interest and told them that may be I will come back later. This was the easiest option. After some time I was back in the room. Neeru told me that another friend Anil who was staying in the same hotel wanted to take us to Hard Rock Cafe for a drink. We decided to take his offer. Whilst we came out of the lobby I was walking a few steps ahead of everyone, one of the characters thought that I was a loyal customer and had genuinely come back to take their offer. I looked at him sheepishly and told him not now. We all had a hearty laugh.

With nothing specific planned in the morning, we decided to explore the city and local markets on our own.

We were walking near Pratunam Market and Indra square. A lady who spoke good English and looked very friendly walked upto us. She said that she liked to meet people from abroad and specially Indians. I asked her as to what she was doing. She said that she was working for Standard Chartered Bank. Old habits die hard. I flashed all my cards including Standard Chartered bank cards and told her that I was a loyal customer of Standard Chartered Bank and was very impressed with their service.

A narrow escape

While we were talking to her she did mention that a sale of rubies was going on. When you are travelling with your wife you have to show interest when it comes to jewellery, gold, diamonds and special stones. We did say good bye and crossed over to the other side by the pedestrian overbridge. We stopped by at a small shop. One gentleman whom I did not know introduced himself as Captain Prasong; he spoke fluent English. He said that he did all his shopping by credit card. He also mentioned that there was big government aided ruby sale going on. Not wanting to spend much time talking to him we walked away.

As both of us were walking another gentleman came up to us and wished us. By then I realized and sensed something was not right. Thanks to mobile phones they were communicating with each other. He said that he lived in Australia and originally he was from Thailand. He mentioned that he visited Thailand a couple of times in a year and bought rubies and precious stones from here and sold them in Australia making huge profit. By now the story was getting interesting and I was getting even more suspicious of the whole plot. He said that it was the last day of ruby sale in Bangkok and that he could take us to a place where we could pick up genuine rubies, gemstones and jewellery. By now I had understood their game. I told Neeru as to what the plot could be.

In a short while he took us to a jewellery show room. It was a huge place with few staff and two shoppers ie Neeru and me. They started showing some gemstones and Jewellery. Jewellery apart, the place did not look or feel very safe. While all this was going on I indicated to Neeru we should run away from this place without giving any hint. That is exactly what we did. I pretended to be talking on my mobile and we rushed out of the showroom and took a Tuk Tuk from the other side of the road. We thought that was safer unless one amongst the gang was waiting just outside and we would still be in a trap.

A boat cruise to remember

In the evening we came to River City Pier to embark the boat for Chao Phraya Dinner cruise. It is an unforgettable both romantic and cultural experience. The Chao Phraya river by night is a charming place not easily forgotten. The Chao Phraya river, also known as the River of Kings, is one of Thailand's major rivers. It originates in North Western Thailand and is almost 400 kilometres long. It flows through Bangkok and ends into the Gulf of Thailand.

During the cruise we could see the traces of Thai history dating back to the time of the Rattanakosin era when the capital of Bangkok was established in 1782. In those days people used to settle by the Chao Phraya river and on the many canals spreading out further away from the river.

As the boat cruised we could see both old architecture like the Santa Cruz Church, Kalayanamit Temple and Bang Khun Phrom Palace and modern architecture like Rama VIII bridge, the Oriental hotel and the Shangri-La hotel. It was a contrasting style of architecture both ancient and modern.

With an expansive spread of international buffet, drinks and music playing it was an entertaining evening.

We arrived at Chiang Mai Airport on another trip in November 2011. It was a rare experience that happened at the Airport all because my friend Nuch had requested me to get a statue of Lord Buddha from India. She did not ask me for anything else and I was naturally obliged to bring it along for her.

As is the case in most airports baggage is sent through the x-ray machine and more often than not it is done at random. My baggage after passing through the x-ray machine was taken out and it was checked thoroughly. I was a confused and a worried man as to why this was being done. The customs officer looked very disturbed, annoyed and furious. Of all that there was in my bag he took out the statue of Buddha and asked me what it was. I told him that it was the statue of Lord Buddha. He said this was no Buddha. I told him that although I was a Hindu by religion, I had a lot of respect for Buddha and was also a Buddhist in faith. For some reason, he was not convinced that I had faith in Buddhism. It was getting difficult for me to explain it to this gentleman that it was only a gift that was bought for my friends. He even remarked that my friends were not Buddhists, and they would probably display the statue in their bathrooms. I had to tell him that I was from a military background and disciplined would not do anything wrong. Thereafter, he probably got the point and understood what I was trying to convey. He took me to his office.

He showed me the customs book that showed that exporting of Buddha's statue in fragmented form ie bust etc was illegal. I had brought a bust of Buddha. Luckily I was only bringing it in. He showed me a safe where there were a number of fragmented Buddha statues confiscated and kept. Anyway, he let me take it away.

My hosts were waiting outside for a long time and were worried due to the delay. I was the last person to walk out after the flight's arrival. I told them the complete story; they felt embarrassed and profusely apologized for putting me to such inconvenience.

Later in the day when I visited my friend's home, I was pleasantly surprised that the bust was displayed on the dining table in her house.

The initial impression of Thailand would be of a place which has beaches, rivers and plain landscape. But there is more to Thailand. Chiang Mai is a city located in mountainous northern Thailand. It was founded in 1296 and was the capital of the independent Lanna Kingdom until 1558. Its old city walls do tell about the historic grandeur although today they are in ruins. The city has over three hundreds temples Wat Chiang Man being the oldest; also the 14th century Wat Phra Singh, 15th century Wat Chedi Luang, and Wat Phra That Doi Suthep are some of the older ones.

In recent years there are more people coming here, but this place still has its own charm.

Wat Phra That Doi Suthep is one of the most important temples in Northern Thailand and at the same time one of the most beautiful. The temple is referred to as Doi Suthep *"doi"* meaning mountain. It is said that in ancient times a hermit called Suthep lived on the mountain much before the temple was built. The mountain was named after him.

The locals say that in case you have not visited Doi Suthep then you have not been to Chiang Mai.

In the 1300s a monk named Sumanaost found an intriguing relic believed to be part of Buddha's shoulder bone. The monk believed the relic had special powers and hid it in a series of silver Chinese boxes which he put into a bronze casket. With the relic in safe keeping Chiang Mai's King Kuna built Wat Suan Dok to house it. While moving the relic into Wat Suan Dok it miraculously divided itself into two pieces with each piece growing back to the size of the original.

While the one half of the newly split relic remained here at Wat Suan Dok, the King felt the second half needed its own temple. King Ku Na declared that a new temple needed to be built to honour the miracle but he wanted divine guidance on where to build it. The King placed the second half of the relic onto one of his White Elephants and sent it off into the jungle. The White Elephant climbed and climbed until he reached the peak on Doi Suthep Mountain then trumpeted three times, made three counterclockwise circles and laid down refusing to go any farther. This was the sign the King needed and Doi Suthep Temple was built on this site in 1383.

On reaching the temple you are greeted with a daunting 306 steps which are guarded by stone statues of giant snakes (*nagas*). These huge snakes run the entire length of the steps and are truly one of the highlights of the visit. For those having difficulty walking up there is funicular available for going up.

A gala time with elephants

There are a couple of elephant parks in Chiang Mai. We visited Elephant Nature Park located about 60 kms from the city. It was established in the 90s as a rescue centre for elephants and has been a sanctuary for numerous distressed elephants from all over Thailand. The place has been developed and maintained by mainly the entry fees collected from hundreds of visitors every day. There has been a growing movement to protect elephants and Elephant Nature Park has been the biggest elephant rescue organization in Thailand. They also have cats, dogs, buffaloes and many other rescued species. Activity at the park includes spending the day with elephants, feeding them, bathing them in the river and watching them roaming around freely.

The park encourages people to volunteer to work here but to do so one must plan well in time.

We arrived at the park in the morning; our guide took charge and we were assigned a place to sit and keep our belongings. After settling down and picking up a drink we moved to the elephant feeding area where they were all lined up for their meal. We were assigned the elephant to feed and were given a bucket of watermelons. We all fed them one by one and got our photos taken.

Once we had finished feeding, our guide gave us a lecture on elephants, the difference in elephants from African and Asian continents, their eating habits, life span, etc. We walked around the sanctuary and he kept telling us about the elephants and their traits.

Subsequently we had some time to relax and enjoy the sumptuous lunch.

It was afternoon and bathing time for the elephants. Slowly the elephants made their way to the water. Children and elders all enjoyed giving them a bath by splashing and pouring buckets of water over them.

Since we had some spare time our guide took us around and we stopped by the kitchen where food for elephants was being prepared. The park has received numerous awards; it has been featured in many international publications including *National Geographic* magazine as well as documentaries and film production companies like Discovery Channel, National Geographic, Animal Planet, BBC, CNN, KTV, RAI, major Thai language TV channels, print media and radio stations.

Having seen plenty of elephants in India and elsewhere it was indeed an experience to visit a sanctuary in Thailand.

We spent some time at the gift shop and then took the bus to go back to the city.

In the evening we visited the night market in Chiang Mai. Night market is a hub for shopping and hyper activity although this night market as compared to the one in Bangkok is really small. It still is the main venue for shopping in Chiang Mai. Ground zero of the market is located at the intersection of Chang Khlan Road and Loi Khro. Shops open early in the evening and close much later in the evening. It is also a good meeting point. There are plenty of knick knacks that can be picked up here. Over all it is a good way to spend the evening here and interact with the locals. Haggling to purchase any items is a must and is done through calculators.

There are plenty of adventure options available like zip lining, trekking and responsible eco-tourism activities in Chiang Mai.

We visited one of the schools where children suffering from HIV were being kept and taken care of. This was one of the most touching visits; there were these young children looking so pretty and giving a spectacular dance performance. The children did not know what they were suffering from. The whole organization has a major support base of committed donors.

Next day early in the morning even as the sun came up, we went to the base of Chiang Mai Hill; we could see the monks walking down to collect alms for the day. We were briefed about the procedure and we were ready for giving alms to them. In Thai it is called "Tak bat" meaning presenting food to monks. It is a Buddhist ritual and an important part of Thai culture. Giving alms is a virtue and is an ancient Buddhist tradition. We stood by for them whilst they were descending and offered them fruits and food. It was a solemn ceremony.

After performing this charitable act which made us feel good, we were on our way to the next destination- Chiang Rai. It was a three hour scenic drive through multiple hills continuously shifting between winding roads and flat plains.

Chiag Rai is popularly known as the Golden Triangle where Laos, Myanmar and Thailand meet.

We visited Wat Rong Khun located on the outskirts of Chiang Rai popularly known as "the White Temple" it is one of the most recognizable temples in

Thailand and the most visited attraction. It is a unique temple that stands out because of the white colour and pieces of glass shining in the sun. The white colour symbolizes the purity of Buddha and white glasses wisdom and dharma.

At the end of 20th century the original Wat Rong Khun was in a very poor state of preservation. Restoration work on the temple started but had to be halted due to a lack of funds.

Chalermchai Kositpipat, an artist born in Chiang Rai decided to completely rebuild the temple and fund the project with his own money. He built the temple to be a centre of learning and meditation and for people to gain benefit from the teachings of Buddha. Kositpipat considers the temple to be an offering to Lord Buddha and believes the project will give him immortal life.

Ubosot, the main building at the white temple is reached by crossing a bridge. In front of the bridge are hundreds of outstretched hands that symbolize unrestrained desire. The bridge proclaims that the way to happiness is by foregoing temptation, greed and desire. Next to the lake stand two very elegant Kinnaree, half-human and half-bird creatures from Buddhist mythology.

The Golden Building, a structure that stands out because of its colour, is the rest rooms building. Another very ornately decorated structure this golden building represents the body whereas the white ubosot represents the mind. The gold symbolizes how people focus on worldly desires and money. The white building represents the idea to make merit and to focus on the mind inwards instead of on material things and possessions.

The long necked tribals

We then visited Karen Long Neck Village which was an experience in itself. I had only seen women with long necks in pictures and had no idea where exactly they existed and the tradition behind it.

The Karen are a tribal group who have historically lived in the hills in Myanmar side of the Thai border. They are recognized by their elongated necks. They wear heavy brass rings around their necks, forearms and shins.

In the village there were bamboo houses. There were a couple of small booths selling handicrafts and other textile items. Each household had their small booths to sell the merchandise. They were a simple lot of people who did not push the visitor to buy anything but once you asked them they felt obliged to sell the stuff. We did pick up some items basically with the idea of helping them out.

Thousands of Karen have had to flee Myanmar over the decades due to political unrest. However, they would not get Thai citizenship; but still they are in a much better state having taken refuge in Thailand.

It simply is a tradition that Karen women put themselves through the neck lengthening routine. There are a number of them who are sticking to the tradition of keeping long necks; being refugees at least they can make some money and survive and some do it to keep up their heritage. It is said that the practice of long necks and keeping brass rings round them was to protect them from tigers. Slowly the tradition is being broken with the younger generation keeping fewer rings round their neck.

Undoubtedly the main tourist attraction among the hill tribes of Thailand is the Karen Long Necks (*Paduang*). There are a couple of other groups living in Thailand for centuries like the Big Earring (*Akha*), Yao, Palong, Kayor, and Hmong (*Meo*). These other groups largely have better-established villages than the Karen Long Necks do but are still known for their own unique traditions. These traditions range from heavily belled clothing to large gauge earnings stretching out of their earlobes. The Hmong people have many large villages.

There are various schools of thought regarding visiting tribal villages. I have always thought that it is always a good thing to do; visiting them helps them survive better. Tourists do tend to pick up products made by them and see their culture and lifestyle.

The Golden Triangle

The Golden Triangle is an area of around 350,000 square kilometres that overlaps the mountains of three countries of Myanmar, Laos and Thailand. The Golden Triangle designates the confluence of the Sop Ruak River and the Mekong river.

The next day we wanted to complete the visit of the golden triangle. We took a boat from the jetty underneath the statue of Golden Buddha at Sop Ruak meaning Golden Triangle to Don Laos Island. We spent a couple of hours here looking around the island. There are some restaurants and shops selling souvenirs, textiles and jewellery. It was an easier way to set foot on another foreign country. After spending a couple of hours here we took the boat back to Sop Ruak. After a short drive from Sop Ruak we were at Tachilek in Myanmar's southern most region. It may not be real Myanmar; but at least coming here we did get a flavour of this place and time to interact with the locals. It is a peculiar border trading town and is being upgraded as a town at the heart of Golden Triangle.

Development work by MFLF

We had the opportunity to visit and learn about one of the most successful Sustainable Alternative Livelihood Development projects run by Mae Fah Luang Foundation (MFLF).

In 1972, the late Her Royal Highness Princess Srinagarindra (Princess Mother) founded the Thai Hill Crafts Foundation to offer market access for craft-making to villages in the Northern highlands. It was later renamed the Mae Fah Luang Foundation in 1985 after the name given to the Princess Mother by the ethnic minorities, meaning "royal mother from the sky." The new name indicates the growing scope of social development efforts the foundation was assuming based on the ideas and philosophy of the Princess Mother.

In 1988 the MFLF initiated its flagship project in Doi Tung area with the goal of providing people with sustainable livelihoods and to tackle opium cultivation at its root cause, poverty and lack of opportunity. The MFLF developed the Sustainable Alternative Livelihood Development (SALD) model, which emphasizes thorough understanding of the needs of the local people and their socio-geographical realities, as well as integration and involvement of all levels. This model has been replicated in its projects in Thailand, Myanmar, Afghanistan and Indonesia.

Over a period of decades the Mah Fah Luang Foundation implemented the Doi Tung Development project after Thailand's Princess Mother pledged to address poverty in the marginalized region. The programme worked in stages; first alleviating immediate poverty through healthcare and basic education, then working with communities on new entrepreneurial opportunities. Its ongoing final stage developed growth opportunities and a recognizable local brand, Doi Tung. The initiative built upon government projects that had been preventing growth of the opium cultivation and use through law enforcement and welfare committees since the 1950s. Between 1991 and 2000 annual opium production in Thailand dropped from 23 to 6 tons with an eradication rate of between 800 and 1,000 hectares a year. The Doi Tung Development Project works in 29 villages benefiting 11,000 people and has been recognized by the UN Office of Drugs and Crime as one of the best examples of Sustainable Alternative Livelihood

Development in the world. Thailand's successful efforts to eradicate opium harvesting have made the country a leader in the global fight against the drugs trade.

Focusing on the hilly areas of the north where marginalized tribal populations have been harvesting opium for centuries, Thailand's campaign against opium has developed income streams in tourism, coffee and fruit farming. Running in various permutations since the 1960s, it has been made possible by long term cooperation between the royal family, government and small communities.

We visited the hub of activity Mae Fah Luang Art and Culture Park. It is a landscaped garden and museum, housing the region's largest collection of Lanna arts, including the teakwood exhibition, a botanical collection, and the largest collection of art items from the Lanna culture or Tai culture. They are minorities who can be found in northern Thailand, China's southwestern region or Yunnan, eastern Myanmar or the Shan States, north western Vietnam and western Lao. It started first as the office of the Thai Hill Crafts Foundation. Through purchasing and marketing handicrafts, the Thai Hill Crafts Foundation helped preserve the traditional skills and support the livelihoods of ethnic minorities. The Golden Pavilion that the people of Chiang Rai built was presented to the Princess Mother in honour of her 84th birthday.

Hall of Opium was created to reduce the demands of drug abuse through knowledge and education. While the DTDP tackles the drug problems from the supply side this centre tries to solve drug problems from the demand side. A result of almost 10 years of research the exhibition at the Hall of Opium conveys the history of opium and its trade across the globe as well as provides a comprehensive source of knowledge on opium, opiates and other narcotics. The exhibition also presents current issues regarding the efforts to control drugs and the impacts of drug abuse with the belief that education would deter drug abuse.

Mae Fah Luang Foundation had a great impact on us. Interestingly, we flew back home from Chiang Rai International Airport which is also named "Mae Fah Luang."

Chapter 12

Brazil and Fiji – A Taste of Diversity

Within a period of about a year, ie from April 2011 to April 2012, I visited two countries very different in every way but fascinating – Brazil and Fiji.

Brazil – Land of Carnivals

I reached Rio after flying for 42 hours from Delhi, transiting through Chicago, New York and Sao Paulo. A visit to Brazil had been in my bucket list for many years. So it certainly was worth taking such a long flight in the April of 2011, although the flying time could have been much shorter had I flown through the middle-east.

It was my first landing in Brazil and in fact in South America. South America is a large continent and distant from India. Brazil is a country of colour, life and music. Inspite of the problems it faces, people from all over the world visit this great country, which covers half of South America. Whether looking for wild pristine beaches, incredible surf, huge modern cities or charming colonial towns in a part of the world this large, it truly does have something for everyone.

Spanish is the official language in all South American countries except Brazil, Guyana, Suriname and French Guinea and is spoken in countries that are not historically Spanish. Portuguese is the official language of Brazil. Brazil is the only Latin American nation that derives its language and culture from Portugal. For me language has never been a barrier for communication. I have always found my way and received great help from locals even without knowing a word of the local language.

After leaving the airport I felt quite at home traversing through the busy traffic. After almost an hour's drive from the airport I reached Sheraton

Grand Rio Hotel & Resort located in Leblon. The hotel was busy and full due to a major event. Every one was keen to check in and frequently kept asking for rooms to the front office staff. Something that I have realized over a period of time is that when the hotel staff are doing their job and trying to help out and they are genuinely busy, by repeatedly asking them the room does not get ready faster. I gave them my voucher and showed them the place where I would be sitting in a corner. After about 45 minutes they gave me a suite on one of the higher floors with a wonderful view of South Atlantic flanked by towering mountains. This is something I was rewarded with for being patient and my room was upgraded. From the balcony there was the beautiful view of Copacabana Beach and statue of Christ the Redeemer. There could not be a better location of the hotel between trendy Barra da Tijuca and famed Ipanema Beach.

Rio is truly a magical city, known for its Copacabana and Ipanema beaches, the Christ the Redeemer statue atop Mt Corcovado, Sugarloaf Mountain and its Carnival festival; the seaside city is lively. Copacabana, is Rio's egalitarian and eclectic neighbourhood. The very name itself provokes images of beauty, sand and ocean. The magnificent jungle-clad mountains rise from the ocean and seem to blend into the beautiful bend of Copacabana Beach, now a world renowned hotspot for tourists from around the world. The Copacabana Beach stretches for over five kilometres and beckons one and all to its alluring waters. Sun, sea and beautiful bodies are what represent the pleasure-seeking side of the neighbourhood. Copacabana is renowned for excellent hotels, bars and restaurants.

I do remember my Norwegian shipmates who I had worked with in the oilfields in India; some of who had also worked in Brazilian oilfields had told me that one must be very careful in Brazil and that chances were very likely for one to get mugged. They would normally keep a few dollars in the wallet and rest of the money in their socks. In case they landed in a difficult situation the best option was to give their wallet away. I was lucky not to encounter anything like this. Of course I did not venture out alone at odd times and in unfamiliar places.

The first night I was taken to the nightlife district of Lapa by my hostess, Ana. It was once a seedy area but now had changed into fun option of nightlife. It is something one has to experience first hand; it is famous for the aqueduct arches built by the indigenous people to bring water to the city in its early stages. At night the place is full of thriving nightlife, bright with colours, food and carts carrying drinks. There was Brazilian music playing from crowded clubs, which can be heard from dusk to dawn in the streets. Locals, tourists both young and old, were merrily dancing here. After spending some time and enjoying our drinks it was a bit late and my hotel was at a distance. I asked Ana to hail a cab for me instead of dropping me back to the hotel. The ride back was quite an adventure, the taxi driver was honking, driving full speed and cutting lanes. But I did not find this a problem being used to it back home. The only difference was that the road signs were in Portuguese. No wonder a study by Dutch transport technology company TomTom has revealed that Rio de Janeiro has the third worst traffic in the world.

I started the following day with a visit to Christ the Redeemer, a colossal statue of Jesus Christ located on the summit of Mount Corcovado. The statue is the largest Art Deco-style sculpture in the world and is one of Rio de Janeiro's most recognizable landmarks. It is ideal to visit the statue of Christ the Redeemer in the morning before the rush of tourists build up; we did exactly that. Within a few minutes taking escalators and panoramic elevators we were on top at the base of the statue.

On reaching the top to my pleasant surprise heard the song "JaiHo" composed by A.R. Rehman, a famous Indian composer, singer and music producer. This song was composed for the film "Slumdog Millionaire". There was a group of young boys and girls, dancing and exercising in perfect co-ordination with this song.

Ana having spent her childhood in Rio insisted that I should visit garden Jardim Botanico. Respecting her sentiments I took the offer and the visit was no disappointment as it is a beautiful garden; we enjoyed a relaxed walk away from the hustle and bustle of the city.

It is a botanical garden that was formed over 200 years ago in 1808 and opened to the public in 1822. The garden is spread over 50 hectares and it was originally intended for the cultivation of imported spices; it now contains over 6000 species of indigenous and foreign plants and trees which includes over 900 varieties of palm trees. The famed 750 metre long avenue of royal palms leading from the entrance to the gardens is simply impressive. The cultivated garden is less than 50% of the parkland with the rest of the land taken up as forest land all of which lies within the heart of urban Rio and was designated a biosphere reserve by UNESCO in 1992. The garden has a huge collection of cacti, orchids, bromeliads, spices, herbs and other rare Brazilian plants, whilst the park itself is home to about 140 bird species such as the toucan, guan and the endangered white-necked hawk, as well as to capuchin monkeys and marmosets.

We drove to the Sugarloaf Mountain a little late in the aftenoon. On the way it was a wonderful sight to see the followers of Hare Krishna movement, dancing and chanting Hare Krishna in the streets. There is an Iskcon Temple in Rio; interestingly members of this movement are professionals, company executives and even scientists.

We went up by the Sugarloaf Cable car which opened in 1912; it has been in continual use since then and was even the site for the 1979 James Bond film, *Moonraker.*

Ana told me that one can visit the Sugarloaf mountains at any time of the day. However she took me around sunset; it was a magnificent view, when the sunset covers the neighbouring hills, the port and the ships anchored in the Bay of Guanabara and the silhouette of Jesus Christ himself that stands out in different shades as light changes. There is no better view of Rio than from Sugar loaf mountains.

The last day in Rio I spent time leisurely. It is amazing to see people running, exercising and playing on the beaches. There were so many people on the beaches that it looked as if the locals had left their homes to be here. Rio's beaches are world renowned for their clean soft sand and their convenient accessibility from most hotels and hostels. Along Copacabana beach there was a plethora of rental tents and chairs, wet trails, free showers, bars and cafes. Although Ipanema and Copacabana beaches are busy and popular, I spent the morning swimming at Leblon beach which is much quieter and had a direct access from the hotel I was staying in.

The next day I left Rio by the afternoon flight for Foz du Iguacu, the International Airport for Iguazu falls. After reaching the hotel, I was told at the reception that there was a bus going to the duty free zone at Puerto Iguazu and if I desired I could hop on. For me, more than shopping I did not want to miss a chance to set foot on Argentinian soil. I quickly put my bags in the room, picked up my passport and got on the bus. Puerto Iguazu indeed is an organized shoppers' paradise; one can buy virtually anything, from simple utensils to computers, perfumes and designer clothing.

The following morning I went on a tour of Iguazu Falls. The name of the falls originates from the Tupi or Guarani language, and means "big water". While the ancient Brazilian tribes knew of its thunderous beauty, it was only officially discovered in 1541, when the European explorer the Spanish Conquistador Alvar Nunez Cabeza de Vaca came across its awe inspiring magnificent spectacle.

In fact the Iguazu Falls are what divides the river of the same name into its upper and lower portions, a fact that has given rise to several myths and legends as to their origin. This river forms the boundary between Brazil and Argentina making it a significant part of the political and geographical structure of the continent of South America. The Iguazu Falls and Iguazu National Parks in Brazil and Argentina are two UNESCO World Heritage Sites.

It was a spectacular sight to see Iguazu falls, which is taller than Niagra Falls and more than twice wide. On arrival I embarked to take the boat ride in Iguazu Falls with other visitors. We were asked to put all our important items in the water proof bags and were given a set of rain coats each. The boat was rolling and pitching. It was a wonderful experience. Water was dropping all over us, the climax was getting down to water level beneath the roaring cascades which is a once in a life time experience. Noise of water falling and this experience was so awesome that we kept admiring it all through the boat ride.

I spent time on the walkways that have been built around the falls to have a close look at mesmerizing waterfalls and hear the thunderous noise of water.

Before I came to South America a friend had sent me a video clip of a helicopter ride over the falls. He did not know much about my travel plans apart from the fact that I was going to South America. There were some helicopters parked. I bought a ticket to take this marvellous helicopter ride. It was amazing to fly over one of the most beautiful landscapes in the world and take in its immense size. It was a memorable ten minute ride, where the pilot gives a running commentary, explaining some vital aspects about the falls and the park. The flight starts with flying over the Visitor's Centre and then heads over the National Park and I could see the jungle deep inside Brazil, Argentina and Paraguay. Then he flies close to the falls, where I could see the falls both from the Brazilian and Argentinian side, as well as Devil's Throat (the largest waterfall in the region), San Martin Island and San Martin Waterfall (the second largest). The pilot took the helicopter around the falls for us to take photos. These were certainly one of the most memorable ten minutes in the air.

After dinner in the hotel, with some friends whom I had met during the visit to Iguazu Falls we decided to go to a bar for a drink which was quite busy, lively and had Brazilian music playing. It was a wonderful and relaxed evening. I was carrying my camera strapped on my belt. We were having fun and enjoying our evening and talking about our experiences of travel and for some reason I unstrapped the camera tied to my belt and kept it on the table. After spending some time here in a happy mood we took a taxi to the hotel which was some 15 minutes ride from the bar. On reaching the hotel, I realized that the camera was not with me. Obviously I had forgotten it on the table. I called up the bar from my room to tell them that I had forgotten my camera; they said that every one who had ever left anything there always got it back and they would keep it safe in case they found it. I called them up in the morning and was told that the camera had been found. On reaching the bar, the girl on duty came with a camera cover and nothing in it! May be this is what they kept as a sample for cameras lost there to be shown to guests. It was not the first time that I was losing a camera! There are times when one must leave photos behind and keep them etched in memory.

Fiji: Heavenly Islands in the South Pacific

Fiji, literally is in the other part of the world. New Delhi and Suva, the capital of Fiji are over 12000 kilometres apart. This was a place which I knew a bit about. Apart from visiting Fiji, the other attraction of my going there was to spend some time with my friend Udai and his family, who was there on an assignment.

Fiji is an island country in Melanesia, part of ocean in South Pacific Ocean. It consists of an archipelago of more than 300 islands.

My flight landed a bit late in the evening at Nadi, which is also the gateway of Fiji. I was welcomed with the warm greeting *"Bula"*. It is the Fijian word for "hello". *"Ni sa bula vinaka"* is the full and correct greeting meaning, "a warm hello," but *bula* is more commonly used. The Fijian people are exceedingly warm and friendly and they love to express their love of life and their genuine hospitality with infectious and enthusiastic *bulas.* The word is also used as a blessing when someone sneezes.

I spent the night at a hotel in Nadi before going to Suva the next morning. The first impression of Nadi was that of a laid back place and I could hear Indian and Fijian music playing all over. The hotel staff are a mix of people; a large number of staff were of Indian origin.

After a quiet night, in the morning I drove to Suva. It was a fascinating drive taking in the Coral Coast, Sigatoka and Pacific Harbour regions route. It is probably one of the most driven roads on the main island of Viti Levu, Queens Road, between Nadi, home to the international airport and Suva. This scenic highway takes in the island's western and southern coastlines and passes through the renowned resort areas of the Coral Coast and Pacific Harbour via Sigatoka. It was a comfortable drive from Nadi to Suva and it took about three hours.

Suva, the capital, is the heart of Fiji, home to half of the country's urban population and the largest city in the South Pacific. It's a lush green city on a hilly peninsula and has a vibrant cultural scene. It has been the capital of Fiji since 1882, and many buildings date back to the colonial era.

With Ezna, a friend, I visited the Fiji Museum, which is located in the heart of Suva's Thurston Gardens. The museum holds a remarkable collection, which includes archaeological material dating back 3,700 years and cultural objects representing both Fiji's indigenous inhabitants and the other communities that have settled in the island group over the past 200 years.

Thurston Gardens have a lot of history attached to it; originally located near Waimanu Road, a Botanical Garden was first established in Suva back in 1881 by the Colonial Secretary Sir John Bates Thurston, a knowledgeable amateur botanist. In 1913 the Botanical Gardens was moved to their current location and eventually renamed Thurston Gardens in 1976.

The drinking fountain was established by Henry Marks for the use of the public visiting the gardens in 1914 and shortly after that the Marks family presented the octagonal bandstand with its classical, columned clock tower. The clock tower and bandstand were officially opened in 1918 and were often used for musical concerts.

A visit was organized for me to the office of *Fiji Times* by Ezna. *Fiji Times* is a daily English newspaper published in Suva; it was established in Levuka on 4 September 1869 by George Littleton Griffiths. It is Fiji's oldest and most prominent newspaper and is still published. The newspaper's masthead states that it is "The First Newspaper Published In The World Every Day". It is owned by Motibhai Group of Companies.

I had a meeting with Rakesh Kumar, a senior reporter of *Shanti Dut* (messenger of peace) which is an award winning Hindi language newspaper published weekly. This is also a part of *Fiji Times* and with the same ownership. It was a pleasant surprise and nice to know a Hindi weekly was published so far away from India. Interestingly, it is the people of Indian origin, who have kept it alive.

We had a long discussion about India, Fijians and those of Indian origin. India's links with Fiji Islands commenced in 1879 when Indian labourers were brought here under indentured system to work on sugarcane plantations. The first ship load of 498 labourers arrived in Fiji on 14 May 1879. Between 1879 and 1916 (when this system was abolished) around 60,000 Indians were brought to Fiji. In popular parlance, indenture was known as 'Girmit' — a distortion of agreement and those taken under it the 'Girmityas'. Despite maintaining minimal contacts with India, ethnic Indians here have retained their religion, culture, tradition and language. They speak Fiji Hindi, a mixture of Awadhi and Bhojpuri. They are also great fans of Bollywood and one can hear Hindi songs in a lot of places. Hindustani is recognized as one of the three official languages, besides English and Fijian, as per 1997 Constitution. Hindi is also taught in schools. Owing to 1987 and 2000 coups, a large number of Fijians of Indian origin emigrated from Fiji, mainly to Australia, New Zealand, US and Canada. This included many doctors, engineers, professionals, skilled personnel, senior officials, businessmen and also students.

Rakesh interviewed me regarding India, tourism, cultural exchange and trade between the two countries. The same was covered extensively in the subsequent issue of *Shanti Dut*.

While travelling I do not crave for Indian food. The main criteria is that it should be vegetarian and there is always a chance to try out something new. Suva has plenty of dining options available that range from affordable eateries to high end restaurants. Indo Fijian and Chinese food is the most popular but at the same time there is a good selection of cafes, bistros and restaurants specialising in Italian, seafood and Japanese cuisine. Shopping malls also have plenty of dining options and there are a couple of Indian Restaurants. In the evening Suva's nightclub district comes alive with a number of great bars, pubs and clubs to choose from. Most of the bars are within Victoria Parade vicinity. People from all over, locals and tourists can be found here merry making till late in the night. We did a bit of bar hopping.

Udai had organized a meeting one morning with Ayaz Sayed-Khaiyum who was holding a couple of port folios including that of Tourism Minister. I reached there a few minutes before the scheduled time. His secretary offered me a cup of coffee and said that the minister would be arriving anytime and may take a few minutes. He was there at our appointment time and was very happy to meet me. He was down with viral, inspite of that he made to the office to keep the appointment. Being of Indian origin, he had a lot to discuss about both the countries. He gave me an insight into the plans of Fiji, he said that there were only about 2,000 Indians who had visited Fiji. He wanted the number to increase. There should be a greater exchange of people travelling and more from India, as India was a growing economy and there were more Indians travelling abroad with disposable income.

The next day I drove back to Nadi and visited Denarau Island; it is is a small private island located five kilometres north west of Nadi. It is connected to the mainland by a short causeway.

Denarau is a luxurious island and all famous international chains have hotels and resorts here. Some of them who have their properties here are Sheraton, Sofitel, Radisson and Hilton. There are residential, commercial and retail precincts here. The island boasts of 18-hole Denarau Golf course and beautiful beaches.

Denarau Marina provides sea transfer services to the island chains of the Mamanucas and the Yasawas.

The Marina, is a place for shopping and has variety of restaurants, a supermarket, bakery, and other amenities. It is a great place to be at, any time of the day.

The development of Denarau Island started in 1969, when American developer Dennis McElrath purchased the land. The first hotel, the Regent of Fiji now the Westin Denarau, opened in 1975.

Between 1988 and 1991, Japanese property developer EIE International purchased all of Denarau in stages and started on a $200 million development project and building an 18 hole golf course, a marina and more hotels. After EIE went bankrupt in 1995, the resort was purchased by a consortium of investors.

Fiji has a lot of islands; some could take hours to reach. Naturally, the best islands are further away and more time is required to reach them and explore. There are a couple of tours by ferry to islands close by. I decided to choose one of the closest islands to Denarau. I took a day trip by ferry to South Sea Island. It is peppered with palm trees and surrounded by a coral lagoon; the uninhabited South Sea Island is one of the treasures of the Mamanuca Islands. Crystal clear waters, coral reefs and thousands of colourful tropical fish surround the tiny island.

South Sea Island is a 30 minute ferry ride from Denarau Marina. Being a close location to Denarau, it is a small island; it is only a few minutes walk from one end to other but it offers a lot of activity. Sail boats and kyaks are available here. One can swim, snorkel or go diving in clear waters.

It was a day well spent; having been a sailor and fond of the sea I did not miss out on any of the water sports activities.

Although the island is uninhabited, one can still get a taste of Fijian culture with a traditional Meke performance and craft market on week days. Meke performances embraces traditional song and dance to conjure up the legends, love stories, spirits and history of Fiji through symbolic movements. Music is a favourite pastime of Fijians and at the same time it is important part of their rich culture.

At lunchtime, everyone gathered around the tables at the open air restaurant to watch Fijian performances and enjoy a delicious buffet lunch with beer, wine and soft drinks flowing.

Time just flew and soon I was on my way back from this beautiful island to spend a day in Nadi.

Nadi due to its close proximity to Denarau Island and its wide range of quality accommodation also makes it an ideal base to discover the rest of Fiji.

Affordable hotels along the main road in Martintar and Namaka provide ideal pre or post flight accommodation. In Nadi town, there are plenty of affordable eateries offering Indian, Chinese and Western cuisine.

Nadi has plenty of activities; water sports are available on most resorts. Also there are other adventure activities available like off road vehicle tours, skydiving and zip lining.

Later I visited the local fruit and vegetable markets Namaka and Nadi. Whenever I am in a new place I have always liked to visit the local markets. These markets really give a pulse and feel of the local people be it vendors or those locals coming for shopping. Enthusiastic and at the same time calm, there were a lot vendors selling a variety of fruits and vegetables like pineapples, kava roots, papayas, brinjals, chillies and spices. There were also fishmongers.

My trip thus coming to an end, I prepared for my return home.

Chapter 13

Experiences in Greece and Turkey

It is popularly said that Thessaloniki is a city easy to fall in love with. It is one of the most beautiful cities in Greece. The city brims with romance and lovebirds from all over the world find it an ideal destination to spend a romantic getaway. In March 2013, Roxani a friend of mine invited me to visit Thessaloniki. I landed at Makedonia Airport in Thessaloniki, a port city in Greece where my friend lives. Roxani, received me at the airport with a warm hug. Soon we were chauffeured in a limousine and drove to the hotel, admiring the architecture and ancient archaeological remains on the way. Roxani kept briefing me about Thessaloniki and mentioned that the city is renowned for its historic sites, festivals and is considered to be Greece's cultural capital.

After a short drive I was at the Mediterranean Palace which is a luxury hotel and is located in the centre of Thessaloniki at the commercial, business and cultural heart of the city, next to one of the most picturesque districts of the historic Ladadika. Due to it's central location most important places can be reached in a few minutes on foot, be it Aristotelous Square, Ladadika or Tsimiski Street, the city's busiest shopping street. I checked in and soon I was in my beautifuly furnished room with elegant furniture, with an astonishing view of the the Thermaikos Gulf overlooking the harbour.

Thessaloniki lies on the northern fringe of the Thermaic Gulf on its eastern coast and is bound by Mount Chortiatis on its southeast. In the old town and literally the Upper Town, it is easy to find one's way; most roads in the city centre are either parallel or perpendicular to the sea. It is a simple rule here; in case a street is going downhill and you keep walking, one would land up near the sea.

Thessaloniki was founded in 315 BC by King Cassander of Macedonia. It rapidly became a very important centre and one of the major cities of the kingdom during the Hellenistic era with limited political autonomy.

Thessaloniki's unique personality is mostly due to its people, where there are many ethinic minorities who were offered asylum, a place to call home. Thessaloniki is known by Greeks as the "Mother of Migration," due to its centuries-long history of providing refuge to those fleeing persecution and conflict, from Sephardic Jews in the 1400s to Greek refugee returnees in the 1900s. Today, Thessaloniki hosts asylum seekers and refugees from Syria, Afghanistan, Iraq, Turkey, South Asian and African countries.

It is a city full of stories that have been unfolding over 2300 years. They are the stories of her people, visitors and friends.

After the fall of the Kingdom of Macedon in 168 BC it became part of the Roman Republic and was further developed into an important trade centre actually connecting Europe with Asia through the Roman empire via Egnatia.

During the first century AD and afterwards, the city became one of the first early Christian centres after Paul the Apostle preached here and laid the foundations for a new religion.

During the Byzantine era the city was further developed and became even bigger being the second most important city of the empire after Constantinople itself. Wonderful churches and other buildings were built in several areas while extended defensive constructions were also erected.

In 1204 AD, during the fourth crusade the city fell into the hands of the Crusaders and thus the Kingdom of Thessalonic was created. In 1246 though, the Byzantines managed to recover the entire area.

After 1430, the Ottomans conquered Thessaloniki, under the command of Mourad II. During the Ottoman occupation period, the city once again rose to prominence as the most important commercial and trade centre of the region and was considered of great strategic importance due to the trade routes established.

During the 19th century while the Ottoman empire was making extensive reorganization and modernization efforts several wonderful new buildings were built or redisgned; Aristotelous Square was redesigned, Ladadika was transformed with renovations of several neoclassical buildings and Nedekou Mansion was constructed. The gradually expanding use of steam and the wider spread of the railways transformed Thessaloniki into the largest industrial centre in the Balkans.

On 27 October 1912, during the first Balkan War the Greek army liberated the city, while in 1917 the city faced what was perhaps its greatest disaster ever as a huge fire destroyed almost three quarters of the centre which had various consequences in the following years. Serious efforts and proposals were made by famous architects like Ernest Hebrard in order for the city centre to be rebuilt like a modern European capital.

Today Thessaloniki is a modern European city, as always an important trade and transportation centre connected to all the Balkan countries. It was nominated as the Cultural Capital of Europe in 1997.

In 2004, during the Athens Olympics, the city hosted a number of athletic events while being designated as one of the Greek Olympic Cities.

In the evening Roxani came to meet me at the hotel; we walked across to Ladadika which was full of people enjoying music in the local taverns. We went to a restaurant and found a place for us to sit; it was a bit early and we were told by the Manager that there was a booking for some other guests at nine for the table. We ordered our dinner with some Greek wine. We had enough time to chat and enjoy our dinner. It was a lovely evening. Ladadika remains quite busy till late night and it was nice to see people in a cheerful and happy mood.

Next morning we had a lovely Greek breakfast. Roxani had planned to show me Thessaloniki which for me was a godsend, having a local to escort me around her city. We walked to Aristotelous Square which is the beating heart of Thessaloniki. Lined with shops, restaurants, bars and hotels, it's the perfect place to get a feeling for the pace of life in this city. Stretching down to the waterfront, the square opens up to reveal beautiful views of the Thermaikos Gulf. Cafes were full of people from all walks of life.

After spending some time here we walked on Tsimiski Street. It has many boutiques, fashion shops, delicatessens, large bookstores and errant vendors; we stopped at Trigona Elenidi to eat trigona panoramatos. This sweet cream-filled pastry is said to have originated in Thessaloniki and was absolutely yummy.

We later walked to the White Tower which is perhaps the most recognizable spot in Thessaloniki. Depicted on all types of souvenirs and favourite clothes, photographed from all angles, in all seasons and at each hour of the day, it has come to be imprinted and recognized as the city's trademark.

The White Tower, apart from being a great architectural monument, is a vital reference point in Thessaloniki. Dominating the shore, it has become a meeting point and a good place for a walk. The White Tower is used as an exhibition centre. Under the auspices of the Museum of Byzantine Culture a permanent exhibition is on display dedicated to Thessaloniki, which allows the visitor to acquire a detailed knowledge of the successive historical periods of this great city. One can enjoy romantic walks in the town and stroll through the stunning monuments of Thessaloniki.

We walked past an impressive statue of Alexander the Great on his horse Bucephalus located near the archeological museum and the white tower in the water front. He is overtly heroic in pose, drawn sword held with his right hand and reins in left hand. He is wearing the typical Macedonian armour. On the way we came across a public park named Whatsapp!!

We stopped by a local restaurant for a quick lunch but it lasted for over an hour and a half. Roxani told me that Greeks like to enjoy their food. For me it was almost like a gastronomic tour.

One is very relaxed while walking in Thessaloniki due to the beautiful walking areas and architecture. After a leisurely walk we reached Atatürk Museum, a historic house museum. The house is the birthplace of the founder of modern Turkey, Mustafa Kemal Atatürk, who was born here in 1881.

In 1935, the Thessaloniki city council decided to give the building to the Turkish State which afterwards converted it into a museum dedicated to the life and achievements of Mustafa Kemal Atatürk. Mustafa Kemal Atatürk was the founder and leader of the modern secular Turkish State and is considered to be one of the most important and historic personalities of Turkey.

Next few days we spent time visiting places at our own pace and get immersed in the city. Despite its rich history, Thessaloniki refuses to be locked in the past. It has a modern, cosmopolitan feel, a busy cultural life with 30 museums and galleries, including the State Museum of Contemporary Art, which houses the Costakis collection. The Archaeological Museum of Thessaloniki is considered one of Greece's most important museums. Its collection includes important artefacts from the local area and wider northern Greece.

We enjoyed an opportunity to walk along the beach, which is about five kilometres in length, from the Concert Hall to the port. The beach of Thessaloniki has a linear front with relatively limited depth and long length, which gives the characteristics of a narrow coastal front.

Interestingly, Thessaloniki has almost twenty military and historical cemeteries. The oldest cemetery open to visitors, dates back to 8 BC. There are cemeteries and individual graves from the time of the Macedonian Dynasty, Hellenestic and Byzyantine period, Muslim and Jewish cemeteries. The most modern cemeteries are the cities religious cemeteries and the military cemeteries of World War 1.

We visited the Indian Cemetery which is located in Thessaloniki and not many people are aware of this. It is the final resting place for the Indian soldiers who fought and died during World War I in this theatre of war. It is located along side the railway tracks near Monastiriou street covering an area of 0.55 hectares. The inscription on the monument reads:

"To the glory of God in honoured memory of the one hundred and sixty three Indian soldiers, followers and labourers of the British Salonika Force and of the Army of the Black Sea, whose names are here recorded".

It is not only 163 Indians who are buried here, but a total of 520. They were soldiers who lost their lives fighting side by side with the allied forces to repulse Bulgarians and Germans. They were part of the multinational Army of the orient, for most part poor and illiterate. They fell defeated by the enemy and weather and were buried thousands of miles from home.

This cemetery contains the graves of 384 Hindus, 107 Muslims, 26 Sikhs, and a few Christians. There is also a Hindu Memorial which holds the ashes of 220 fallen soldiers, a memorial of 130 missing soldiers of the Salonika Front and 33 missing Indians of the British Royal Navy. It is a unique cemetery created in the panic of the period, burying all non-Christians together regardless of their religion. Innovative artist Leda Papa-Costantinou was so impressed by the Indian cemetery that the part of her work "in the name of", presented in 2007 at the 1st Biennale of Contemporary Art in Thessaloniki, was dedicated to it.

One afternoon I was walking in the port area and met a smart polished Greek gentleman. He came up to me and greeted me. We got into an interesting conversation. I gave him some details about my background and he told me that he was from the Greek Navy and retired now. As I was already close to the hotel and said bye to him. He was insistent that I should meet him at a café when I was free. I told him it was not possible this time and perhaps we could catch up another time. After about an hour

I came out of the hotel and found him hanging outside the hotel. I was not comfortable with him for some reason and anyway sat down at a café on his request. There were some people who were walking behind us and I could see them near the café as well. The restaurant Manager probably being nice indicated to me to come near him and he whispered in my ear that the person was part of a gang of scamsters operating here and I should quietly leave. I got up and pretending to be talking to someone on my mobile started walking away. He insisted that I should sit down as he was ordering some food. My suspicion arose further as he and a few others later started following me. As the hotel was across the road I ran to the hotel and once inside did not look back.

A day before departure it was Roxani's birthday. A positive, empathetic and vibrant person, who was looking at an exciting journey ahead. She had created a wonderful life and a beautiful family. On this occasion she organized a party at home with family and friends, with a big spread of Greek food and wine, which was really touching, delightful in every way and made it an evening to remember.

Turkey: Between the Sea of Marmara and the Black Sea

It is said about Turkey that it is a European country, an Asian country, a Middle Eastern country, a Balkan country, a Caucasian country, a neighbour to Africa, Black Sea country, Caspian Sea, all these.

It was in February 2014 that I flew from Delhi by Turkish Airlines and landed at Istanbul Atatürk International Airport to visit a country with stunning scenery and rich history.

Turkey is located between Europe and Asia, the Anatolian peninsula in western Asia, with a small enclave in Thrace in the Balkan region of southeastern Europe. Turkey is bordered by the Mediterranean Sea in south and east and by the Black Sea in north, by Armenia, Iran and Azerbaijan in the east, by Georgia in north east, by Bulgaria and Greece in north west and by Iraq and Syria in south east.

Turkey covers an area of 783,562 square kilometres and has a population of 80 million. It has a GDP figure of US Dollars 859,449 million. Industries include textiles, food processing, automotive, electronics, tourism, mining of coal, chromate, copper and boron, steel, petroleum, construction, lumber, and paper.

The history of the Turks covers a time frame of more than 4000 years. Turks first lived in Central Asia around 2000 BC. Later, some of them left Central Asia and spread around establishing many states and empires independent from each other within a vast area of Asia and Europe. These empires included The Great Hun Empire (established during the 3rd Century BC), the Göktürk Empire (552- 740), the Uygur Empire (741- 840), the Avar Empire (6-9 Century AD), the Hazar Empire (5-10 Century AD), and the Great Seljuk Empire (1040- 1157), apart from some others.

Turks started to settle in Anatolia in the early 11th century by way of continual migrations and incursions. Later Turks fully conquered the whole of Anatolia and established the Anatolian Seljuk State there (1080-1308).

The Seljuk State rapidly declined with the Mongol invasion of Anatolia which started in 1243. During the period of the decline of the Anatolian Seljuk state and after its disappearance, many Turcoman principalities were established in Anatolia towards the end of the thirteenth century. One of these was the Ottoman. It expanded rapidly throughout the 14th century and thus arose the Ottoman Empire which lasted until the end of the First World War.

The weakening of the Empire continued until World War I. The Ottoman Empire entered the First World War in 1914 on the side of the Central Powers and was defeated. Under the Mondros Armistice treaty, the territories of Ottoman Empire were occupied by Britain, France, Russia, and Greece. This was the end of the Ottoman Empire.

Kemal Atatürk started the Turkish National Liberation War after the occupation of the Ottoman Empire. After signing the Lausanne Peace Treaty on 24 July 1923, Turkey obtained independence and became a Republic on 29 October 1923.

Mustafa Kemal Atatürk (Atatürk meaning "Father of Turks") became the first President and introduced a broad range of reforms in the political, religious, social, legal, economic, and cultural spheres, designed to convert the new Republic of Turkey into a secular, modern nation.

Istanbul—blending the East and West

Istanbul is a city of unparalleled social and cultural richness. Napoleon Bonaparte said about Istanbul "If the Earth were a single state, Istanbul would be its capital." It not only joins continents, it also joins cultures and people. It is as fascinating and historical as it is dynamic and modern. Serving as the capital of two mighty empires incessantly for centuries, Eastern Roman or Byzantine and Ottoman and set squarely between two continents, Istanbul has cultures and traditions that blend East with West and Mediterranean with Anatolian. Each civilization that has made Istanbul its home has left its mark in sublime and splendid ways. It is one of the most visited places in the world and a central hub connecting Asia and Europe.

A habit that I have is to explore a place without wasting any time after arrival even if I am tired or not rested at all. The thought of missing something always bothers me. I had an early dinner and I went for a walk to Taksim Square, since the hotel I was staying in was also at Taksim. Taksim is the busiest part of Istanbul with many hotels, restaurants and shops. In every nook and corner of Taksim there is entertainment with street artists performing soothing music. All this makes Taksim square a must-visit when you are in Istanbul. Even strolling around the Taksim square and appreciating the lively atmosphere is simply a great experience.

I was walking around and enjoying the vibrant place, I met Ekrem a friendly guy. He got into a polite conversation. Generally enquiring were I was from and giving a brief detail about his family, he said that he was fond of talking to tourists and it gave him a chance to learn and improve his English. We were talking and walking down the street and sat at a nice Italian restaurant, which was quite busy and had a violinist performing. Ekrem offered to have dinner with me which I declined. All that I had was an espresso.

After having dinner Ekrem went down to the washroom, I also went down with him. Before I could think of anything else, I found myself in a nightclub and he asked me to accompany him. Thanks to his hospitality I was there! We sat down and he offered me a drink. Meanwhile, some women came and joined us; he told me that they were his friends. Playing safe I ordered for plain water. After the first drink for the group that had gathered the waiter would on and off ask me, "Sir, a drink for the lady?" By then I did guess what the game was.

After a long journey and jet lag I was too tired. Being in a foreign country, it is not easy to walk away. I already knew that I was in a trap and in any case surrounded by some of them. I had already spent a long time here and told Ekrem that I should leave. A few minutes later a waiter came and asked me as to how I would like to pay the bill. This did not come to me as a surprise. I told him that I had come to this place as Ekrem's guest and there was no question of my paying. Meanwhile, Ekrem pretended that he had no money with him and the card he was carrying there had no limit left to make the payment. Meanwhile, the manager came to me and said that the bill needs to be cleared. I told him the same thing that I was Ekrem's guest. I certainly was in a trap. The manager requested me to come to his office and asked me to clear a USD fifteen hundred bill. Preference was for cash payment but otherwise I had the option of making the payment by a credit card. I told him that I had no money and was not carrying any credit cards. He insisted that cash/card should be in my room. I told him that I had come as some one's guest in Istanbul and was being looked after by him. I gave him my wallet which had around 50 US dollars. He took the amount and let me go. I had only had a galss of water; instead of paying USD 1500, paying USD 50 was not a bad bargain!

During breakfast I had met Zaki who was from Lahore in Pakistan and was also a guest staying in the same hotel. We had a lot to talk about. Interestingly he too had worked in the oilfields like me. His family had moved to Pakistan during partition of India and Pakistan. He said that he would be coming to Delhi soon as his daughter wanted to do all her wedding shopping from Chandni Chowk in Delhi. I did mention about the previous night's encounter with Ekrem and the night club.

After the previous night's encounter I decided to stroll around Taksim Square during the day. The atmosphere is a bit different from the night; at the same time it was quite busy. There were people all over and with a lot of activity as in a way it is a central meeting point. Istiklal Street is a popular street and has many traditional shops selling Turkish items. I bought some saffron and dry fruits. It is a pedestrian street, hence easy to move around.

The Independence Monument in Taksim square is the most important and eye catching landmark. The monument was made by the Italian sculptor Pietro Canonica; it was inaugurated on 8 August 1928 with huge fanfare. It portrays the founders of the Turkish Republic including Mustafa Kemal Ataturk, Ismet Inonu, Fevzi Cakmak, as well as the other characters that symbolize the Turkish nation and the military aid of the Soviet Union during the Turkish War of Independence between 1919 and 1923. Most official ceremonies are held here.

In the afternoon, my guide Demir was there to take me around. Demir was a retired engineer, who out of personal interest had undertaken the assignment. He was a true copy of my father; when I told him so he was quite amused. I was at Golden Horn Districts and saw the centuries old city walls of Istanbul; these walls were built to protect the acropolis. The second set was established by the Roman Emperor Septimius Severus. They extend for 22 kilometres, stretching from the Sea of Marmara to the Golden Horn and demolished only twice in all their history. It was demolished by the Latin Crusaders who were supposed to be heading toward the Holy Land in 1204 and again in 1453 by the Ottoman Turks who tried to conquer the city of Constantinople. The walls had geopolitical importance. Every one struggled to take this city.

It was nice to see the Jewish quarters; the place looked very traditional with shops. It is a charming and wonderful area with cafes and restaurants.

I went upto Pierre Loti Hill by cable car . From top one has a breathtaking view of Halic and Istanbul. The name has originated from the French Pierre Loti novelist and naval officer. In 1876 he wrote passages in his diary dealing with some experiences at Istanbul.

I boarded a boat to take the Bosphorus cruise along the Bosphorus, the winding strait separating Europe and Asia. This cruise is one of the best ways to discover the elegance of Istanbul. Bosphorus joins the Sea of Marmara to the south with the Black Sea to the north of Istanbul. Bosphorus coastline is a delightful mixture of the past and the present where one can enjoy the grand splendour and quaint beauty of the ancient wooden mansions, palaces of marble, fortresses and small fishing villages.

The boat sailed past imposing Rumeli Fortress, located on a hill at the European side right on the banks of Bosphorus at the Sariyer district. It was built in 1452, before the conquest of Constantinople by the Ottoman Sultan Mehmed II in order to control commercial and military traffic. Inside the walls there are three big towers that were named after the three viziers of Mehmet, Sadrazam Candarli Halil Pasha (larger tower), Zaganos Pasha (south tower), Sarica Pasha (north tower).

The boat sailed past Leander's Tower also known as "Maiden's Tower," located on a tiny islet near Uskudar on the Asian side of Istanbul with a history spanning over 2500 years. It is truly a beautiful landmark which symbolizes the city of Istanbul. According to history, the first structure on the island was a mausoleum and later it was used as a customs office to control the movement of naval ships passing through the Bosphorus Straits.

Over a period the tower was also used as a prison, radar station and cyanide warehouse. Like many of the buildings in Istanbul, Leander's Tower succumbed to natural and man made disasters including an earthquake in 1509 and a fire in 1716. The fire completely destroyed the Tower and it was rebuilt in 1725.

In the evening I went to the famous Sultana's belly dancing show. The show is a lot of fun and some of the world's best belly dancers perform here. Interestingly, on the tables for dinner, they had put flags of countries that one belonged to. I was at a table with some Japanese; it had both Indian and Japanese flags. The singer made sure he sang in as many different languages as he could depending on the nationalities watching the show.

The show got over a bit late in the evening. While coming back to the hotel I met Zaki. He asked me if I would like to go for a drink, which I agreed to. Both of us being sailors our eagerness for adventure would never end. He told me that he had met a Pakistani gentleman, who was the Manager of a night club and had insisted that he should visit that. We looked for the place as he had also not been there before. We finally located it and it was the same place that I had been to the night before. I told Zaki that I was certainly not going in with him. Since he insisted and said that if things did not look good we would walk out.

His friend welcomed us at the same time the Turkish Manager and some other staff recognized me. The evening was enjoyable and we were looked after like VIPs by them. They promised me that they had given me an honourary membership of the club and that I would not be taken for a ride again. The place was almost empty and we asked for the bill but they would not present one. Jokingly Zaki said I hope they were not planning to give us a hefty bill and only preparing us for the same. Finally, the Manager appeared and said that it was all taken care off. As we insisted they gave us a token bill.

On our way back to the hotel from the night club one guy walked upto me and enquired, how I was doing. I asked him to go away. Zaki told me that I must be a popular person that some people already knew me in Istanbul. I had to tell him that it was Ekrem the same character who had taken me to the club the night before.

There were some others who approached us. Zaki would just say "Seychelles" a few times and the person would walk away. Have now tried this a number of times when travelling abroad in case some one keeps following me and pesters me. I just keep repeating "Seychelles"and it works very well.

Next morning after breakfast I started tour of Istanbul with Demir for the places that were still left to be visited. First stop was St Sophia, the great church of the Byzantine capital Constantinople (Istanbul) that took its current structural form under the direction of the Emperor Justinian I. The church was dedicated in 537 and was the pride of the emperor. The daring engineering feats of the building are well known. St Sophia is the symbol of Byzantium in the same way that the Parthenon embodies Classical Greece or the Eiffel Tower typifies Paris. It is one of the finest architectural wonders of the world.

Byzantine Hippodrome, the former centre of sports and political activities in Constantinople was next on our agenda. Byzantine Hippodrome, in which stands the 3500 year old Egyptian granite obelisk of Theodosius and the Serpent Column taken from Delphi by Emperor Constantine is a wonder to behold.

The Blue Mosque (Sultan Ahmed Mosque) is an historical mosque in Istanbul. The mosque is known as the Blue Mosque because of blue tiles surrounding the walls of interior design. This mosque was built between 1609 and 1616 during the rule of Ahmed I. Just like many other mosques, it also comprises of a tomb of the founder, a madrasa and a hospice. It is still used as a mosque and is a popular tourist attraction.

The last place we visited was the Grand Bazaar which dates back to 15th century. It is one of the oldest and largest covered markets in the world with over 4,000 shops under one roof and covering a total area 30,700 square metres. The main area of the Grand Bazaar boasts a total of 64 streets and 22 entrances; however the entire section around the historical bedesten is also considered to be a part of the market. You can get everything that a tourist would be looking for from ceramics, Turkish lamps, evil eye ornaments, Turkish delight, scents, tea, spices and rugs. The shopkeepers were friendly and waiting to welcome visitors. It is an easy place to get immersed into. Haggling is a way of life here to get a good price.

After having done most that I could do in Istanbul and enjoying Turkish coffee, Turkish delight, it was time to go to a Turkish Bath (Turkish Hamam). Turkey is synonymous with *hamams*. Turkish Bath is a form of public bathing whose origins can be found in the culture of the Ottoman Empire. These were established because of commercial, cultural and religious reasons

On recommendations of my guide Demir, I went to Aga Hamami an authentic Turkish hamam. It has a lot of history. Mehmed the Conqueror (the 7th Ottoman Padishah) constructed this building as a hunting house in 1454. It underwent a large-scale renovation in 1844 by Abdulmecid (the 31st Ottoman Padishah). It was used by the Padishahs and their sons until the final years of the Ottoman Empire. With the foundation of the Republic of Turkey in 1923, the Ottoman Empire ended. An Armenian woman bought the Aga Hamami and it then opened to public.

The staff from the time I entered made me feel comfortable and were absolutely hospitable. I was directed to the changing room, where I took a shower and wiped myself dry. I was advised to drink water before entering the Hamam to avoid dehydration, due to high temperature and steam. Inside the Hamam, the average temperature is 45° C and the humidity rate is almost 100 percent. The high temperature warms up the body, which starts producing sweat as a self-defence measure from the heat. Sweating promotes the elimination of toxins and uric acid, fostering renal activity and hydration of the upper respiratory tract.

After relaxing and spending about 30 minutes in the Hamam, masseur Mustafa did body scrubbing with Kese, which is a special bath glove. As the skin gets softer as the result of perspiration in the hamam, with the help of a kese dead skin is removed and skin pores are opened up. This is followed by foam bath which cleans the body. Finale was a massage and with a tasty apple tea to sip. It was a wonderful, memorable and relaxing experience. At the end of it I felt as if I was in seventh heaven. There could not have been a better way to unwind myself after such a fascinating trip.

Zaki and I met for dinner and spent a quiet evening in the hotel discussing our ventures and fond memories of Istanbul. Later, we both prepared ourselves to start our journey back.

Chapter 14

Argentina and the End of the World

In April 2015, I got an opportunity to visit Argentina, which remains etched in my mind for many reasons, apart from being a distant place from India.

Argentina is a huge country which stretches 4,000 kilometres from its sub-tropical north to the sub-Antarctic south. Its terrain includes part of the Andes mountain range, swamps, the plains of the Pampas and a long coastline. A country rich in resources it is one of South America's largest economies. But its political life has been troubled by military coups and the vagaries of the populist Peronist movement, while the economy has been prey to dramatic booms and recessions.

I flew from Delhi to Buenos Aires via Dubai by Emirates Airlines; it was a long haul flight. After a short drive of less than an hour from the airport I reached Hotel Madero, a luxury hotel located in the exclusive neighbourhood of Peurto Madero. My room had a beautiful view of the port; what else could a Mariner ask for.

Next morning Marcela Ramirez, a journalist friend took me around Buenos Aires. It was a marvelous way to explore the city, with a local and a knowledgeable person. Buenos Aires is a city and a fascinating destination all on its own.

We first went to Plaza de Mayo (May Square). It is the oldest public square in Buenos Aires, and has been the scene of many of the most important events in the city's history, from the second founding of the city in 1580, through the revolution of independence, to more recent political demonstrations.

The square is named after the Argentine revolution, which began on 25 May 1810. Around the square are several important buildings: the Cabildo, the Metropolitan Cathedral, where Pope Francis conducted mass for 20 years, the Casa Rosada, seat of the national government, the national revenue office (AFIP), the national bank and the intelligence secretariat.

Apart from being the site of the May revolution, the square was also the location for Argentina's first political rally in 1890. It has remained the focal point for public gatherings, either in support of or to protest against successive governments ever since, a tradition that reached its apex with the crowds that came to hear Eva "Evita" Perón speak from the balcony of the Casa Rosada in the late 1940s. The famous song "Don't cry for me Argentina" celebrates the the life of Evita and the charismatic persona she created in the public mind.

We walked across to San Telmo; it is the barrio that lies six blocks from Plaza de Mayo, the oldest barrio in Buenos Aires. It dates back to the 17th century, when it was first home to dockworkers and brick-makers and later became an industrial area. It is blessed with cobblestoned streets and many good places to eat and drink — a barrio not to be missed.

San Telmo was a poor area, and one attempt to address this was the establishment of the Parish of San Pedro González Telmo in the area in 1806. 'San Telmo' is the patron saint of seafarers, and he is of course the namesake of the barrio today.

San Telmo began to attract the well-to-do after the establishment of gas mains, lighting, sewers, running water and cobblestones, which led to the construction of many mansions and imposing homes and establishing the area as a hotspot for the tango.

Being a Sunday, San Telmo was full of activity, with lots of street and antique shops set up and opportunity to buy souvenirs and mate cups and plenty of street performers with some doing the Tango dance .

The evening before I had picked up a conversation with Ferdino on duty at the Front Desk of the hotel and enquired from him, where were the Polo Grounds located in Bs As. He said that he had no idea about polo; in Argentina they only know football. No wonder they say that Argentina is a catholic country and their real religion is football.

I made a quick visit to La Bombonera Boca Junior's home, located in La Boca itself. The stadium has a capacity of 60,000 and is usually full for Boca games. The most dedicated Boca Juniors´ fans are known as "La Doce" (the twelve), and the Xeneizes (the Genoese) because the team was founded by

Italian immigrants who populated the La Boca neighbourhood in the early 20th century.

Boca Juniors is the biggest soccer team in Argentina and is well known around the world. It's Diego Maradona's favorite team and Diego himself played for Buenos Aires' Boca on two different occasions.

Although Argentina is obsessed with soccer but the sport in the country that truly dominates is polo.

The 'sport of kings' is played professionally only in 18 countries. Argentina is universally recognized as polo's mecca, with several thousand active players.

Over half of the sport's top pro players hail from Argentina, including Adolfo Cambiaso of La Dolfina and Facundo Pieres of Ellerstina (his brothers, Gonzolo and Nicolás are also pro players).

Marcela, who mainly covers polo events, took me to the Argentine Polo Association, which is the guiding entity of the game of polo in Argentina.

I visited Campo Argentino del Polo which is a multipurpose stadium once mainly used for polo matches. Today, it is also used for other sporting and performing arts events.

The Campo Argentino de Polo can hold over 30,000 people. Several important tournaments take place here. It hosts polo, pato and field hockey matches. The best known polo tournament in the country, the Compeonato Argentino Abierto de Polo takes place here annually since its inauguration in 1928.

The game here is so popular that it was nice to see two teams of girls playing chukkers; a rare sight anywhere in the world.

Since I was staying in Puerto Madero, I spent a lot of time, exploring the area.

Peurto Madero is one of the finest neighbourhoods in Buenos Aires; its history goes back more than a hundred years. Although Buenos Aires is conveniently located right on the banks of Rio de la Plata, the shallow waters of the river have always prevented cargo ships from docking directly. All cargo and passengers had to be offloaded to smaller barges and ferries in order to be transported onto land. In 1882, the Argentine government contracted local businessman Eduardo Madero, in whose name the port is named, to make a new port that would resolve this docking problem.

Peurto Madero was constructed in a period of ten years. Construction began in 1887 and was completed in 1897, although the installed fittings had been partially operative some years before completion of the port. It was a costly project and an engineering landmark at the time but ten years after its completion the appearance of larger cargo ships made Puerto Madero obsolete. Subsequently, Puerto Nuevo was constructed, whose first section opened in 1911 and is in use even today.

After the construction of Puerto Nuevo, Puerto Madero was not in use and was neglected for a long time. Inspite of various efforts by the government, nothing substantial happened. Towards end of the last century and beginning of this century, there was a total change. The area became one of the most sought after neighbourhoods from residential to commercial buildings. Be it restaurants, cinemas and luxury hotels.

Each street in Puerto Madero is named after famous women from Argentine history. One of the main attractions is Puente de la Mujer, a footbridge, representing a couple dancing the tango.

In the evening Marcilez took me for the Tango Show at El Querandi, the historic venue in San Telmo.

The exact origins of tango, both the dance and the word itself, are lost in myth and an unrecorded history. The generally accepted theory is that in the mid 1800s, the African slaves who had been brought to Argentina or their descendants began to influence the local culture. The word "tango" may be straightforwardly African in origin, meaning "closed place" or "reserved ground." Or it may derive from Portuguese (and from the Latin verb *tanguere*, meaning to touch) and was picked up by Africans on the slave ships. Whatever its origin, the word "tango" has acquired the standard meaning of the place where African slaves and free blacks gathered to dance.

With beginning of 20th century, tango spread worldwide throughout; the dance appeared in movies and tango singers travelled the world. The tango came to be a fundamental expression of Argentine culture.

I spent the evening, knowing the history, music and the traditions about the tango dance. The show takes you from 1860 to the present, highlighting the history of tango and Buenos Aires. While musicians sing and play the accordion, piano, violin and bass, couples show their tango skills. It was a spectacular performance of sensuous and passionate dance. I spent a memorable evening enjoying our dinner with Argentine wine.

The following day, in the morning, after an hour's drive from Bs As I reached Estancia   (South American Cattle Ranch), "El Ombu de Areco", located near San Antonio de Areco, a small village, a typical countryside village full of history and gaucho tradition of Pampas land. The magnificent "casco", a house built by Lieutenant General Pablo Riccheri in 1880, opens its "tranquera" every single day to offer its guests an unforgettable visit. The estancia was purchased in 1934 by Enrique Boelcke, Cristina and Eva's grandfather and Diego and Juan Pablo's great grandfather, who are the present owners. It was the first Estancia which decided to receive tourists in 1993.

It has more than 350 heads of cattle (Aberdeen Angus) and 70 horses grazing in its fields. There is also soya, corn, oat or pastures, depending on the season ploughed in its fields. Diego, a fabulous host received us and took us around the property and offered us a sumptuous Argentine meal, everything fresh from the ranch.

After seeing the beautiful horses I was tempted to request Diego whether I could go for a ride. Of course I did tell him a bit about my riding experience. He asked the Gaucho to get me a horse. Gaucho is the cow boy of Argentina, but also of Uruguay and South Brazil, who takes care of cattle in the Pampas fields. The gaucho is an iconic figure that represents the value of bravery, honour and freedom of the rural man. Being brave, good horse rider, a land expert, he proved to be a valuable soldier in the past.

Soon Gaucho and I were riding towards the cows that were grazing in a marshy area. Gaucho was wearing a ceremonial dress , leather boots with spurs, baggy trousers, a belt ornamented with coins, a dagger and a beret. It was a wonderful ride; for a change I also felt like a gaucho, rounding up cattle. We both rode back to the stables after a while.

The following day after a three hour flight from Buenos Aires, I landed in Ushuaia, the southern most city in the world.

Ushuaia is located on the Tierra del Fuego archipelago, the southernmost tip of South America, nicknamed the "End of the World." It is the gateway to Antarctica.

I was received at the Airport by Bronco, my guide and taken to Los Cauquenes, where I spent the next few days. It is the only high-end Resort & Spa on the Beagle Channel beach, with the snowed peaks of the imposing Andes mountain range behind it.

Later in the afternoon Bronco took me for a trek to Martial Glacier, a few kilometres from the hotel, which is one of the most outstanding natural attractions. The trek was easy and comfortable and I walked at my own pace. Bronco explained a lot about the glacier, nature, plants and trees growing in the area. Martial Glacier was named in honour of the explorer Luis Fernando Martial, leader of the French scientific expedition which arrived in 1883.

On reaching the top, we found there was tea, coffee, sandwiches, fruits and juices available for visitors in a small tent.

Walking back was comfortable; on the way back we tasted some fruits, growing in the wild called Indian bread fruit, a bit placid but nice.

Next day I took a helicopter ride by Heli Ushuaia with some other vistors; it was a ride to remember. Nichola, the pilot of the helicopter gave brief safety instructions. Soon we took off towards the Andes over flying the Valley of Encajonado, appreciating the view of Beagle channel, Ushuaia bay, a beautiful city framed by the imposing Andes Martial Glacier, the Monte Cinco Hermanos and the iconic Monte Olivia.

After a magnificent helicopter ride we landed on snow on top of the Andes mountain range. We walked around in the snow; it was a fantastic and memorable photo opportunity. The flight back was even more exhilarating, flying through the valley and the mountain range. Soon we landed at the helicopter base.

In the afternoon I walked around the city. For a very long time, only the Selk'nam and Yahgan *(Yamana)* indigenous tribes lived in this remote part of the world. British missionaries arrived in the early 1830s and established the first European settlements. I visited the Thematic Gallery (Historia Fueguina); it is an area in which a group of figures and replicas of historical value have been created but there is more to it.

Willing to go through this experience, I moved around the different spaces where 36 pictures were hung on the walls in chronological order. There were also 120 life-size figures representing a faithful reproduction of the composition of human groups, their characteristics and ways of survival. Very interesting material about the history, customs and events that shed light over the different periods of the past has been collected. A Scotsman named Ernest Shackleton (1874-1922) was one of the many explorers who had worked in the region and has left the imprint of his incredible exploits in Antarctica.

A section covers the Beagle Channel from the moment it was discovered, the difficult conditions to navigate it and the multiple expeditions that have crossed it. Likewise, the Prison at the World's End and the train that led the prisoners to the wood to collect firewood have their own corner inside the museum.

After completing the visit to the Thematic Gallery and a walk around the fascinating city I went for dinner to the renowned Adnino Gourmet restaurant. To my delight some vegetarian dishes were made for me in a mutton, beef and fish eating country.

For a long time, Ushuaia was little more than a remote outpost. After the British came here, it was then used by the Argentinian government as a penal colony. All types of offenders were sent there and later those who opposed the regime. The city grew around it to host the families of those manning the prison. It was closed in the middle of the twentieth century. The prison now hosts the Museum of the *Ex-Presidio*. Prisoners' stories are told on the walls of their cells and there's a replica of the End of the World lighthouse in the gardens. Well-documented and highly interesting, the museum is an absolute must-see in town.

Ushuaia itself is modest and unassuming, with just one main street and the star of the show, its waterfront.

Next day in the afternoon I embarked on a small boat from the pier. Bruno welcomed the guests for a tour of the Beagle Channel, which is a 240 kilometre passageway, sailing towards Paso Chico pass, following the route of the explorer Charles Darwin across the Beagle Channel. It was from this body of water that separates Ushuaia and Antarctica that Charles Darwin saw his first glacier. Our boat captain brought the boat very close to Sea Lion's island where we saw both South American sea lions and South American fur seals. It was a great photo opportunity. Although the weather can be unpredictable, the captain of the boat told us that we were lucky to have such a great weather, which is not more than three to four days in a year.

We sailed past Les Eclaireurs (the Scouts) Lighthouse which stands on a small island guarding the entrance to the Bay of Ushuaia. It is a working lighthouse dating to 1920.

On the way, we stopped at the Bridges Island. Bruno took us on a short trek, warning us not to step on the plants since these need to be protected. Here we saw how nature is preserved, despite plenty of visitors coming here. He spoke about the cushion plants which are usually found much higher in the mountains, but for some reason this mini ecosystem has survived on Bridges Island for centuries outlasting even the original inhabitants.

When we first stepped onto the island it looked like rocks covered in moss, but on closer investigation we saw several plants that co-exist on the moss like surface. This unique species only grows an inch in a year and then only during the warmer months making the Bridges Island a fragile but well protected island in the Beagle Channel.

The original inhabitants of the Bridges Island were the Yamana, a nomadic tribe that moved between the islands by canoe. The Yamana developed a natural resistance against the sub-Antarctic climate by smearing their bodies with seal oil which may have been the reason why their body temperature was 1 degree higher than humans today. The region was named the Land of Fire (*Tierra del Fuego*) by the early European explorers who saw the dotted Yamana camp fires on the islands throughout the Beagle channel.

Isla de los Pajaros(Birds' Island), so called due to the large number of birds dwelling on it, is ideal to appreciate King Cormorants which look like penguins.

After a refreshing cup of coffee and some snacks, we disembarked from the boat and said good bye to Bruno and the Beagle Channel. As usual I did not miss the opportunity to drive the boat, which the captain of the boat was kind enough to allow me.

The next day in the morning we ventured on a tour of the Andes with our guide cum driver Felipe who picked us up in a 4x4 Land Rover. We started from the city and soon we were in the mountains. The terrain was mixed but navigating with a 4x4 vehicle was an experience and showed his expertise to manoeuvre and go up and down the difficult terrain. Felipe told me that please tell Mr Tata not to stop manufacturing this vehicle! I was surprised to know that he knew about the ownership of the Company by TATAs. We visited lakes Escondido (Hidden Lake), where we did kayaking and saw the spectacular Lake Fagnano (Big Lake). It was a good learning about southernmost corner of Argentina and its history, geology and wildlife. We had lunch on the way back to Ushuaia.

It was cold, we had Mate; it is probably the most popular beverage in Argentina. Dried and crushed up leaves of the yerba mate are placed into a hollowed out gourd and drunk through a screened straw called a bombilla. We passed it around and it was very refreshing and quite addictive.

One evening we had dinner at La Cravia Restaurant in Arakur Hotel. The restaurant serves Argentinian and international cuisine. Non vegetarian food has plenty of options and variety of dishes. Restaurant did serve me some vegetarian food. It was delicious pumpkin soup, salads, pasta, ice cream and Argentine wines. With a lot of Italian influence, Italian cuisine is easily available in most places. Italian is the largest ethnic origin of modern Argentines. Today, Argentina has 30 million Argentines with some degree of Italian ancestry in a total population of 40 million. We enjoyed our dinner with an amazing view of the Beagle Channel.

On that last day, we took "The End of the World Train" from end of the world station. One relives the last 7 kilometre trip convicts used to make when the train left from the prison located in the town of Ushuaia towards the slopes of Mount Susana in order to obtain different materials for construction. On board we could hear the story and were delighted with the magnificent landscape comprising the zigzag Pipo River, Macarena cascade, the tree cemetery, the beautiful forest, and travelling through part of the inaccessible Tierra del Fuego National Park. The train is driven by a steam locomotive.

After getting off the train we spent some more time in Tierra del Fuego National Park. The park is remote with stunning natural beauty and wildlife. We walked around the park and visited the museum highlighting the indigenous Feugan culture.

Our last stop was Unidad Postal Del Fin Mundo, the post office at end of the world. From there you can send mail. Some of us got our passports stamped from the Principality of the country of Redonda Island.

After a quiet dinner I packed my bags. Next morning it was time to leave End of the World. I left with a heavy heart dreaming of that day when I would return to sail to Antarctica from the port of Ushuaia.

Author in the Centre at the Statue of Christ the Redeemer atop Mt Corcovado, Rio De Janeiro(Brazil)

Author second from left with Roxani, extreme left and friends in Thessaloniki (Greece)

Author and Marcela at Argentina Polo Association, Buenos Aires(Argentina)

Author on top of Andes on landing by helicopter in Ushuaia (Argentina)

Le Eclaireurs Lighthouse, Beagle Channel, Tierra del Feugo (Argentina)

Lake Wanaka, Otago(New Zealand)

Author on right at Te Puia Thermal Reserve, Rotorua (New Zealand)

Author at Sky Tower, Auckland

Goats on top of Argan Trees on the way from Marrakech to Essaouira
(Morocco)

Mohammad AlAmin Mosque (Blue Mosque), Beirut

Author with Lu Mon and Sandi at Shwedagon Pagoda, Yangon
(Myanmar)

Ketchikan, Alaska

Cruise ship alongside in Juneau port(Alaska)

Author with group sitting front row extreme left with group at the
Citadel, Amman(Jordan)

Author second from right with group at Lawrence of Arabia's rock carving, Wadi Rum(Jordan)

Author second row extreme right with group at Jericho, Palestine

Author and Neeru at Dome of the Rock, Jerusalem

Wailing Wall, Jerusalem

Kalia Beach, Dead Sea (Israel)

Author third from right with group at Cape of Good Hope, Cape Town(South Africa)

Yurts in Steppes of Kazakhstan

Rider with a Falcon at Sunkar Falcon Farm in Almaty(Kazakhstan)

Author (wearing hat) with group at Jomo Kenyata International
Airport,Nairobi

Maasai Tribe, Maasai Village, Amboseli National Park (Kenya)

Chapter 15

New Zealand: The Thrill never ends

My trip to New Zealand took place in June 2015. It was the beginning of winter in New Zealand and after a long flight I along with some colleagues reached Christchurch.

New Zealand is located in the southwestern Pacific Ocean, just south of Australia. It has been its own country since the late 19th century. Before that, the country was actually considered to be part of the United Kingdom and was under the laws and jurisdiction of the crown. New Zealand is actually a number of smaller islands, with two main islands the North Island and the South Island that comprise most of the land mass of the country. The first people to arrive in New Zealand were ancestors of the Māori. The first settlers probably arrived from Polynesia between 1200 and 1300 AD. They discovered New Zealand as they explored the Pacific, navigating by the ocean currents and winds.

Christchurch is the third largest city in New Zealand bordered by hills and the Pacific Ocean; it is situated on the edge of the Canterbury Plains that stretch to the Southern Alps. Internationally famed as 'The Garden City', it has well-established expansive parks and public gardens. An earthquake in 2011 left the city devastated. It caused widespread damage across the city, especially in the central spots and eastern suburbs. It is estimated that the total cost for Christchurch's reconstruction will exceed 40 billion NZ dollars, which equals approximately 10 percent of New Zealand's gross domestic product (GDP).

After resting a bit we drove to Terrace Downs Resort for lunch. It is located in the shadow of the majestic Southern Alps and in the heart of the picturesque Canterbury region. It is perched on the edge of the spectacular Rakaia River; the resort boasts a stunning view up to Mt Hutt and is within close proximity to various ski fields. It also has a golf course and boasts of various other activities.

After a sumptuous lunch, we tried our hand at Claybird shooting and archery.

Later in Christchurch, we visited the transitional 'Cardboard Cathedral'. After the earthquake caused catastrophic damage to the iconic Christchurch Cathedral, Japanese architect Shigeru Ban designed one of his famous "Emergency Architecture" buildings and the transitional 'Cardboard' Cathedral project was well underway. Constructed from a series of 96 cardboard tubes and framing, this is an exciting symbol of innovation, hope and inspiration for the city for the next 50 or so years.

The following day we visited the International Antarctic Centre; it is Christchurch's leading attraction and is located right next to Christchurch International Airport. Experiences at the Centre include the 'Antarctic Storm', the amazing Hagglund all-terrain vehicle and the 'Penguin Encounter'. We experienced the new 4D "Extreme Theatre" featuring an exhilarating 3D movie with 4D special effects, perhaps the only one of its kind in the world.

We wore protective clothing and entered the Storm Dome, which is chilled to minus 5° celsius, swept through by minus 18°C wind, buffeted by a realistic Antarctic storm. We found this tough for a few minutes. This is what the scientists and explorers have to go through for days in the Antarctic. The next day we took a flight from Christchurch to Queenstown.

In the afternoon we went on 2.5-hour 4WD adventure journey, which offered Wanaka's finest lakeside scenery through a real alpine, mountain farm. We got an opportunity to watch closely red deer, angus cattle, sheep and horses. We had coffee and snacks at alpine café. After that we went on a short nature walk.

From the top it was a breath-taking panoramic view of snow-capped peaks, glaciers and Lake Wanaka far below. It offered unique insight into Wanaka's rich history, heritage, incredible scenery and modern-day farming life. Gigantic glaciers created the neighbouring lakes of Hawea and Wanaka over 10,000 years ago, long before humans entered into the history of Wanaka. The first human settlements near these lakes were Maori summer campsites known as 'kianga'.

Next morning was well spent with Oxbow Adventure, something not to be missed in Wanaka. It was absolutely an amazing experience at Oxbow with Darb, Tim and an interesting team - a great place for thrill seekers. It offered rides on the jet sprint boats, clay bird shooting, golf and offroader truck. We went smoothly through the terrain with steep climbs, slopes and hurdles on the offroader. Jet sprint ride was quite an experience for which we wore helmets and put on the seat belt. In no time the boat accelerated and was moving full speed, carrying out various manoeuvres around the bays. I had never experienced such an amazing control of the sprint boat. It is said that this is the only jet sprint boat, the only commercial one of its type in the world and can go from 0-100 km in 0.5 seconds. This adventure was conducted with complete safety checks and multiple safeguards. Interestingly, Oxbow owner Darb Richmond is also the in-house helicopter pilot.

After a short drive we reached the Gibbston Valley Winery. It is world renowned for crafting award winning Central Otago Pinot Noirs. The winery is also home to New Zealand's largest wine cave and one of the region's finest dining experiences.

We had wine tasting; we were told about the finer points of tasting wine from current releases to select vintages at their Cellar Door. We also learned about the timeless traditions and vineyards that create the winery's premium handcrafted ranges, as Central Otago's founding winery. A little later we enjoyed excellent Italian cuisine in the restaurant and finest of wines.

Later we went to the Bungy Centre, which is the only bungy site in Queensland. Kawarau Bridge is home to the world's first and most famous of leaps over the Kawarau River. Here one can bungy forwards, backwards, by yourself, or with a friend, it's up to you. One can choose to bob above the water, touch it, or get fully immersed! Located at the gateway to Queenstown, it's an essential component of every one visiting New Zealand.

We were at the AJ Hackett Kawaru Bungy Centre that represents the ultimate in innovation and commitment to excellence in adventure tourism. Inspired by the vine jumpers of Vanuatu, pioneers Henry van Asch and AJ Hackett have won international acclaim for turning Bungy jumping into a distinctly New Zealand tourism phenomenon. The first commercial Bungy site opened at the Kawarau bridge site in Queenstown in 1988 and the first Queenstown Sky Swing was opened on the Ledge site in 2000. Today the exploits of AJ Hackett Bungy of New Zealand are renowned the world over. Some of us did the Bungy jumps; it starts and finishes in a few seconds.

Adventure never ends in New Zealand. Soon we were there to enjoy the thrill of a ride on the world famous Shotover Jet. Since it was cold and we were told that the jet boat would be moving at great speed, we covered ourselves with warm clothing - jackets, warm head gear, gloves and scarves.

It was an ultimate jet boat experience. It was a unique breathtaking ride through dramatic and narrow canyons, the jet boat moving upto 90 km per hour. As it took 360 degree spins and skimmed around boulders, we were holding on tight to the rails. Shotover jet is owned by Ngāi Tahu, the Māori people, their connection to the Kimiakau (Shotover River) goes back centuries.

The following day we flew from Queenstown to Rotorua via Christchurch. After putting our bags in the hotel we headed for Rotorua Gondola base. We went up to the summit of Mt Ngongotaha in a eight-seater gondola enjoying panoramic view over the region and came racing down on a luge cart. A world first proudly designed and built in Rotorua, the luge is a three-wheeled cart with a unique braking and steering system that gives riders full control. We came down full speed doing some wild steering. We returned to the top on double-seater chairlifts. We had lunch in the restaurant with a lovely view over the city.

Soon we were again out for some adventure with Off Road NZ, located on a beautiful native bush-clad property on the Mamaku Plateau, just 20 minutes north of Rotorua City.

There are plenty of activities here, which include Raceline Karting – we were all briefed and prepared to drive state-of-the-art, 4-stroke 390cc Sodi karts. We went zooming past and took a number of rounds on the track; we were given points throughout the race. Everyone on the track felt like a formula one race driver. 4WD Bush Safari was another great adventurous experience; we encountered a difficult terrain, being behind the wheel, all under expert guidance. We did some very interesting manoeuvres.

Rotorua is a magical city on the shores of Lake Rotorua in the Bay of Plenty in the North Island. Rotorua is also seeped in Māori history and culture. There is no better place to witness both the natural wonders of the area and learn about Māori ancestral history than Te Puia. Te Puia is a living Maori cultural centre set on 60 hectares of land in the Whakarewarewa geothermal valley.

We were welcomed by Shannon, our guide, a Maori, who took us around Te Puia. He briefed us about the area and told us that Te Puia Springs was one of the best Rotorua tourist attractions. Not only does it boast of the New Zealand Māori Arts and Culture Centre, it also has a live Kiwi enclosure, it is home to the magnificent Pohutu Geyser and contains over 500 natural geothermal wonders. The entrance of Te Puia sets the scene, as twelve celestial guardians watch over you.

It was dark and our guide made one of us the group Chief for us to be accepted by tribes. The tribes challenged us, displaying their art and asked whether we came as friends or foes. We told them that we came as friends and we were accepted as friends and allowed entry. Shannon did all the translation for us.

Maoris have been living in this area for almost 700 years. We discovered how the Māoris have used the geothermal areas for cooking, preserving food and bathing. With steam coming from all over, the chef prepared for us dhokla (It is made with a fermented batter derived from rice and split chickpeas, a vegetarian food item that originates from the Indian state of Gujarat), and idlis (a type of savoury rice cake), popular as breakfast food in southern India and among Tamils in Sri Lanka.

At the Maori Arts and Crafts Institute many traditional art forms have been preserved and passed on to new generations of artists from all over New Zealand because of the amazing work of this institute.

Located at Te Puia is also the famous natural wonder, the Pohutu geyser. You can walk upon the earth, where legend has it, Pohutu is the largest active geyser in the southern hemisphere. She erupts once or twice every hour and sometimes reaches heights of 30 metres. Apart from being a spectacular sight, Pohutu is the most reliable geyser on earth. Eruptions can last from a few minutes to much longer. About 15 years ago, Pohutu erupted for over 250 days. Pohutu has been visited by royalty and many other famous people. However, because nearby residents used bores to tap into the valley's geothermal resources, Pohutu was once at grave risk of losing its power. Fortunately, a programme to close bores has ensured that today Pohutu continues to impress visitors once or twice an hour. There are six other natural geysers in the area.

The finale in the evening was a Maori cultural performance over dinner, inside the beautifully carved *wharenui* (meeting house). We were all made to take part with the performers; it was interesting and interactive.

Kapa haka (Maori performing arts) is an avenue to express and showcase their heritage and cultural identity through song and dance. The art dates back to pre-European times and involves singing, dancing and movements associated with traditional hand-to-hand combat.

The next day we went to the world-renowned Agrodome in Rotorua; it is an extraordinary experience for anyone interested in farming and agriculture. Located in the heart of 350 acres of lush farmland, we had to get aboard the all weather, all terrain vehicle to take a tour of the farm. We saw all sorts of friendly animals, including Romney sheep, cattle, deer, llamas, ostrich, pigs and alpaca. We also visited a fruit orchard and olive grove. There was an interesting show with dogs performing and keeping sheep and ducks in line.

In the Woollen Mill at the farm there was an authentic Platt wool carding machine dating back to 1906. We saw sheep sharing. The Woollen Mill sells a range of homespun, hand knitted/woven garments along with handcrafted footwear, rugs, knitting and weaving kits.

Later in the evening we went to the Polynesian Spa. Its geothermal hot mineral waters are sourced from two natural springs and feed into 28 hot mineral pools. The slightly acidic Priest Spring waters relieve tired muscles, aches and pains while the alkaline waters of the Rachel Spring nourish the skin due to antiseptic action of sodium silicate. An old local belief is that those who swim in the Rachel Spring water will receive ageless beauty.

We relaxed in the hot mineral pools at Polynesian Spa, gazing at the hills in the distance and reflecting on this tranquil volcanic landscape. For 130 years people have come to the site to try the geothermal therapeutic waters. It was voted among the World Top 10 Spas by the Conde Nast Traveller in 2011.

The Spa Essentials store offers one of the most comprehensive ranges of spa body and skin care products. Nearby the indoor/ outdoor Hot Springs Cafe provides a tempting selection of light cafe food, beverages, fruit platters and juice.

The following day we went to Agroventures, a Premier Adventure Park and home to five unique adventures, all in one location. It has the world's only Shweeb, one of the fastest and only jet sprint experience, swing towards the earth at 130 kmph with the giant Swoop, Rotorua Bungy and outdoor wind tunnel. We took part in some of the activities.

Later we went to H2OGO Sidewinder Track; it was a different experience. We were put in a big inflatable plastic ball, called Zorb, and since it was cold some hot water was put inside. We zorbed down the track, laughing and rolling all over. We were going in different directions in the ball, zig zagging our way down in a wash of water. A bit of craziness but good fun. We came down covering a distance of almost 250 metres down hill.

Later in the evening we went to Hobbiton, something that we were all eagerly looking forward to. It was a magical evening at the Hobbiton Movie Set from *The Lord of the Rings* and *The Hobbit* film trilogies. The set has been completely rebuilt for *The Hobbit* and remains as it was seen in the films. It is the only remaining full movie set location from the Lord of the Rings and Hobbit films that still exists.

On arrival at Hobbiton we were met by our guide Howard, who gave a brief introduction about Hobbiton. We made our way through the Alexander farm to the movie set, enjoying a beautiful view across the rolling green hills of the Waikato. It was a memorable journey through Hobbiton, viewing the Hobbit Holes. Along rolling hills of Hobbit shire, there were so many hobbit holes in different sizes; some big, some small. The hobbit holes are just facades with less than 4 feet of standing room in the interior. Laundry lines with washing hung out to dry. A picnic set up on the dock. Moss and lichen growing on the fences while brooms and gardening tools could be seen near hobbit doors. It was a great photo opportunity for all of us.

The mill and the double arch stone bridge, all were kept as they were during filming. The tour culminated at The Green Dragon Inn and the Hobbit market place, where we joined the festivities. We had a few drinks in the market place.

The Green Dragon Inn featured in The Lord of the Rings trilogy as the local meeting place for all the residents of Hobbiton. It is the perfect place to satisfy the thirst, enjoy the meal and ale hotpot and numerous other goodies fresh from The Green Dragon kitchen. A hobbit feast was arranged by the open fire place; the feast was designed to incorporate everything that keeps a Hobbits cheeks plump and as is the tradition in the Shire, second helpings were encouraged.

Next morning we departed for Auckland via Wiatomo by road.

We were overwhelmed by the guided tour of majestic Waitomo Glowworm caves; these caves were formed over 30 million years ago. We walked through the caves, with an informative commentary and listening to the many legends. It is a huge cavern filled with enormous stalagmites and stalactites, ornate cave decorations- the deep limestone shaft known as the Tomo and the equally magnificent Cathedral cavern known for its world-renowned acoustics, the home of where New Zealand's own opera diva Kiri Te Kanawa once performed.

It was dark and fluorescent glowworms were dotted over the cave walls and gave a feeling as if we were gazing in the night sky. Photography is not allowed inside the caves due to environmental safeguard policies.

After a brief tour of the cave, we took a boat ride, which goes along an underwater river; it took us into a cavern twinkling with a constellation of glowworms. As we gazed up in wonder at the starry ceiling we learnt how these tiny, luminous insects belonged to a species only found in New Zealand. It was a majestic sensation of floating slowly through the magical cavern before returning to the world of daylight.

After days of adventure and being close to natural attractions, we were in a big city, Auckland. Situated in the north of North Island it is the largest city and commercial hub. It is home to more than a third of the country's population. The city is a combination of skyscrapers, the harbour, restaurants and the quiet suburbs.

We went by Waiheke Island by ferry. The island is located approximately 18 kilometres east of Auckland and is probably the most popular holiday and weekend destination for the inhabitants of Auckland. With regular ferry sailings, Waiheke is the perfect place to escape to for the day, or even just the afternoon. With pristine beaches, world class wines, and fantastic cuisine, it's easy to see why Waiheke Island is considered the jewel in the Hauraki Gulf's crown.

In Auckland we stayed at SKYCITY Hotel; it is one of New Zealand's most popular hotels and offers a place to relax and unwind in the heart of the city, with entertainment right on your doorstep. From the world class casino to a selection of restaurants, bars and cafés, live entertainment and the spectacular views across Auckland from the 328 metre high Sky Tower, there really is something for everyone.

It offers Sky jump and Sky walk from the Sky Tower. We offered to take the latter, viewing Auckland while walking around the 1.2 metre wide platform, a dizzying 192 metres high. A full body harness and overhead safety lines keep you safe as you walk the edge of Sky Tower's pergola. Some of us were quite comfortable to seek this adventure. We leaned out and the safety guide told me that I could lean out, but would have to come back on my own. I did that, a great experience and view of the city.

The following day we spent some time at Viaduct harbour. The harbour itself is packed with fancy boats and yachts of all shapes and sizes. With plenty of restaurants and bars it is a superb place to stroll, dine, relax and watch the world go by. The harbour is a bit upmarket, but a great place to spend time.

In the evening my friend Dr Mona Verma based in Auckland offered to take me out for a drive. I asked her to take me to Achilles Point or Te Pane o Horoiwi meaning 'The head of Horoiwi'. It is a scenic lookout point found along Cliff Road, a few minutes drive from Mission Bay and just past St Heliers Bay.

It was a nostalgic visit to Achilles Point, which takes its name from the HMNZS Achilles, a Leander Class light cruiser, which in 1939 defeated the German battleship, Admiral Graf Spee. After Second World War service in the Atlantic and Pacific, she was returned to the Royal Navy. She was later sold to the Indian Navy in 1948 and recommissioned as INS Delhi. I was privileged to have done my sea cadet's training on this famous ship.

Achilles Point provides a viewing platform with fantastic views of the Hauraki Gulf, Brown's Island, Rangitoto Island and a distant view of Auckland City. Mona dropped me back to the hotel after this outing.

At night I packed my stuff in order to depart. The following day it was time to say good bye to this enchanting country. Perhaps I will return again one day.

Chapter 16

My Experience of Morocco, Lebanon and Myanmar

etween November 2016 and November 2017, I visited three countries. While many thought there was not much to see in Morocco, some friends definitely felt my plan to visit Lebanon and Myanmar was too risky. However, in each case I had local contacts I could trust and I knew most fears were exaggerated and fanned by people who had never gone to such places.

Morocco- My trip to Marrakech

I had planned to visit Morocco from Milan, where I had gone for some work in November 2016. I had known Fadel and some other Moroccans for quite some time. It was because I sensed the warm and friendly nature of these people that I wanted to visit Morocco. Marrakech was a viable option for a short trip as it is an exotic city with a mix of European, Middle Eastern and African culture. On landing at the Marrakech Menara Airport Immigration officer Adil, welcomed me with "Namaste" and I wished him in French "Bonjour" and we exchanged some pleasantries. Gradually all the passengers moved out from various immigration counters. I was there for over thirty minutes or more and could not figure out what the delay was about. After sometime, his senior came. I was told that they had fed passport number of my old passport and he was trying to rectify it. The senior officer was very apologetic for the undue delay I had to suffer.

After clearing immigration, the driver Ali, whom my friend Fadel had sent for me to be picked up, expressed his unhappiness for the long wait. Anyway, it was a lovely drive to the hotel cruising through the pink city Marrakech, the city of colour. It is called pink or sometimes red due to the colour of the city walls. Finally we arrived and I checked in at the Hotel Le Vizir.

Morocco is a magical country, rich in culture and history, with a wonderful cuisine, clean hilltop towns, walled cities with labyrinthine old medinas, laidback cities with Art Deco architecture and diverse landscapes. It is located in Northern Africa; it is bordered by the Atlantic Ocean in west, by the Mediterranean Sea in north, by Algeria in east and in south by Western Sahara, the non-self-governing territory claimed by Morocco. Morocco shares small borders with Spain by the Spanish exclaves of Ceuta and Melilla; it has borders with Mauritania in the Moroccan-controlled part of Western Sahara, and it shares maritime borders with Portugal. It covers an area of 446,550 square kilometres (excluding Western Sahara).

The culture of Morocco is as diverse as its landscape. Apart from the Berbers, the culture of Morocco has been influenced by the Arabs, Phoenicians, Sub-Saharan Africans, and the Romans among other groups. The Berbers are native to North Africa; the majority live in Morocco and Algeria. The history of Morocco is tied up with Berber people who repelled the ancient Roman colonialists and later survived several Islamic dynasties. The culture may differ from one region to another and is particularly evident in cuisine, art, clothing and music.

Morocco recognizes both Modern Standard Arabic (Darija) and Berber (Amazigh) as its official languages. French is the country's primary language of economics, culture, commerce, medicine, and sciences and it is used in government and schools. Nearly five million of Moroccans use Spanish particularly those residing in the northern region.

In the evening I joined my host Fadel for dinner at the La Maison Arabe, an opulent place. The hotel is elegantly done in Moroccan style.

After dinner we went to the Djama El Fna Square, which is the beating heart of the city, full of life and one could watch the entertainment of jugglers, story tellers, snake charmers and acrobats. One of the young restaurant owners, came upto me and spoke to me in Hindi, which he had learnt from watching Indian movies. He asked me to tell him the meaning of "*Dil Diwana hai, Kuch Kuch hota hai*" and other filmy titles and sang some lines of songs from Hindi movies.

We stopped at a restaurant overlooking the square to have green tea. Issam the restaurant owner explained that in Morocco, brewing and drinking tea is a much-loved tradition that signifies hospitality and friendship and is carried out with great care. Using green tea as a base, with mint leaves and sugar, Moroccan mint tea is served throughout the day and particularly at mealtimes. While food preparation is the domain of women, the tea is often prepared by the male head of the family and is considered to be an art passed down through generations. Hot tea was very refreshing, specially having it in the winter.

Next morning, after a leisurely breakfast, Bouchra, the guide came to pick me up from the hotel to take me on a tour of Marrakech.

She was a pleasant person, with in-depth knowledge and a good sense of humour; she had spent a couple of years in Italy after graduating from Cad Ayyad University in Marrakech. I couldn't have found a better person to take me around, someone who had spent time in one of my favourite countries, Italy. In fact I started calling her Moroccan Italian much to her amusement.

We started our tour walking through the alleys and streets. Sometimes it felt like I was in some place in Rajasthan in India, looking at the colour and artefacts. We walked in the Medina; the walls surrounding the Medina were built in the 12th century to protect the people who lived there. There are plenty of shops and restaurants in the Medina. We hired a horse-drawn carriage for some time to see part of Marrakech. It is mesmerizing to watch the city as the sun sets and slowly changing the hues on the red clay walls. We visited Koutoubia Mosque, the largest mosque in Morocco, located in the district of the south-west Medina. The mosque is decorated with curved windows, a strip of ceramic, pointed merlons and decorative arches and has a large square with gardens. The minaret, 77 metres high, includes an arrow and orbs. It was completed under the reign of the Berber Almohad caliph Yaqub al-Mansour. This was followed by a visit to the Bahia Palace consisting of rooms decorated with stunning stuccos, paintings and mosaics.

Later we went to the Majorelle Garden designed by the French Artist, Jacques Majorelle in 1924, the result of forty years of passion and dedication to create this enchanting garden in the heart of the "Ochre City".

In 1980, this was purchased by Yves St Laurent and Pierre Berge, the famous French fashion designers. They bought this garden to avoid the land being used to make a hotel. Collections of cacti, exotic plants and trees are landscaped to emphasize each one's unique beauty. It houses some three hundred species of plants from five continents, including cacti, palms and other plants. Jardin Majorelle finalized a long anticipated project and opened its Berber Museum. Housed in a painting studio designed by Paul Sinoir in 1931 for Jacques Majorelle, it presents Pierre Berge and Yves Saint Laurent's personal collection to the public. The *Imazighen* (singular *Amazigh*) or Berbers, are among the original peoples of North Africa. Their myths, legends and history span 9,000 years, and can be traced to the Proto-Mediterraneans. They have achieved unity by maintaining their unique language and culture which are like their land, both African and Mediterranean.

Yves St Laurent passed away on 1 June 2008 in Paris. His ashes were scattered in the rose garden of the Villa Oasis; a memorial is built in the garden, designed around a Roman pillar which was brought from Tangier and set on a pedestal with a plate bearing his name, so that visitors can remember him and his unique contribution to fashion. After Yves died, Pierre Berge donated the Jardin Majorelle and the Villa Oasis to the foundation in Paris which bears both their names.

In the afternoon, Fadel invited us for lunch to his luxurious farm. We had a few drinks and couscous for lunch and enjoyed the warm Moroccan hospitality of the family. From the farm, we had a beautiful view of the blue mountains of High Atlas. To express my gratitude I had carried some Indian tea for Amina; she was very touched and promised to see us in India, a country that she had always wanted to visit.

Later part of the afternoon we spent walking through the streets of Marrakech, which left me mesmerized while Bouchra explained everything so eloquently.

In the evening we went for dinner at Les Jardin de Bala restaurant located in the hotel Les Jardins de Koutoubia close to Jemma El Fna square. The restaurant has a stunning view of Koutoubia. We had Indian food, which was very authentic. Marie and Bala run this restaurant. Marie was a perfect hostess and new enough about India and her cuisine. At the entrance there was a painting of Shri Arvind Singh Mewar, Maharana of Udaipur, whom I have known personally. To my utter surprise Marie knew a lot about the Maharana and the history of Udaipur.

After dinner we went to Palais Jad Mahal. I would call it more of a night club, although it does have a restaurant. It is owned by Andre and Adriana Ohanian. The decor wavers between India and Morocco with wide colourful areas. We had a few glasses of champagne, discussing about Morocco, its people and life in general. The performance by Oriental dancers was fascinating; all in all a classy evening I thought should never have ended.

Next day we drove from Marrakech to the fishing port of Essaouira. The driver was Ali who had by now become more friendly with me and Bouchra. It was a smooth drive and with no traffic on the road. Interestingly, I was very impressed with the driver who would follow the speed limits indicated on sign boards and while crossing a village would reduce speed as indicated. At the same time the police would be ready with speed cameras to catch errant drivers. Not sure whether it was his disciplined driving skill or the fear of being fined by police, but he did not take any chances. Being a local, he certainly knew the way to cut corners but he did not. We could see locals moving on donkeys from one place to another.

After some time Bouchra told me about Argan trees which we could see on the way. These grow between the geographical area of Marrakech and Essaouira; it has grown here for thousands of years. Argan trees have long been known by locals for their medicinal properties. From the nuts, oil is extracted and traditionally this job has been performed by Berber women. The local Berber people have known about the medicinal properties of the oil extracted from Argan trees for centuries. It was used as a folk medicine for heart disease, rheumatism, and skin conditions, as well as a deliciously nutty food oil although only in its raw form as it doesn't resist heat. Now it has been brought to cosmetic use also. There are plenty of co-operatives run by women, which is a good source of income and employment for them. We stopped by one of the co-operatives and it was interesting to see local women totally engrossed in their work and the co-operatives being run professionally.

We saw some Argan trees with goats climbed up on them and grazing on the branches. It has now become more of a tourist attraction. May be the goats are also made to climb up and their legs tied. It is nice to take pictures and the goat herders do expect a tip. I obliged a few of them and gave some Dirhams.

Before entering Essaouira, we saw boys standing on the road side, shaking keys to tourists, for renting out apartments. After almost three hour's drive we reached the pretty white walled town of Essaouira on the Atlantic coast.

We parked our car near Skala du Port. It provides a picturesque view over the fishing port and the Ile de Mogador. In 1766, Sultan Sidi Mohammad ben Abdallah engaged Theodore Cornut, a French architect, to design the new city. He worked three years on constructing the Scala of the port and the Scala of the Kasbah.

It is a busy port filled with little blue fishing boats, which is a site peculiar to this place. These boats are unique to Essaouira.

We made a short visit to Sidi Mohammed ben Abdallah, since we had spare time in hand. It has a collection of weapons, traditional dresses and old musical instruments.

We walked around the medina which is small. The traffic free streets are lined with small shops selling handicrafts and colourful rugs and is a great place to pick up souvenirs. After spending a relaxed day, we drove back to Marrakech.

Next morning I had a stroll in the hotel; it had beautiful lawns and large area to walk around and did some outdoor activities, since the hotel had plenty of them to offer. After breakfast, I was picked up from the hotel to go to the airport. I bid goodbye to Bouchra and thanked her for making my trip so fascinating. I also profusely thanked my friend Fadel for without him I would never have been here.

Like all good things this trip had to come to an end and shortly I was on my way back to Milan.

Lebanon - Paris of the Middle East

It was in May 2017, I set foot in Lebanon. Even before I started I faced a deluge of questions from friends and acquaintances. "Is Lebanon safe? Why are you going there? There are plenty of other places to visit". Having been in the travel business for a long time, I do make it a point to talk to local people even before landing there. If one totally goes by the media reporting, there are very few places left in the world where one can set foot. At the same time I do not mean that one should be foolhardy to venture out to war torn or terrorist infested areas. Unless of course you are in the military or professional commitments take you there. In that case you are well equipped or protected and certainly you are not on a vacation. Areas on the east and northeast, close to the Syrian border could be avoided, due to certain spordic violence. In case we all lived in fear and avoided travelling to places, the world would become a dangerous place to live in. Even those who live in so called dangerous places in the world are people like us. Visiting places encourages local people and helps the locals and their economy. One of my very close friends, Olivier, an American architect, would rave about Beirut, since he had spent a lot of time there and had done some important projects. He would be regularly travelling there and I had the latest updates from him.

Before applying for a visa I was told that my passport should not have an Israeli visa stamped on it, otherwise I would not be given a visa to enter. Although I had visited Israel earlier, luckily this passport did not have an Israeli visa. Trying to rush through, since it was taking some time to get a visa from Lebanon, I chased the Embassy in Delhi. I got the visa stamped in my passport and another one came by mail. By now I had two visas. I decided to use the visa stamped on my passport on landing. I was allowed to safely pass through the immigration.

Not that I am much of a movie fan but some famous films that have been filmed here are *24 Hours to Kill, The Message, Death of a Princess, Carlos* and the famous James Bond movie *Man with Golden Gun* was partly filmed here. Ian Fleming being one of my favourite authors, it was a good enough motivation to visit Beirut.

After World War II, Beirut became a major tourist destination and financial capital. It was called "Paris of Middle East". This was due to the French influence, vibrant culture and intellectual life.

It all changed; a beautiful country was ruined by the civil war that lasted from 1975 to 1990, resulting in almost 120,000 fatalities. The civil war erupted because the Phalangists, a Christian militia, clashed with Palestinian factions over the latter's armed struggle against Israel from Lebanese territory. But the conflict changed rapidly into a fight over the Lebanese state and its political system. A 34-day war took place in 2006 between Hezbollah and Israeli defence forces. What ever be the cause, the country has suffered. I got into a conversation with a Lebanese passenger on the flight, Henri, a youngman, an engineer by profession. I asked him what it was like to live in Lebanon. He said, "It is getting better, but my parents say it can never be what it was like before".

In about 20 minutes drive from the Airport I reached the luxurious Le Royal Hotel in Beirut which is a member of the leading hotels of the World chain. It is a huge property and has a panoramic view of the Mediterranean sea. My suite was spacious and comfortable with spectacular view of the Mediterranean sea. The gymnasium and the indoor pool had a high and large facade overlooking the sea.

The following day I took a walking tour with a charming and knowledgeable guide by the name of Elizabeth Abou Nafeh. She was my guide for the whole tour. She gave a brief background of Lebanon and Beirut, its history and culture. She explained about the civil war that the country was embroiled in for almost 15 years and how Beirut had been rebuilt. She also said that Beirut is best seen on foot.

We walked through a heavily secured area, the old Jewish quarter of Beirut and saw one of the only synagogues in Beirut. No Jews are left here, the last one known as 'Liza the Jew', passed away in 2009. This area was heavily bombed during the war by the Israelis.

We walked to the heart of downtown and saw the old Roman ruins. Next to the Mohammad Al Amin Mosque there are the remains of the ancient Roman Cardo Maximus. Cardo Maximus can be considered the main road of any Roman town or city.

Beirut was named Berytus in Roman times. It was conquered around 64 BC. In modern-day Beirut, you can see the remains of five columns still standing tall at the ancient market place and central road across Beirut. One cannot go down to the ruins but you get a pretty good view and impression from the street level.

We walked to the main circle which was full of rich French colonization history, which had been raised to the ground. Now the area has been rebuilt and brought to its original shape. Later we took a break at the Central Clock Tower. It was beginning of Ramadan; unlike rest of middle- east, there was no restriction on eating and the country had a liberal look. Elizabeth asked me if I was fasting. I told her I was not a Muslim and Hindus did not not have any special month or period for fasting. Elizabeth told me she was a Christian; that gave me clarity with her name, she was an Arab Christian. One does not see any kind of discrimination and it is a very open and modern society.

We stopped at the Martyrs' Square, which is an iconic landmark. Named in 1931, it was set up as a tribute to martyrs executed during the Ottoman rule. The martyrs were protesting to end the Ottoman rule over Lebanon in favour of Arab Nationalist movements. Originally it was an open space beyond the Ottoman city's walls and was named "Sahat Al Burj" because it was marked by 'Burj Al Kashef'. Under the French mandate, however, it became a modernized meeting place with kiosks, a tramway and souks. In 1930, a sculpture of a Muslim and Christian woman holding hands over a coffin adorned the square. The statue was designed by a local artist Youssef Hoyek as a testament to people coming together at a time of strife. The four metre high statue of the martyrs that adorns the square was created by Italian artist Marino Mazzacurati and inaugurated by President Fouad Chehab in 1960. It was damaged during the civil war and restored later.

The bullet scarring on the statue was kept as a purposeful show of the monument's history.

During the civil war, the square was used as a point that divided the city into East and West Beirut to indicate opposing sects. Subsequently, the spot was completely destroyed as buildings and statues fell to ruin under the rain of bullets and bombings. Like a lot of Beirut, not much survived in the wake of 15-year civil war. After the assassination of then Prime Minister, Rafic Al Hariri, one of the main contributors to Downtown Beirut's renovation, the square once again became a popular site for political activity and protest as people came together year after year to remember the late politician. Nowadays people come together here, such that their voice can be heard.

We later headed for the National Museum of Beirut. We spent some time there. It is located on the former infamous Green line, which was once one of the most dangerous places on earth. It was closed during the Civil War, for over two decades as a result of the bloody Lebanese Civil War. The building was occupied by snipers and militia men, the museum building was a wreck, with bullet holes peppering the facade and holes in the walls and roof caused by shelling. The museum was constructed between 1930 and 1937 to house a rich collection of artefacts from pre-history to the Ottoman period, all discovered on Lebanese soil. Its magnificent collection of archaeological artefacts offers a great overview of Lebanese history and civilization that impacted its cultural crossroads. Every Lebanese can be proud of their rich heritage.

Downtown Beirut has been nicely restored, leaving a few patches from the past and restored to its original glory it has become a major tourist attraction. It is a wonderful place for the locals to meet.

I am not much of a gambler, but have never missed an opportunity to visit casinos. In the evening I visited Casino du Liban, located in Maameltein, Jounieh in Lebanon, 22 kilometres north of Beirut. Although I am more of a disappointment to Casino Staff and those especially at the gaming tables, I do remember an anecdote of my visit to Atlantic City in USA, a place full of casinos. I was curiously watching a girl playing some game and suddenly a lot of coins dropped down from the machine. She would not let me walk away from there and said I should not move as I was bringing her lots of luck! There was an old lady with hearing aid on a wheel chair with her credit card connected and payments being made for gambling. I am not sure what she would have lost or made. There are all kinds who are casino lovers. I have enjoyed the ambience, light, energy and food in casinos.

Casino du Liban is huge with an area of 35,000 square metres, with around 400 slot machines and 60 gaming tables. It has a showroom, night club, theatre, banquet facility and five restaurants. The casino was first opened in 1959. It closed in 1989 and reopened in 1996 after a fifty million dollars reconstruction and refurbishment project. Casino du Liban was the only casino in the Arab world in the 1970s.

On the terrace of the Casino, overlooking the beautiful bay of Jounieh we had our dinner, a lovely spread of Lebanese food. It was an entertaining evening with musical performances by various artists. The climax of the evening was performance by world renowned pianist, Guy Manoukian, a Lebanese-Armenian musician, composer and pianist. His fusion of oriental melodies with modern arrangements has taken him all over the world. Music was absolutely mesmerizing. At the end of the show he made a statement: "At the stage that I have reached, I could probably stay anywhere in the world, but I choose to stay in my beautiful country; there is no better place than Lebanon".

Lebanon itself is a small country and one can travel from Beirut to North or South in a few hours. Since there was limited time in hand and I was told that northern part would be more interesting, I decided to cover the northern part.

We stopped on top at a strategic point at the northern road for panoramic stop to view the Kadisha Valley, to take some memorable pictures. Kadisha Valley, Romanized as the Qadisha Valley and also known as the Kadisha Gorge or Wadi Kadisha, is a gorge that lies within the Becharre and Zgharta districts of the North Governorate of Lebanon. The valley was carved by the Kadisha River, also known as the Nahr Abu Ali when it reaches Tripoli. Kadisha means "Holy" in Aramaic, and the valley, sometimes called the Holy Valley. It has sheltered Christian monastic communities for many centuries. The valley is located at the foot of Mount al-Makmal in northern Lebanon.

The Kadisha Valley is near the Forest of the Cedars of God, survivors of the ancient Cedars of Lebanon, the most highly prized building materials of the ancient world. The forest is said to contain 375 individual trees, two claimed to be over 3000 years old, ten over 1000 years, and the remainder at least centuries old. The Lebanon Cedar (*Cedrus Libani*) is described in ancient works on botany as the oldest tree in the world. It was admired by the Israelites, who brought it to their land to build the First and the Second temples in Jerusalem. Historical sources report that the famous cedar forests were beginning to disappear at the time of Justinian in the 6th century AD.

After about two hours we arrived at the Cedars of the Lord. Suddenly from the warm climate it was cold here. We were in the mountains; anticipating this, I had kept a jacket, and thus while there were others suffering due to the cold, I was very comfortable. We walked inside the forest, enjoying the fresh air and the serene atmosphere.

The Cedars of God is one of the last vestiges of the extensive forests of the Lebanon cedar, that once thrived across Mount Lebanon in ancient times. Their timber was exploited by the Phoenicians, Egyptians, Assyrians, Babylonians, Persians, Romans, and Turks. The wood was prized by Egyptians for shipbuilding; the Ottoman Empire used the cedars in railway construction.

As mentioned above, the forest is unique. There was a sculpture made in natural shape on one of the Cedar trees depicting Jesus Christ. There were shops selling handicrafts. I bought a sculpture of St George riding a horse.

So much is the importance of the Lebanon Cedar, it is there on the National flag of Lebanon. I carried a small cedar tree home.

We stopped at Ehden, a beautiful mountainous town. Ideally placed along the slopes of Mount Makmal, which is a part of the Mount Lebanon Range. Ehden makes the ideal place for those looking to enjoy the best of nature. The town is historic and has served as hometown to some of the well-known people of Lebanon like Youssef Bey Karam.

The town is best known for its restaurants, cafes and lively atmosphere. The Horsh Ehden Nature Reserve around Ehden is a must visit for every traveller. Apart from being an important natural attraction, the Nature Reserve is also of cultural importance to Lebanon. It is a part of the remaining forest of Cedar of Lebanon.

We had a sumptuous lunch at Al Ferdaous Restaurant, serving authentic Lebanese food. The owners were there to make sure that we were looked after.

After lunch we left Ehden, heading to Batroun city, a coastal city in northern Lebanon and one of the oldest cities in the world with a history of human occupation going back to at least 5,000 years. Batroun is a major tourist destination in North Lebanon. The sea wall at Batroun was originally a natural structure composed of petrified sand dunes. This was reinforced by the Phoenicians with rocks and the process went on until it took its present shape in the first century BC. The wall is 225 metres long and 1 to 1.5 metres thick. Parts of it has crumbled but the remaining still stands strong and proud in Batroun's bay, and is a must see for an authentic piece of Lebanon's ancient history. The town boasts historic churches from Roman Catholic to Greek Orthodox. The town is also a major beach resort (knowing that Batroun is one of the cleanest rock and pebble beaches in Lebanon) with a vibrant nightlife that includes pubs and nightclubs. Citrus groves surround Batroun, and the town has been famous (from the early twentieth century) for its fresh lemonade sold at the cafés and restaurants on its main street. In 2009, the Batroun International Festival was born. It started hosting leading local and international artists. The festival takes place usually in July and/or August of each year in the old harbour area.

After a short drive, we were back in the hotel.

In the evening we went to the Music Hall, which is the most happening place in town. Described by international media as "the place where the heart of world fusion music beats", the Music Hall is not just a theatre venue and much more than a club. There was a musical performance and dance show by renowned artists. Elefteriades Productions launched the first Music Hall in Beirut in 2003.

Music Hall has hosted many famous international artists such as Nigel Kennedy, Roberto Fonseca, Paolo Fresu, Jane Birkin, Olivia Ruiz, Bernard Lavilliers, Yann Tiersen, and Grand Corps Malade Souad Massi, among others.

We spent the evening dancing, enjoying snacks and choicest of drinks. It was rather late at night and we thought that the night should go on but sadly all good things must come to an end as they say.

After coming back to the hotel, I got ready to embark on the early morning flight back home.

Myanmar: Experiencing Yangon (Rangoon)

I planned a short visit to Yangon in Myanmar in November 2017. This was the only neighbouring country that I had not been to. In 1989, the ruling military government changed the name from Burma to Myanmar after thousands were killed in an uprising. The city of Rangoon also came to be known as Yangon. Yangon served as the capital of Myanmar until 2006. It was thereafter replaced by Naypyidaw, officially spelled Nay Pyi Taw.

Myanmar is home to over 130 ethnic groups spread all over the country. Although eight major national races are residing in the respective States and eight Regions, some tribal groups are scattered in sub-regions of each State and Region. Each one has its own tradition and culture and thus the diversity of cultural background has been flourishing in this land. There are a total of 111 languages spoken by the people living in Myanmar. Among them, the top language groups are Myanmar (Burmese), Shan, Kayin (Karen), Rakhine, Mon, Chin and Kachin.

This land has long been recognized as having religious freedom. However, since the inception of Myanmar's political establishment in 11th century, owing to strong cultural interchange with India, Buddhism has been predominant though Christian, Muslim and Animist are also found in smaller numbers. It is also the world's greatest propagation centre of Theravada Buddhism. Theravada Buddhists comprise over 85% of the population.

Myanmar was a British colony from 1824 to 1948. Over the course of this century Yangon was an important commerce hub and also the capital of the country. After the dire years of the military rule much of its former glory has faded and now that it's not the capital anymore it seems much of the structures are also left to crumble, except for the "Secretariat" building, which is currently undergoing constructions and should become a museum at some point.

I was picked up early in the morning from the hotel by my friends Lu Mon and Sandi to see Yangon. Both of them are trained doctors but had got into a couple of businesses including hospitality. They had advised me that it was better to start early for Shwedagon Pagoda to avoid the crowds.

Shwedagon is the religious, cultural and touristic centre of Yangon. It's hard to grasp the size of the pagoda from photos, but it's height of 95 metres is quite impressive. New gold coating is done every few years. It is one of the holiest of places for Buddhists in Myanmar; so they all try to make at least one pilgrimage every year to Shwedagon.

A tradition at Shwedagon Pagoda is to pour water over your 'planetary post' indicating the day of your birth. All Burmese Buddhists know the day of the week that they were born on. Burmese people believe that the astrological day a person was born is a great determinant in his or her personality and life. It is believed by the Buddhists, that there are eight days in the week, with Wednesday split into two days, with morning and afternoon. Each day is represented by different animals for the eight-day week. Inside the pagoda, there is a corner with a post, or alter for each day of the week. I found my planetary post Tuesday covered in flowers and prayer flags. I poured water over my planetary post and over each Buddha and animal statue.

Gold dominated the intricate buildings. Beginning in the 15th century, the monarchs gave their weight in gold to the pagoda. Traditionally donating gold has been a way to earn merit. Queen Shinsawby was reportedly the first to donate her weight in gold; this happened some 600 years ago. She reportedly weighed a total of 88 pounds. King Dhammazedi gave four times his weight to outdo her. Over the years the weight of all this gold is said to have reached 45 tons.

After a few minute's drive from Shwedagon Pagoda we reached Sule pagoda, which is located in the centre of town. It is surrounded by busy streets, markets and colonial era buildings like the Supreme court building and Yangon city hall.

According to legend the pagoda was built during the lifetime of the Gautama Buddha, about 2,500 years ago. The pagoda was much smaller at that time. It has been renovated and enlarged several times by later Kings. The paya reached its present height when it was renovated halfway in the 15th century.

The Sule pagoda is named after Sularata, the *Sule Nat* (spirit) who lived at the spot where the pagoda now stands. According to legend Sularata, a Nat millions of years old found the spot where relics of the three reincarnations of the Buddha were buried. Nat spirits have been worshipped for centuries in Burma, even before the arrival of Buddhism. The Sule pagoda is highly revered because it enshrines a hair relic of the Buddha.

We visited the century old Bogyoke Aung San Market, where you'll find black market money exchanges, a growing art scene and rows of rare gems and jewellery shops. Towering ceilings, clean floors and semi-orderly shops make for a relatively serene experience. Bogyoke has long been a centre for selling jade, rubies and other rare gems.

Some people still call Bogyoke "Scott market" as it was named during colonial times, but after independence in 1948, the market was renamed in honour of General Aung San.

Although Yangon has a couple of museums, we visited the National Museum. The National Museum of Myanmar was founded in 1952 with its premises at what was once the Jubilee Hall. The National Museum is now located on Pyay Road in a splendid five-storey building constructed for the purpose in spacious and specially landscaped grounds. Priceless ancient artifacts, works of art and historic memorabilia are on display in 14 halls on four floors. Three halls on the ground floor hold exhibits on the evolution of the Myanmar script and alphabet, apart from the Lion Throne Room and Yatanabon period pieces.

We drove to ChaukHtatGyi pagoda; it has a very impressive 65 metres long and 16 metres high Buddha statue. The statue is wearing a golden robe, the right arm of the Buddha is supporting the back of the head. It is decorated with very expressive colours, white face, red lips, blue eye shadow, golden robe and red fingernails. A prominent part of the statue are the soles of his feet containing 108 segments in red and gold colours that show symbols representing the 108 'lakshanas' or auspicious characteristics of the Buddha.

The next day I took a stroll around and came across a Kali Bari Mandir located very close to the hotel that I was staying in. I stopped by to have a look from outside. One elderly gentleman, Mr Ghosh saw me and invited me to come inside. He was in his eighties and was born in Myanmar; he took me around the temple and I offered my prayers. Mr Ghosh gave me the background about his life in Myanmar. He spoke about the changes that had taken place over a period of time. During the conversation he did make a special mention of Admiral Katari when he was the Indian Ambassador in Myanmar in 1964 and the great work he had done for the Indian community here.

We soon became good friends. He offered to take me around to all the religious places which were a few minute's walk. We went to the Arya Samaj Mandir; my father had been a staunch follower of this sect. Caretakers of the Arya Samaj Mandir presented me with a souvenir of the Arya Samaj, interestingly published in Hindi. It was followed by a visit to the Gurudwara, where recitation of Guru Granth Saheb was going on. The Gurudwara was founded in 1942 by Sardar Jagat Singh Granthi; this is the only fuctional Gurudwara in Yangon. Later Mr Ghosh took me to Immaculate Conception Cathedral or Saint Mary's Cathedral; it is an architecture marvel; the exterior is of red brick, and consists of spires and a bell tower. It was designed by the Dutch architect Joseph Cuypers.

We walked past the Secretariat, a colossal colonial building which was under renovation. It is also known as the Prime Minister's Office; built in the late 19th century it is more than 120 years old. Standing at the heart of the city, the elegant Victorian-style building served as the seat of government for the British in Myanmar until the country's independence in 1948. The historic building was also the site where Bogyoke Aung San and six cabinet ministers were assassinated by political rivals on 19 July 1947. The building is now open to visitors and regular tours are conducted here. Also souvenir shops, a coffee shop and an art gallery have been opened at the Secretariat.

For his age Mr Ghosh was quite enthusiastic taking me around. We shook hands as I thanked him and then we parted.

Later, I visited Inyalake; it is one of the nature spots in Yangon and the biggest lake here. It was created artificially by the British to offer water supply to the city. Its function has transformed over the years and it's now used for sailing and rowing.

A visit to the tomb of Bahadur Shah Zafar was sombre occasion. He was the last Mughal emperor who had the reputation of being a talented Urdu poet and had succeeded his father Akbar II. Following his involvement in the Revolt of 1857, the British exiled him to Rangoon in 1858 in British-controlled Burma, after convicting him on conspiracy charges.

Zafar died four years later in 1862 and he was buried on the same day. The British wanted his tomb to be lost and forgotten. In February 1991, workers who were digging for a drain discovered a "brick lined tomb". On top of it was an inscription and soon the body was identified. After a few years, a dargah was built. The dargah is now a place of pilgrimage. It is also visited by politicians and senior officials as a mark of respect, and those interested in the history of Raj.

These couplets written by Bahadur Shah Zafar, the last Mughal Emperor describe his feelings in his final days:

"Kitna hai bad naseeb zafar, dafn keliye

Do gaz zameen bhi namilikoo-e-yaar me"

How wretched is your fate, Zafar!

That for your final berth

You couldn't get in your beloved's land

Two meagre yards of earth.

In the evening Mandy Walters, a US diplomat friend of mine invited me for dinner at the famous Rangoon Tea House. The interiors, ambience and the service were great in the restaurant. I tried some Burmese food. Since we were meeting after many years it gave us time to talk about all that happened between now and our last meeting. The first time I had met her in Delhi she had come on a short project with the embassy and was now a career diplomat. She mentioned that she was enjoying her stay here although in certain aspects it was not very different from India. After a wonderful evening and dinner she dropped me to the hotel.

The next morning, I had reached the airport quite early to take a flight for Kolkata. I had time to look around for some last minute shopping. I bought some bracelets made of tiger's eye gemstones as a memory of my visit to Yangon. It is said that wearing tiger's eye is beneficial for health and spiritual well being. Legend also says it is a psychic protector, great for business and an aid to achieving mental clarity. I put the bracelet around my wrist and bid goodbye to Myanmar.

Chapter 17

Alaska - The Last Frontier

Having sailed on warships and merchant ships, going on a passenger ship on a holiday was a totally different experience.

Once when I was a Master on a Shipping Corporation of India vessel I was discussing with my colleagues that I would like to take a vacation on the passenger ship being operated by our company. They thought I must be crazy to do that, having spent so much of time at sea and then to go on a holiday on a ship. Obviously I did not do that.

Later I took some short cruises on passenger ships. One place that we were keen to travel to was Alaska and there is no better way than to do it on a cruise ship. In May 2018 with Ved my brother and Neeru we proceeded to Vancouver from where most of the cruise ships operate for Alaska.

Some facts about Alaska; it was owned by Russia at one point. Russia lacked the financial resources to support major settlements. Permanent Russian settlers in Alaska never exceeded more than four hundred. Russia offered to sell Alaska to the United States for USD 7.2 million. Alaska was formally transferred to the United States on 18 October 1867.

Skeptic's termed Alaska as Seward's folly, since Secretary of State, William Seward was instrumental in signing of the Alaska Treaty. The Alaskan story changed when a major gold deposit was discovered in the Yukon. The rest is history.

We came a few days earlier and spent some time exploring Vancouver before commencing the cruise. Vancouver, a bustling west coast seaport in British Columbia, is among Canada's densest, most ethnically diverse cities. It is surrounded by mountains and also has thriving art, theatre and music scenes. Vancouver Art Gallery is known for its works by regional artists, while the Museum of Anthropology houses preeminent First Nations collections.

There are various cruise ship companies that operate in Alaska like Princess Cruises, Holland America line, Disney, Royal Caribbean, Celebrity, etc.

We chose the cruise ship *Emerald Princess* from the fleet of Princess Cruises, which commenced sailing on 13 May 2018 from Vancouver. The ship has a Gross Registered tonnage of 113,561 tons, with a capacity of maximum 3,573 passengers and a crew of 1,227. It is registered in Hamilton, Bermuda.

Choice of this ship was more for the convenience of dates as our plan was to disembark in Seattle and continue our further travel in the United States.

We reached the embarkation point Canada place at the cruise terminal where hundreds of passengers were waiting to embark on the ship. Although it does take some time, it was a very well organized procedure, from the handing over of the baggage, where tags are put with cabin numbers, followed by customs and immigration.

After clearing US immigration we were on board in our cabins and the baggage was already there outside our cabins. Before the ship set sail, we all gathered at the assigned emergency stations, with our life jackets. We were given a briefing on the action to be taken during an emergency and our assigned boats. This is a mandatory exercise on all ships due to safety considerations.

In the evening we commenced our journey from Vancouver, casting off from the jetty and leaving behind the beautiful skyline. The ship later lined up to pass under the Lions Gate Bridge with which we had a clearance of approximately 7 metres. Throughout the evening Emerald Princess negotiated a number of traffic separation schemes (shipping lanes designed to improve traffic flow in busy areas) under the guidance of two British Columbia pilots, who had boarded in Vancouver and remained on board till the next morning. It is mandatory to have pilots on board to sail and guide the ship through congested tricky areas.

The ship was in command of Captain Todd McBain. He didn't see his first ocean or ship until joining the Royal Canadian Navy. He worked first on destroyers, then later in the Merchant Navy on tankers and cargo ships and later he moved to passenger ships including command of various passenger ships in the Princess fleet.

Ved had never been at sea and specially on such a long trip. On the first day he was not very happy and wondered why he had come with us on this cruise, but from the following day he was comfortable and a changed man involved himself in every activity and started enjoying every bit of the trip. It was the same person who later said it was a great experience and no one should miss it. He was already planning a cruise holiday with his grandchildren.

With plenty of activity on board, our cruise started off on a good note, with Neeru winning a package for photographs to be taken during the cruise. Our photographs were taken at every place and on all occasions; it was like having a personal photographer on board. Photographs captured were very good memories onboard. At the end of the cruise we were given a CD with our photographs and the prints that we needed.

Apart from the ship having a swimming pool, jogging track, putting, SPA and a gym, it also had 24 hour dining.

Every night we would get the programme and details of activities for the following day. There were options to purchase excursions on board; these could also have been booked before as well. With limited time in hand at the ports, we booked most excursions before hand to save time.

The following day the ship sailed along the coast for the complete day for the next port of call named Ketchikan

During the day there were various activities on board like movies, shopping, casinos, shows, art auctions, Jewellery shopping, briefing on Alaska and its destinations etc. Similar activities were on board practically every day.

During the cruise there were various excursions depending on the Port of call like local tours, visit to museums/important tourist sites, helicopter rides to Glaciers, whale watching, boat cruises, salmon tasting, horse riding, dog sledging, train journey, Great Alaskan Lumber Jack show, visit to glaciers, etc.

The highlight of the evening was the Captain's Dinner. It was a formal affair for which everyone was elegantly dressed. There was a Champagne Fountain, various heads of departments, including the Captain were introduced to all the guests on board.

After an overnight sailing we arrived at Ketchikan, which is Alaska's First City; it was founded in 1883, has a population 8,142 and is known as the "Salmon Capital of the world".

After disembarking from the ship it was nice to see some young boys and girls controlling traffic with sign boards. I think the rush of pedestrians on the road was from the ship itself!

There are various excursions that can be taken here; the Great Alaskan Lumber Jack Show is very popular. It gives an insight into the working of lumberjacks. It is the location of the original site of the Ketchikan Spruce Mill built in 1903. The mill served the needs of seven canneries that were producing 1.5 million cases of salmon yearly and was the heart of ever-expanding timber industry in Alaska. The mill closed in 1974 and was idle till 2000 when it was converted to the Great Alaskan Lumber Jack Show.

Each year the Mill sponsors on 4th of July, a Timber Carnival that gathers all the loggers from Southeast Alaska and Canada to crown the "Bull of the Woods". At the Great Alaskan Lumberjack Show this tradition lives on.

We had the privilege of meeting Rob Scheer, the founder of the show on board, listen to him and had an opportunity to interact with him. He rarely sails on board. A tough guy who at the age of 59 can still hold his own with 20 year old competitors, he is the first man to win the title of Iron Jack and is a 3 time World Champion. It is a show with hyperactivity; there are two teams formed of Canada and United States, each trying to outperform the other in various competitions.

With nature in abundance one can enjoy a walk around Ketchikan and there are lots of options for shopping. We visited the Totem Heritage Museum which is a must. It has the largest collection of unrestored 19th century totem poles, but that's just the beginning of what it has to offer. Also displayed are baskets, masks, regalia carvings and incredible photographs of the old villages where the poles were retrieved. There are many carvings and totem poles outside the building too.

Ketchikan boasted of some 30 brothels; Dolly's House still exists, which is now a tourist attraction. It is written outside "Where both men and Salmon came to spawn". In the old days before video games, single young men in Alaska had a different idea of after work entertainment; hard liquor and a certain type of female companionship. These loggers, miners and fishermen worked hard in the woods, the gold camps or at sea. When they got back to town, Creek Street and its brothels were waiting.

Dolly's House, the only "den of iniquity" still stands today. One cannot miss Number 24 Creek Street, for its green doll house appearance looks much like it did during its heyday. Inside there are photos of Dolly adorning the walls, the cabbage rose wallpaper she favoured, and the "secret closet" in Dolly's bedroom, where she stashed contraband liquor during the prohibition years.

Here we learnt more about Dolly and the other women of the red light district, who were only allowed to shop on certain days so that proper ladies could avoid them. Dolly's place was shut down for good in 1954.

There were plenty of shops here selling local handicrafts and jewellery. Most of the shops selling jewellery are owned by Gujaratis from India.

An interesting part of the cruise is the choice of traditional dining at the assigned times every day at the same table. It would be the same stewards serving every night, with the same table mates. Thus Jonathan, a Filippino, was always at our table with his team to make every evening memorable. Service was excellent and we were expected to be in formal attire for dinner. They were very particular to meet special dietary requirements if any. The options in menu were varied from continental to Italian to Indian.

At night the ship sailed for Tracy Arm Fjord. In the morning the ship was to arrive at Tracy Arm Fjord for scenic cruising. The Captain made an announcement to passengers that due to ice conditions at Tracy Arm Fjord, the ship would instead proceed to Endicott Arm. The ship passed through the narrow entrance of three cables or about 500 metres. Large ships do not normally venture here. It is marked by rugged mountains, deep u-shaped valleys and towering waterfalls. At the head of the fjord is a tidewater glacier. The ship passed Wood Spit Light and Endicott Arm bar.

The ship came close to Daws Glacier and we could see plenty of icebergs floating. Being a huge ship, it needed support of tugs to remain in position and to turn around. The ships pontoons were lowered and rigged to accommodate the transfer of passengers on tour boats to take them on a scenic tour. During scenic cruising the ship went close to land which required sharp navigation skills on the part of the crew.

The ship proceeded through Stephens passage, heading past Admiralty island and entered Gastineau Channel; after passing Sheep Creek it entered Juneau Harbour in the afternoon and secured alongside the Alaska Steamship Dock.

En route to Juneau we had a get together of veterans in the bar. It was a nice gesture where we got to meet veterans from various nationalities inlcuding Australia, United States, New Zealand, Canada, United Kingdom and others countries. There were also veterans from India who we met here;

some of them were former colleagues. It was a great interaction and indeed nice to have exchanged our memories in and out of uniform.

Juneau, the State Capital of Alaska, has been home to Tlingit, Haida and Tsimshian people for thousands of years. Juneau is famous for the bald eagle and this is the place to see them in their natural habitat. They are like crows here. Boasting one of the highest concentrations of bald eagles in North America, estimates say there are anywhere from 15,000 to 30,000 here. Population of Juneau is around 32,000.

We rode the Mount Roberts Tramway which was a few minute's walk from where the ship was berthed; it is essentially the Eiffel Tower of Juneau. On top is the panoramic vantage point, 1800 ft above ground level. It also has a museum, restaurant and a theatre. From here we had a panoramic view of the city and its surrounding channels and islands. We were able to spot our cruise ship, which looked tiny from the top. But no landscape is more powerful or strange to behold than a glacier carving through sharp-ridged mountains.

Our driver cum guide Giuseppe, an Italian, who had served in the military and had got married to a local, was very pleasant and knowledgeable. Enroute to Mendenhall Glacier, which is 12 miles long and half a mile wide, he told us about Juneau and its flora and fauna. It was a short drive from downtown. Here you see a giant white sheet of ice, slowly flowing downhill from high up in the Coast Range mountains behind Juneau right into Mendenhall Lake. The enormous weight of the glacier compresses the ice and forces out air bubbles, giving it a deep blue colour visible in the cracks on its surface. It is one of 38 large glaciers that flow from the 1500 square mile expanse of snow and ice known as the Juneau Icefield. As the glacial ice accumulates seasonally, gravity pulls the ice down valleys. We went close to it; there are nicely marked trails. Mendenhall Glacier is melting faster than it grows and receding back into the mountains, a process that's speeding up due to climate change. Soon it will no longer carry ice chunks into Mendenhall Lake.

After an amazing walk in the park close to the glacier we were back at the Visitor Centre, where we watched a movie "Landscape of Change". It has a small museum, which tells us about the glacier, surrounding landscape and wildlife. It also has a book store.

Late at night we sailed for Skagway. Through the night the ship continued to sail southeasterly direction through Gastineau Channel before making a large alteration of course to Mamion Island into Stephens Passage.

Early morning the ship being in Stephens Passage, crossed Admiralty, Shelter and Douglas Islands.

At 0700 hrs the ship arrived at Skagway. Skagway has a population of 1036 which doubles during the tourist season. It is said that history, beauty and adventure meet here. It is Alaska's first incorporated city and the Gateway to the Klondike Gold Rush of 1898. This in fact was the turning point in the history of Alaska.

Skagway's history and spectacular setting create unparalleled sightseeing and recreational opportunities. There are plenty of options available; one can explore on one's own or take tours. It has five churches, one library and one financial institution. A portion of the Skagway downtown area has been designated as the Skagway Unit of the Klondike Gold Rush National Historical Park.

There are shops where local handicrafts can be picked up. Needless to mention, the latest variety of jewellery is available here. It is a good place to purchase Ulu knives. Of all the innovative tools that came from the Eskimo culture, one is the foremost, the Alaska Ulu knife. The ulu knife was their main cutting tool. It was originally made from flat, thin, rocks, slate, or even jade. The Ulu Knife dates back to 2500 BC and said to contain ancestral secrets and so is often passed down from generation to generation. They have a unique design that increases dexterity and leverage, making fine cuts simple and chopping easier. The blade is made of stainless steel and has a large, easy to grip wooden handle. It has been used by native people of the Arctic for centuries. We picked up a couple of Ulu knives as souvenirs and gifts for folks back home.

We visited the library close by. The library staff was very friendly and helpful. I had a chance to glance through some books and then used the internet facility available here. It gave me a quick chance to catch up with everyone.

The place is so small and everything in such close proximity, that we managed to do a number of things and activities. The National Park Visitor Centre located on 2nd Broadway offers a number of activities. We watched a film about the gold rush and Skagway. We also took a short guided tour of Skagway Historic District.

We then took the scenic train trip to White Pass Summit. White Pass & Yukon Route Rail Road is an International Historic Civil Engineering Land Mark and is known as Scenic Railway of the world. Like every railroad has a colourful beginning and a story, for White Pass and Yukon Route it was gold, discovered in 1896 by George Carmack and two First Nations companions, Shookum Jim and Dawson Charlie. The few flakes they found in Bonaza Creek in the Klondike was enough to trigger incredible stampede for riches that became known as the "Klondike Gold Rush."

The rush for riches was actually predicted by Skagway founder, Captain William Moore. The known route Chilkoot pass was rough and rugged. Moore and Shookum Jim decided to head North over uncharted ground and seek an easier route to the interior. They reached Lake Bennett, near the headwaters of the Yukon River and named the new potential route, White Pass, in honour of the Canadian Minister of the Interior, Sir Thomas White.

The headline of the *Seattle Post-Intelligencer* on 17 July 1897, broadcast the news of discovery of gold in the Canadian Klondike. The newspaper reported that "Sixty eight rich men on the steamer Portland arrived in Seattle with stacks of yellow metal."

The news spread like wild fire. Tens of thousands of gold crazed men and women steamed up the Inside Passage waterway and arrived in Dyea and Skagway to begin the overland trek to Klondike. Some chose the shorter but steeper Chilkoot trail which began in Dyea while others chose the longer, less steep White Pass Trail out of Skagway. Both the Chilkoot Trail and the White Pass Trail were full of hazards and many had harrowing experiences.

Michael J. Heney helped build railroads in Canada, Washington and Alaska, but it was his work as a labour contractor for the White Pass & Yukon Route that brought him wide recognition. The White Pass and Yukon route was built in twenty six months for ten million dollars. The project was the product of British financing, American engineering and Canadian contracting. Tens of thousands of men and 450 tons of explosives overcame a harsh and challenging climate and geography to create the wonder of steel and timber, "The Scenic Railway of the World."

In a three hour journey, the train travels five territories including Canada. It is a fascinating rail journey, through mountains, tunnels and bridges. Seeing wildlife is a possibility. The train crew keep a sharp lookout for wildlife and announce any sightings; we were lucky to sight some bears and mountain goats. The train earlier used to run all year round, when it carried freight. Today it runs early May to end September, coinciding with the cruise season. On return the train stopped on the jetty in front of the ship and we just had to walk across to the gangway to board the ship.

In the evening we sailed for Victoria. We were privileged to meet Jesus and Rosa More. They were the most travelled guests on board who had sailed for 1348 days with Princess Cruises.

We sailed through Chatham Strait and next morning Emerald Princess passed from US to Canadian waters. The day was full of various activities on board. There were some adventurous passengers onboard watching movies on the deck in the night, wrapped in blankets.

Then came the farewell party in the evening. This was again a formal affair, with music, champagne flowing freely and lots of formal photography.

The following day the ship sailed through the Olympic Marine Sanctuary which covers an area of 3200 square miles and is administered by the National Oceanic and Atmospheric Administration (NOAA) for the protection of marine life.

In the evening we arrived at Victoria, the oldest city in Western Canada and also known as the City of Gardens. Considered Canada's most British City, Victoria showcases elegant Victorian and Edwardian-era mansions and impressive architectural landmarks that define the British style.

The stately Legislative Buildings constructed in 1893 in honour of Queen Victoria's Diamond Jubilee is a must see. At the majestic Fairmont Express Hotel we indulged in the ultimate British tradition, high tea. The hotel has a breathtaking lobby and overlooks the beautiful harbour. The places around the inner harbour are beautiful. It is a nice walk to the second oldest Chinatown in North America, the ornate "Gate of Harmonius Interset"; the historic passage has remained untouched since early days.

At night we embarked on and sailed for Seattle on the last leg of the Alaskan Cruise.

The next morning at 0700 hrs we arrived at Seattle. All guests onboard disembarked from the ship in a very orderly manner in various groups. It was finally the end of the famous Alaskan cruise. We parted with fond memories and from friends we made onboard.

As we had some time before taking our flight to San Diego we took a short tour of Seattle. Seattle is surrounded by water, mountains and evergreen forests, and contains thousands of acres of parkland. It is Washington State's largest city and home to a large tech industry, with Microsoft and Amazon headquartered in its metropolitan area. We visited the Space Needle; it was built at the same time as the Monorail for the 1962 Seattle World's Fair. It stands at a height of 605 feet and provides a 360-degree view of Seattle from the Observation Deck. The Needle also features a revolving restaurant five hundred feet above ground called SkyCity.

A must visit place is the Pike Place Market; it is an iconic attraction in downtown Seattle and boasts nine acres of fresh produce, fish, flowers, local jewellery, artwork and gifts. Pike Place Market was founded on 17 August 1907 to provide Seattle citizen's direct access to local producers. That first day, farmers arrived with wagons full of produce and a grand tradition in public markets was born. Even today Washington farmers sell their fresh produce and specialty farm products daily. It is also home to the original Starbucks. The Pike Place Market crafts market began more than 40 years ago and now represents 225 local and regional crafts people. Since its beginnings in the late sixties, this dynamic and diverse group has become an integral part of the Pike Place Market community. Located in the North Arcade, the daily crafts market provides the opportunity to discover unique, local and handcrafted items and is one of the largest and most diverse in the United States. Over 10 million visitors visit Pike Place Market every year.

From Seattle we flew down to San Diego, to spend some time with our friend Kiki in Julian. But that is another story.

Chapter 18

Sojourn to the Middle East — Visiting Jordan and Israel

The Middle-east has been so often in the news for some conflict or the other that it is not exactly on the top as a tourist destination. But in 2018 my wife and I decided that we could go to Jordan and Israel in a group and visit specific places with a good guide. In fact I had been to Israel earlier and the experience whet my appetite for another sojourn in that region.

A Trip to Jordan

With some Rotarians and other friends we visited Jordan and Israel in October 2018. We arrived at Queen Alia International Airport, Amman in the afternoon. We were received at the Airport by Yosef, airport representative from the tour company; after a smooth clearance from immigration, and collecting our bags we moved straight to the hotel.

The Hashemite Kingdom of Jordan is a small country that occupies the ancient land that bears the traces of many civilizations. Separated from ancient Palestine by the Jordan River, the region played a prominent role in biblical history. The ancient biblical kingdoms of Moab, Gilead and Edom lie within its borders. Jordan's significance results partly from its strategic location at the crossroads of what Christians, Jews and Muslims call the Holy Land. It is believed that John the Baptist baptized Lord Jesus in this river.

The first settlers in Jordan were the Amorites in 2000 BC. Many other ancient nations and empires settled here or conquered the land over the years. These included the Hittites, Egyptians, Israelites, Assyrians, Babylonians, Persians, Greeks and Romans. Jordan has been an independent kingdom since 1946. Before that, under the British mandate of Transjordan in early 1920s, it became the Emirate of Transjordan under the Hashemite Emir.

Amman apart from being the capital and largest city of the Hashemite Kingdom of Jordan has a population of more than four million. Amman is a great base for exploring not just Jordan, but the wider region.

In the evening we all went out for a walk near the hotel and had dinner together. It was a great time to catch up and know each other better.

The following day we started our day with our guide Mohammed Ahmed who picked us up from the hotel. He was an elderly, savvy and knowledgeable gentleman, who was with us for rest of the tour of Jordan. He started the tour briefing us about Jordan, its history, formation and the present state.

Our first stop was at the Roman Amphitheatre; it is the most impressive monument of old Philadelphia, as Amman was known when it was part the Roman Decapolis — the cities network on the frontier of the Roman Empire in the southeastern Levant. According to an inscription, it was built during the era of the Antonine emperors, at the end of the 2nd century AD.

Its tiered, semicircular seating space, carved into the Jabal Al-Jofeh hill in three horizontal sections with a total of 44 rows, can seat around 6,000 people.

The Roman Theatre is used for performances, concerts, and events. There are also two heritage museums on either side, the Folklore Museum and Museum of Popular traditions. The Folklore museum showcases a collection of Jordanian cultural heritage items from the desert, villages, and towns including costumes, musical instruments, handicrafts and mosaics.

The Museum of Popular traditions is located to the left from the entrance. The museum exhibits Jordanian and Palestinian heritage, such as traditional costumes and head dresses, weavings and embroideries, jewellery and cosmetic items, and household and food preparation utensils.

The fifth hall, which is in a vault of the Roman Amphitheatre, houses a collection of mosaics from Byzantine churches in Jerash and Madaba from the 6th century AD.

The hilltop holding the Citadel & Temple of Hercules ruins seems unremarkable as far as hills are concerned. Amman is a city comprising seven hills and the one holding the Temple of Hercules isn't especially different from the others. The Romans chose this hill out of the seven to hold the Temple of Hercules and a Byzantine church. Amman's modern appearance, however, hides its ancient history dating to the neolithic period and considered among the world's oldest continuously inhabited places.

The Citadel dates from AD 162 to 166—which puts it smack in the middle of Amman's period of Roman occupation during Marcus Aurelius' time and some say that the structure itself was never finished since there are missing columns and other archaeological evidence missing. The Citadel and Temple of Hercules sit with a gorgeous view of the city.

Citadel Hill (Jabal al-Qal'a) stands out because it's located in what is now the heart of downtown modern Amman but also among the oldest parts of the city.

Archaeologist believe bad luck played in what is left standing today, even if it appears as just crumbling marble columns. Parts of the Citadel complex, including the Temple of Hercules, were likely cannibalized to build the nearby church.

An earthquake is strongly believed to have been responsible for taking down the Statue of Hercules. All that's left of this mighty statue is a set of three fingers crawling over the side of the hill and a huge white fragment of his elbow. The Statue of Hercules would have stood as much as 13 metres high according to archaeologists, which would make it among the largest known marble statues in the world.

It is fascinating to visit the bazaar. The Souk is located in downtown area near the King Hussein Grand Mosque; locals call it the el-Balad. This is the oldest part of the town. The souk has a number of shops selling spices, sweets, dry fruits, fruits, vegetables and local items.

I have firmly believed that shopping is also a great way to give back to the community, buying from independent and locally owned businesses. Locally owned businesses provide many economic benefits to a community. Shopping at local businesses creates more local jobs than shopping at major chains or online companies. Local businesses not only pay their employees, they also spend money at other local businesses. By purchasing food and other goods that are produced locally you stimulate the economy.

Later we visited Madaba; it is best known for its historic churches, historical landmarks and centuries old mosaics. In Jordan there is no other region filled with more historical landmarks than Madaba.

The most well known and a must visit is Mt Nebo. The mount is famed as the biblical location where Moses stood looking out at the Promised Land that he was destined never to set foot in. The Bible tells us that after seeing the Promised Land Moses died here on Mt Nebo. The 1,000 metre high ridge offers a breathtaking view over Jericho, the Dead Sea, the West Bank, the river Jordan and on very clear days even Jerusalem. Mt Nebo has two peaks, namely, Siyagha and al-Mukhayyat; on the summit of Siyagha is the Moses Memorial Church and the remains of a Byzantine monastery and church.

Moses led the Israelites out of slavery in Egypt and through the desert for 40 years. It is believed God showed him all of the Promised Land but told him it would belong to his descendants and he would see it but never cross over into it. Moses was denied entry into the Promised Land because he had struck a rock with his staff to produce water for the people in the desert instead of trusting in God and simply commanding the rock to give water as instructed. The Bible does not specify the location of Moses' burial but Christian tradition holds that Moses was buried on Mt Nebo.

From the early days of Christianity Mt Nebo became a pilgrimage site. Monks and pilgrims from far and wide came to see where Moses had lived out his final days. Third and fourth century Egyptian monks constructed a small church on the mount to commemorate Moses' death. In the 5th century the church was expanded and in the 6th century it became a monastery and basilica with beautiful Byzantine mosaics. The site was abandoned in the 16th century and only rediscovered in the 1930s. In 1993 the Franciscan church bought the site, restored, excavated and preserved what remained of the earlier church mosaics. Careful excavation revealed six tombs in the natural rock structures beneath the church.

The main attraction and reason for visiting Mt Nebo is to enjoy the breathtaking view across the Holy Land as Moses did thousands of years ago. You can see a large portion of the mosaic measuring 9 metres by 3 metres depicting hunting, wine-making, trees and animals. The mosaics are quite magnificent. The original Byzantine baptismal font has also survived. There is the Brazen Serpent Monument – also known as the Serpent Cross; it was created by Italian sculptor Giovanni Fantoni incorporating Christ's cross with the biblical bronze serpent. Here one can also see an olive tree, planted by Pope John Paul II on his visit to the site in 2000. Pope Benedict XVI also visited Mount Nebo in 2009.

The city is famous for mosaics. Decorated with sumptuous interiors, elegant colonnades and various mosaics, the Greek Orthodox Basilica of Saint George hosts the mosaic map of the holy land. With two million pieces of vividly coloured local stone, it depicts hills and valleys, villages and towns as far as the Nile delta. This beautiful church is one of the main places of worship and pilgrimage in Jordan.

The Madaba Mosaic Map covers the floor of the Greek Orthodox Church of St. George, which is located northwest of the city centre. The church was built in 1896 AD, over the remains of a much earlier 6th century Byzantine church. The mosaic panel enclosing the Map was originally around 94 square metres, only about a quarter of which is preserved and can be seen now.

The following day we visited the Royal Automobile Museum, a must visit place for automobile lovers and others; it is one of the most interesting and well organized museums in Jordan. The museum depicts the history of the Hashemite Kingdom of Jordan from the early 1920s until today through cars and motorcycles.

The museum has been developed as a tribute to the late King Hussein. Throughout the museum you get to see rare cars, motorcycles, photos, videos as well as sound bites. On display are a range of vintage and limited edition cars from Aston Martins, Mercedes Benz, Phantom, Lincolns, Cadillacs as well as some beautiful old motorcycles. The museum has about 60 cars and 50 motorcycles; there is a replica of the first motorcycle ever invented dating all the way from 1885 and a replica of the first car ever patented in 1886. The museum covers the Great Arab Revolt era with motorcycles and cars from 1916 to 1923 and onwards to World War II, King Abdullah I and then King Talal and of course King Hussein of Jordan. The newer cars and motorcycles are gifts or loans that the museum has received in the era of King Abdullah II.

While travelling from one place to another when Mohammed was not busy explaining anything, Kamal from our group would keep us entertained and engaged on the way with singing, introducing others or giving short talks. In a way he was the self- appointed Master of Ceremony for the tour.

Although visit to Jerash was not planned, but as we had some free time in hand, Mohammed enquired whether we all would like to visit Jerash. All of us in unison agreed to do so. There were no regrets at all, as we realized after visiting the place. Jerash is considered among the most well-preserved sites for ancient Roman architecture outside of Italy. It lies on a plain surrounded by hilly wooded areas and fertile basins. Conquered by General Pompey in 63 BC, it came under Roman rule and was one of the ten great Roman cities of the Decapolis League. The modern city of Jerash can be found to the east of the ruins. While the old and new share a city wall, careful preservation and planning has seen the city itself develop well away from the ruins so there is no encroachment on the sites of old where so much history is buried.

The amphitheatre, arches and plazas are in excellent condition. It was hidden for centuries under the desert and has only recently been excavated in the past century. It was only rediscovered by the west in the early 1800s and excavations began in 1925.

We entered through Hadrian's Gate, an imposing arch dating back to 129 AD. At its prime, Jerash housed 20,000 people and really began to flourish during the time of Alexander the Great. Located along the trade route, the city thrived and continued to grow until 800 AD.

We saw a bagpipe player and drummers performing at the theatre of the Roman ruins. We could not figure out the significance of this, but it looked different and interesting. Sarathy from our group joined the drummers and gave a striking performance.

We were in time to watch the Roman Army and Chariot Experience (RACE), in the hippodrome. This is performed a few times during the day. RACE is the biggest regular show of any kind in the Middle East and the only large scale Roman re-enactment performance in the world. It started with a performance of twenty-four fully equipped legionaries showing their battle formations and tactics. The narrative explains the history of the Roman army and how the legionaries lived and fought and about their traditions and customs.

Next there is a display of somewhat gruesome gladiator fights with swords. Towards the end is a race with several chariots competing with up to seven laps around the "spina", middle barrier.

Later in the evening we went to the lively Rainbow Street. It is a colourful strip brimming with creative cafes, restaurants and shops. The street is popular with tourists, locals and the city's rich and famous including Jordan's King Hussein and Queen Rania. It was a great place to have some coffee and pick up some snacks. We bought Baklava; it is a rich, sweet dessert pastry made of layers of filo filled with chopped nuts and sweetened and held together with syrup, frosting or honey.

Next day after a three hour drive we reached Petra, hidden in a valley surrounded by stones and desert, an entire city carved out of stone. Immediately after putting our bags in the hotel we went for a nice Mediterranean lunch. It was surprising to find some boys working in the restaurant from the state of Punjab in India.

Petra was built in the 3rd century BC by the Nabataeans, who carved palaces, temples, tombs, storerooms and stables from the soft stone cliffs. Today, it is a World Heritage Site. It was only rediscovered about 200 years back. Petra is without a doubt Jordan's most valuable treasure and greatest tourist attraction. It is a vast, unique city, carved into the sheer rock face by the Nabataeans, an industrious Arab people who settled here more than 2000 years ago, turning it into an important junction for the silk, spice and other trade routes that linked China, India and southern Arabia with Egypt, Syria, Greece and Rome.

As we entered the horse handlers tried to persuade people for a horse ride from the gate down to the dam at the entrance to the Siq – a walk of less than a kilometre. Although a horse ride is included in the entrance ticket, there are few takers for this. I did not want to miss this opportunity. As I had told them that I could ride, they came with offers of giving me a good horse and mentioning names of some famous Indian actors like Shah Rukh Khan and Salman Khan, who had ridden their horses in the past. Mohammed had also briefed us to give them a small tip after the ride, which they would be expecting. I mounted the horse and rode the short distance at a canter. On getting down, I gave a tip to the handler, but he said that it was too little and I should tip him more as I had ridden the horse very fast! Riding horses through the Siq is not allowed, but a horse carriage can be taken all the way through the Siq to the Treasury. Some of us who were not feeling comfortable to walk took the horse carriage.

Walk through this canyon is an exciting and interesting experience. It is because of unique geological landscapes carved out of pale reddish sandstone; the eastern side of this area is bounded by the King's Wall.

Just as one starts to think there's no end to the Siq, we caught a breathtaking glimpse ahead, of the most impressive of Petra's sights, the Treasury, known locally as Al Khazneh. Carved out of iron-laden sandstone to serve as a tomb, the Treasury gets its name from the misguided local belief that an Egyptian pharaoh hid his treasure in the top urn. The Greek-style pillars, alcoves and plinths are truly masterpieces of masonry work.

The Roman theatre at Petra is cut a slope above the riverbed of Wadi Mousa, 600 metres from the centre of the city. Earlier tombs on that cliff were destroyed in order to accommodate the theatre at that site. It is dated to the time of the Nabataean ruler Aretas IV and was excavated in 1961-1962. The cavea (auditorium) and orchestra area were cut out of the rock, while the scaena (stage building) was constructed of ashlar and faced with white-mottled breccia. The theatre faces east and follows the plan typical of the Greco-Roman world, and the cavea seated approximately 4,000 people. The theatre was remodeled during the 1st and 2nd centuries CE, one of the few major architectural changes at Petra made during the Roman occupation.

One cannot miss the unpredictable Royal Tombs that took its name from the rich decoration. To reach them you have to climb a stairway that leads to the famous Urn Tomb, which was used as a place of worship during the Byzantine Empire. Beside the Urn Tomb is a small tomb known as the Silk Tomb. This name comes from the rich colour of the sandstone. Then comes the Palace Tomb, the Corinthian Tomb and the Tomb of Sesto Fiorentino.

The Monastery is probably the second biggest landmark in Petra, right after the famous Treasury. Hidden high in the hills, it is similar in design to the Treasury but far bigger (50 metre wide and 45 metre high); it was built in the 3rd century as Nabataean tomb. This was the very last stop, but there were some small places, where we could get some water and tea. We stopped and ordered some tea; it was served in small glasses without handle called "Istikan." This was a well deserved break after a long walk. We soon started walking back.

The horse handlers were waiting at the Siq with their horses. They recognized me. It was again an enjoyable short ride back. Gave the horse handler a decent tip this time; he had a smile on his face and with a salute he went away, waving at me.

As by end of the day we were quite tired after a hectic and unforgettable day. Some of us decided to rest and others went to a restaurant close by to the hotel for an early dinner . It served nice pizzas, wine and coffee. It was a good way to converse, see the local crowd and generally relax.

The next day on a chilly morning after about an hour and a half's drive we finally made it to the last stop of our visit in Jordan ie Wadi Rum. It is protected area covering 720 square kilometres and is famous for its stunning desert landscape, spectacular sandstone mountains, desert valleys, canyons, dunes, arches. Huge mountains of sandstone and granite emerge, sheer-sided, from wide sandy valleys to reach heights of 1700 metres and more. Narrow canyons and fissures cut deep into the mountains and many conceal ancient rock drawings etched by the peoples of the desert over millennia. Bedouin tribes still live among the mountains of Rum and their large goat-hair tents are a special feature of the landscape.

It is also known as The Valley of the Moon. Wadi Rum has been used as a filming location in 'Lawrence of Arabia', 'Prometheus', 'The Martian' and many other movies.

To safeguard its unique desert landscape, Wadi Rum was declared a protected area in 1998 and an intensive conservation programme is now underway.

We started our visit at the Visitor Centre which provides all the required information, a good restaurant and an excellent view of the rock/mountain. Colonel T. E. Lawrence called it the Seven Pillars of Wisdom, After leaving the Visitor Centre we got in different jeeps and our group formed a small convoy to explore Wadi Rum.

Wadi Rum is well known because of Colonel Lawrence who fell in love with this place; these were the now famous words used by him to describe Wadi Rum: "vast, echoing and God-like".

Colonel Lawrence was a British liaison officer. He served with rebel forces during the successful Arab Revolt against the Ottoman Turks (1916-1918). Many men of the tribe, the Zalabieh, fought alongside with Lawrence. Lawrence wrote an autobiographical book about this period called 'Seven Pillars of Wisdom'. In the 1960s, David Lean made the famous movie 'Lawrence of Arabia' based on this book.

Later we stopped at Lawrence's spring and walked through Khazali canyon. There is a structure, a bunch of unimpressive rubble known as Lawrence house; there are stories that he both stayed and stored weapons here. It is built upon the remains of a Nabataean building. It is uncertain whether this was, in fact, Lawrence's house. Despite all this, it is a place to see. In nearby rocks one can see attractive rock inscriptions.

There are shops owned by Bedouins, the original habitants of Wadi Rum; they sell beverages, souvenirs and dresses and headdresses. With a sculpture of Colonel Lawrence in the background, we all took photos, wearing the Shemagh, the Bedouin male headgear. We bought these from the shops owned by Bedouins. This is the famous, well known traditional headdress of Arabs. It can be worn with or without the agal-rope. It can be tied in different ways according to one's preference. The Jordanian shemagh-cloth is traditionally red and white. The wearing of the Shemagh is a sign of male status. A man who wears it is assumed to be able to uphold the obligations and responsibilities of manhood.

We continued to Anfeeshiah Inscription, Napatean and Bedouin old inscriptions drawn on the mountain. We stopped at the sand dunes and walked up to have a nice view of the desert and take photographs.

After a delightful jeep ride we were back at the visitor centre. We got on the bus to go to our next destination via Allenby border to Jerusalem.

On to Israel: land of Zion

This was my second visit to Israel. Our guide Mohammed assisted us at the Allenby border to be transferred to the Israeli side. It was a smooth transition. Immigration had some questions to ask on the Israeli side, which is quite normal, keeping security in mind. Since it was a group visa we were given entry slips. Our group name was on the screen thus expediting the process at the border.

We had the transport waiting for us outside the terminal and were received by our guide Dalia.

Israel is located on the eastern shores of the Mediterranean Sea and bordered by Egypt, Jordan, Lebanon and Syria. The nation of Israel, with a population of more than 8 million people, most of them Jewish, has many important archaeological and religious sites considered sacred by Jews, Muslims and Christians alike, and a complex history with periods of peace and conflict.

Much of what scholars know about Israel's ancient history comes from the Hebrew Bible. According to the text, Israel's origins can be traced back to Abraham, who is considered the father of both Judaism (through his son Isaac) and Islam (through his son Ishmael).

Abraham's descendants were thought to be enslaved by the Egyptians for hundreds of years before settling in Canaan, which is approximately the region of modern-day Israel.

The word Israel comes from Abraham's grandson, Jacob, who was renamed "Israel" by the Hebrew God in the Bible.

King David ruled the region around 1000 BC. His son, who became King Solomon, is credited with building the first holy temple in ancient

Jerusalem. In about 931 BC, the area was divided into two kingdoms: Israel in the north and Judah in the south.

For the next several centuries, the land of modern-day Israel was conquered and ruled by various groups including Babylonians, Persians, Greeks, Romans, Arabs, Fatimids, Seljuk Turks, Crusaders, Egyptians, Mamelukes, Islamists and others.

How quickly everything changes in this land. From city to desert, from one religion to another, from intense culture to untouched nature this is a land of extremes all packed into a very small space.

After about an hour and a half we reached Jerusalem and checked in Jerusalem Gate Hotel, which was centrally located at the entrance of Jerusalem. It is a hotel with a true Jewish ambiance. Jerusalem Gate Hotel is very popular with Jews visiting from all over the world; it is one of the best glatt kosher hotels in Jerusalem and is under the supervision of *Mehadrin* (most stringent level of kosher supervision) of the Jerusalem Rabbinate. The Jerusalem Gate Hotel is the perfect place for *shabbatot* (Jewish Shabbat days), *simchot* (happy occasions), or a visit to *Eretz Yisroel* (Holy Land Israel).

The following day, with our guide Dalia we visited Jericho in the Palestinian territories, the oldest continually inhabited city in the world. It is said to be about ten thousand years old with evidence of settlement dating back to 9000 BC and urban fortifications dating back to 7000 BC. It is located in a small portion of land, known as area A, which is fully controlled by the Palestinian Authority. This area also includes the cities of Ramallah, Bethlehem, Nabulus, and part of the holy city of Hebron.

Outside the old city of Jericho you will find the road where Jesus is said to have restored the eyesight of the blind beggar, Barttmaeus. Within the old city is the tree where the tax collector Zaccheus climbed the sycamore tree in order to see Jesus as he passed by. Many believe that this is the same tree now over 2,000 years old.

Shops located in Jericho feature Hebron's world renowned ceramics and hand blown glass, a tradition dating from the Middle Ages. Also many products from the Dead Sea are available here.

In the Judean Desert, about five miles from Jericho, is the mountain (Mount of Temptation) where Jesus fasted for 40 days and nights. This is also where he was tempted by the devil. Built atop the mountain and offering a spectacular view is the Greek Orthodox Monastery of the Temptation.

We later drove on to Kibbutz Almog, located near the northwestern shores of the Dead Sea in the Jordan Rift Valley in the West Bank.

Dalia explained about Kibbutz. Kibbutz was a revolutionary idea of a voluntary society in which people live in accordance with a specific social contract, based on egalitarian and communal principles in a social and economic framework. The main characteristics of Kibbutz life were established in adherence to collectivism in property alongside a cooperative character in the spheres of education, culture and social life. With this came the understanding that the Kibbutz member is part of a unit that is larger than just his own family.

The Kibbutz operates under the premise that all income generated by the Kibbutz and its members goes into a common pool. This income is used to run the Kibbutz, make investments, and guarantee mutual and reciprocal aid and responsibility between members. Kibbutz members receive the same budget, depending on family size, regardless of their job or position. In terms of education, all children start equally and are given equal opportunity. The Kibbutz is governed by a system of direct participatory democracy, where the individual can directly influence issues and events in the community. In this mostly self sufficient community, the collective as well as the individual work ethic play a major role.

It was interesting to see how the community lives and works collectively. We were taken around to see the crops and palms grown here. The community also runs a guest house for those interested in staying here and also a restaurant, where we had our lunch. It also has a small museum.

Later we went to Kalia Beach on the Dead Sea. The Dead Sea is the lowest point on earth. The highly saline water of the sea has given rise to the name 'Dead Sea' because no fish can survive in the salty waters. At the same time the salty water of the Dead Sea has health and healing properties. Though well known for years, the Dead Sea shot into global prominence in the early fifties after a Beduin tribesman in 1947 found ancient scraps of papyrus and goatskin manuscript written in a language which was identified as mainly Hebrew and Aramic. These caves overlooking the Dead Sea (the Qumran caves in the Judean desert) were then visited by many experts and the manuscript became famous as the *Dead Sea Scrolls* dated to about 200- 150 years before Christ. Many books have been published and even films were made on this discovery which also created a lot of controversy in the Christian world.

It was a very well organized beach. We were shown the place where lockers were located. We changed our clothes to take a dip in the Dead Sea. It is one of the finest experiences; there is so much of positive buoyancy that it is difficult to go inside the water. I actually lay on my back to see in case I could read a book lying on water on my back. It was possible and comfortable to do so for a short while. It is said that no one can drown in the Dead Sea. Dead Sea mud is used to treat health conditions ranging from psoriasis to back pain. A great deal of research backs up claims that Dead Sea mud can relieve pain, reduce inflammation and more. I did not miss the opportunity, and plastered mud all over my body. After that it was quite an exercise to get it off.

The Dead Sea has a salinity of 33.7 per cent. This is almost 10 times saltier than ordinary seawater. One has to be very careful with the salty water; it gives a burning sensation in the eyes if any water goes in. Swallowing water can be quite toxic. Some over enthusiastic people jumping in the water had salty water in their eyes. They had to rush out to wash their eyes with fresh water to get some relief.

It is an eco-friendly beach. After experiencing the Dead Sea, we had coffee at the lowest bar in the world (at the lowest point on Earth).

In the evening the hotel looked quite busy. There was a Jewish orthodox wedding going on. We were told by Dalia that a wedding would start with a Kabbalat panim, a reception. Men and women hold separate receptions. We could see them dancing in different areas.

The following day we toured Jerusalem starting with a visit to the Mount of Olives; from here was a breathtaking view of the city to the west, and the desert to the east. The mountain was attributed special religious significance and became an integral part of religious services due its proximity to the Temple Mount and especially because of the view that it offered of the surrounding area.

From there we went to the Garden of Gethsemane, located on the foot of Mount of Olives. It is the site where Jesus prayed and his disciples slept, according to Christian tradition, and subsequently became an important pilgrimage site. In addition to its religious significance, a scientific study has shown that the olive trees in the garden are some of the oldest in the world, approximately 2,000 years old. It is believed that Jesus prayed here before the night he was crucified.

We entered the Old City of Jerusalem and walked through the four different quarters located in an area of .9 square kilometres (Muslim, Christian, Jewish and Armenian) viewing the major landmarks of 4000 years of dramatic history.

We entered Temple Mount through Mughrabi Gate and there was proper security at the entrance. Seen as the holiest site for Jewish believers, some parts of the four walls surrounding the Temple Mount date back to the time of the Second Jewish Temple. The walls were built around the summit of Mount Moriah, where biblically, Abraham offered his son, Isaac, as a sacrifice. It is home to some of the holiest sites in Judaism, Islam and Christianity.

The Temple Mount is the third holiest site for Muslims after Mecca and Medina. As per Muslim belief, this is where the Prophet Mohammed made his "Night Journey" to the throne of God. In the seventh century, when the Muslims conquered Jerusalem, they built the Dome of the Rock, the gold-topped Islamic shrine seen in many iconic photographs of the Old City, as well as the Al-Aqsa Mosque.

The Foundation Stone, which is the stone from which Jews believe the world was created, is also the location of the First Temple where the Ark of the Covenant was placed. As a result, this spot has extreme significance for believers as the crossroads between Heaven and Earth.

The Western Wall, a Jewish holy site sits almost literally in the Shadow of the Islamic Dome of the Rock. It's a weird merging of old world and new world – official signs indicate that rabbis have determined that the use of these metal detectors do not violate Shabbat (a day in which use of electricity is forbidden).

The Western Wall is now considered the holiest site for prayer given its proximity to the 'gates of heaven' and the original temple. There are separate sections for prayers for men and women. Visitors are welcome to visit this area and it is open round the clock.

To pray at the Wall, men should cover their head. We covered our heads with Kippahs (skullcaps), which were available from a box kept at the entrance. Women may borrow shawls and short-skirt coverings, but it is best to come with a longish skirt and long sleeves.

There were a number of young soldiers both girls and boys being inducted in the military here. Bar mitzvahs, the initiation ceremony of a Jewish boy who has reached the age of 13 and is regarded as ready to observe religious precepts and eligible to take part in public worship is conducted here. Israel is one of the few countries in the world with a mandatory military service requirement for women.

A tradition at the Western Wall is leaving prayers in notes in the cracks between the large stones. We all did so, by writing on small pieces of papers our prayers and wishes. Hundreds upon thousands of these notes are stuck in every crevice.

The Church of the Holy Sepulchre is the holiest Christian Shrine in the Old City. It is the site of Christ's crucifixion, burial and resurrection. The church is shared by five different Christian communities ie Roman Catholic, Greek Orthodox, Coptic, Syrian Orthodox and Armenian.

It goes without saying that apart from those main sites above, there are plenty of other places to visit in the Old City, such as the markets in each quarter, the rooftop of the Austrian Hospice.

It is the most colourful, impressive, Eastern market. It is spread over many long alleyways, that cross the Old City and crisscross through the different quarters of the Old City - The Christian Quarter, Muslim Quarter, and the Armenian Quarter.

Some areas in the market are tourist oriented and the others are more for the local residents. Each market sells the typical market products. The markets sell everything from souvenirs, fruits and vegetables, food, perfumes, clothes, furniture, stamps and and electronics items. There are food stalls and small restaurants serving all kinds of food. Kamal and Sarathy being philately enthusiasts located a post office and rushed to buy some stamps.

The market maintains the system of streets that used to be here during the Roman and Byzantine periods. The two market walkways are based on ancient streets from the past; the northwestern half of the market is based on the Roman route, while the other half, the north-south axis, is based on the Cardo, the main street of Byzantine Jerusalem, which crossed the city from Damascus Gate to the Zion Gate. Some of us were so engrossed visiting shops and admiring the local crafts, that Dalia lost some of us and but managed to locate them after some effort.

During any of my travels abroad, there never has been a time that I have not come across a Sikh gentleman. I had not seen or met one during this trip. We were near the Zion Gate and to our surprise we saw Capt Amarinder Singh, Chief Minister of the state of Punjab in India who was there on a visit to Jerusalem. We all walked up to him and he was very happy to meet us. Sarathy and I introduced ourselves as alumni of the National Defence Academy. He got out of his car and spoke to us for quite some time. He had also graduated from the National Defence Academy and acknowledged that straight away although he was much senior to us.

The next day we drove to Tel Aviv. The metropolis on the Mediterranean is fun-loving, cosmopolitan, and lively. We first visited the White City. It is located between Allenby street in the south, Begin road and Ibn Gvirol street in the east, the Yarkon River in the north and the Mediterranean in the west.

The White City refers to a collection of over 4,000 buildings built in a unique form of the Bauhaus or International Style in Tel Aviv from the 1930s by German Jewish architects who immigrated to the British Mandate of Palestine after the rise of the Nazis. They had studied in Europe and moved to Tel Aviv. Wanting to recreate the cafe culture of Europe in the hot climate of Israel, whilst integrating the modernist architectural style they had practised, the group utimately created a new architectural language, which is rich and diverse, characterized by its asymmetry, functionality and simplicity. The balconies, building pillars, flat roofs and "thermometre" windows have since become trademarks of Tel Aviv.

We later proceeded to Jaffa — the southern, oldest part of Tel Aviv. The Old City of Jaffa is from the Ottoman period, a few hundred years old. In fact, Jaffa is the root of Tel Aviv, existing for thousands of years before Tel Aviv expanded and grew out of it.

Diana stopped us at Zodiac Bridge in Jaffa hill; it s a wooden bridge that connects the summit garden and Kedumim Square. Before the entrance to the bridge there are 12 signs of the zodiac on a mosiac. The mosiac was created by Varda Gvioli, Ilan Gelber and Nabot Gil. A local legend says that if you describe your sign on the bridge, hold the statues and look towards the sea while you think about your wish - your wish will be fulfilled. Diana ensured that none of us missed an opportunity to fulfill our wishes!

Jaffa is a beautiful touristic place with an artists' colony, shops, restaurants, and can be covered by walking.

St Peter's Church is an important land mark here; it was built in 1654 on the site where Peter stayed when he went to Jaffa; its steeple overlooks the port and inside there are vaulted ceilings, stained-glass windows and a painting above the alter of Peter's visitation by an angel. St Peter's Church also played host to Napoleon Bonaparte, who reportedly stayed in a room in the church when he came to Old Jaffa in 1799.

In the afternoon we spent some time at Carmel Market in Tel Aviv, an amazing place to visit with varied sites, sounds and smells. This market apart from the local flavour has everything to offer from clothes, shoes, fruits, vegetables, bakery items, groceries and souvenirs. Probably anything that a household would need is available here. It was nice to interact with the shopkeepers, each one full of bubbly friendliness.

In the evening we were back in our hotel in Jerusalem. We all reached the restaurant in time for dinner. Dr Prasad, a member of our group, was a shy gentleman. We knew it was his birthday and had organized a cake and wine. He cut the cake; we all wished him and celebrated his birthday. He was pleasantly surprised as he did not know we had such plans for him.

After dinner we went to Mahane Yehuda Market. At night it is a lively, bustling place with plenty of bars. A few drinks down we walked back to the hotel. We bought some local sweet, *Ugat Bisquvitim,* delicious, classic Israeli cheese cake. On the way back we met some Israeli girls, who walked upto us and introduced themselves and spoke in Hindi as well. They had spent some time in India and spoke about their beautiful memories of their visit.

At night we got ready to leave next morning. As our flight was from Amman we travelled back via Allenby border to take our flight back home.

My first visit: a sombre experience

In the earlier trip to Israel in February 2009, I had visited Masada and Yad Vashem Holocaust Memorial Museum, two very important places. I had taken the cable car to go up to Masada.

Masada's legacy is shared primarily through details provided by Jewish historian Josephus Flavius, the commander of the Jewish forces during the First Jewish-Roman War from 66-73 AD. Sicarii were a group of Jewish extremists who fled from Jerusalem and ultimately settled at Masada after taking possession of it following the Great Revolt. More and more of the Sicarii relocated to Masada from Jerusalem in the years after the revolt as they were run out of Jerusalem due to ongoing conflicts with other Jewish groups.

By 72 AD, Masada had become the last Sicarii stronghold in the region and home to almost 1,000 people. With plans to take the fortress back, the Romans constructed a wall and built camps around Masada; they also built a ramp and a tower with a battering ram to breach the walls. As it became clear that the Romans siege would succeed and the Sicarii would be either enslaved or killed, Eleazar Ben Yair delivered speeches to his people and convinced them it would be better to die with honour than it would be to surrender and live in shame and humiliation. Judaism prohibits suicide, and so a small number of people were selected to murder almost the entire community, ensuring only one final volunteer would have to commit suicide. When the Romans arrived, they found the Sicarii destroyed everything except for food, which presumably they intentionally saved to prove they had died not of starvation but because they chose to sacrifice themselves. This comes out in the writing of Josephus in the *War of the Jews.*

The Masada ruins have remains of the Northern Palace, which was constructed by Herod the Great and one of the most impressive sites. The Western Palace is the largest structure. In addition to a large courtyard it has remnants of a public pool and three small palaces. The Byzantine Church is one of the best preserved portions, which features ornate walls and mosaics. The Synagogue was constructed during Herod's reign, which is surrounded by rows of bench seating and was originally used as a stable.

At the breaching point it is still possible to see both the Roman siege ramp and the noticeable hole in the perimeter wall, which was damaged in 73 AD. It's a sobering place to stand; behind you are the remnants of Masada and the spots where so many people died so as not to surrender.

The story of Masada comes to life at the Masada Museum in memory of Yigael Yadin. The unique, dramatic exhibit takes the museum experience to a new level with an innovative combination of archaeological artifacts, theatrical elements, informative audio explanations and a dramatic radio play.

The ancient artifacts that feature in the museum were discovered at archaeological digs at the Masada site between 1963 and 1965. The expeditions were run by the Hebrew University of Jerusalem under the direction of the late Professor Yigael Yadin.

Each of the nine scenes of the Masada story is designed to recreate a slice of history, based on the interaction between the archaeological artifact and the setting. The museum experience begins with a 'meeting' of the legendary historian in his garden in Rome. Then, take a journey back in time, from the ruling period of King Herod, builder of Masada, through the Great Revolt against Rome, when the rebels lived on the mountain top, to the Roman siege and the fall of Masada.

The journey through the Masada story ends in the final space of the museum dedicated to the excavator of the site, Professor Yigael Yadin, the renowned archaeologist who uncovered so many ancient mysteries hidden at the fascinating Masada fortress.

We started the day by visiting the Yad Vashem Holocaust Memorial Museum. It combines the best of Yad Vashem's expertise, the resources and state-of-the-art exhibits to take holocaust memories well into the 21st century. The Holocaust was the systematic state-sponsored killing of six million Jewish men, women, and children and millions of others by Nazi Germany and its collaborators during World War II.

It presents the story of the Shoah from a unique Jewish perspective, emphasizing the experiences of the individual victims through original artifacts, survivor testimonies and personal possessions.

At the end of the Museum's historical narrative is the Hall of Names — a repository for the Pages of Testimony of millions of holocaust victims, a memorial to those who perished. It was very touching to see the suffering of millions of Jews. From the balcony there is panoramic view of Jerusalem.

All in all it was a sombre trip, a mental flipping through the darker pages of history.

Chapter 19

South Africa - A Unique Wildlife Experience

After much persuasion from several wildlife enthusiast friends, in May 2019 Neeru and I finally agreed to accompany the group on a trip to South Africa.

The continent of Africa borders the southern half of the Mediterranean Sea. The Atlantic Ocean is to the west and the Indian Ocean is to the Southeast. Africa stretches well south of the equator to cover more than 12 million square miles making Africa the world's second largest continent. Africa is one of the most diverse places on the planet with a wide variety of terrain, wildlife, and climates.

Africa is considered by most paleoanthropologists to be the oldest inhabited territory on Earth, with the human species originating from the continent. During the mid-20th century, anthropologists discovered many fossils and evidence of human occupation perhaps as early as 7 million years ago.

Africa is a continent with a very high linguistic diversity; there are an estimated 1500-2000 African languages. Around 140 languages are spoken by some eleven million people scattered in Central and Eastern Africa. There are over 3,000 different ethnic groups in Africa with hundreds of tribes. There is abundant cultural diversity in Africa not only across different countries but also within single countries.

The economy of Africa consists of the trade, industry, agriculture, and human resources of the continent. Approximately 1.3 billion people live in 54 countries in Africa. It is a resource-rich continent.

But what attracts millions of visitors every year to Africa is the desire to see its rich wildlife in their natural habitat.

South Africa

South Africa, the southernmost country on the African continent, is renowned for its varied topography, great natural beauty, and cultural diversity, all of which have made the country a favoured destination for travellers since the legal ending of apartheid in 1994.

South Africa is bordered by Namibia to the northwest, by Botswana and Zimbabwe to the north, and by Mozambique and Swaziland on the northeast and east. Lesotho, an independent country, is an enclave in the eastern part of the republic, entirely surrounded by South African territory. South Africa's coastlines border the Indian Ocean to the southeast and the Atlantic Ocean to the southwest. The country possesses two small sub-antarctic islands, Prince Edward and Marion, situated in the Indian Ocean about 1,900 km southeast of Cape Town. The former South African possession of Walvis Bay, on the Atlantic coast some 600 kilometres north of the Orange River, became part of Namibia in 1994.

Cape Town is one of the most popular long haul destinations in the world. Due to its unique topography, it is also one of the easiest places in which to orientate oneself with Table Mountain behind and Robben Island in front on which is located the notorious prison that once held Nelson Mandela. The high-security prison is now a living museum. Cape Town is one of South Africa's most historically important cities. It was here, in the Mother City, where the first European colonists set foot in South Africa, which also marked the beginning of the South African slave trade. South Africa has three capitals, Cape Town, as the seat of Parliament, is the legislative capital; Pretoria, as the seat of the President and Cabinet, is the administrative capital; and Bloemfontein, as the seat of the Supreme Court of Appeal, is the judicial capital, while the Constitutional Court of South Africa sits in Johannesburg.

Transiting via Addis Ababa from Delhi, we landed at Cape Town International Airport. We were received by our guide cum escort Junaid. We checked in at our hotel and freshened up for the evening.

In the evening we drove to Signal Hill, which connects Kloof Nek to Lion's Head in the distinctive shape of a lion's rump and one of the most famous spots in Cape Town. The view from the 350 metre high summit is nothing short of spectacular. This is where the famous Noon Gun is fired every day at 1200 hrs. The sunset view from here is spectacular. There were some paragliders who took off from here, using wind forces to maintain flight.

Signal Hill has a rich and colourful history. It was used as a signaling point; Spanish settlers called the hill "Loma Sental," which translates as "Signal Hill". It is a nice place to take a walk in nature. There is a giant yellow picture frame on Signal Hill, providing a perfect vantage point to take photographs with Table Mountain as the spectacular backdrop. We took a lot of photographs as singles, couples and a group, of course in various poses.

The following morning we went for a scenic coastal drive through Clifton and Sea Point. We drove past the Houses of Parliament, the Castle, the South African Museum, and a few other historical sights like District Six, Bo-Kaap, Slave Lodge and ending at the bustling Greenmarket Square.

Green market is the historical flea market located on a cobbled square and surrounded by historical buildings. This is the ideal place to do your African handicraft shopping ie curios, beadwork, beautifully crafted bowls, sculptures, artwork and jewellery. Like most such flea markets one has to bargain to get a good price. Most of us bought decorated ostrich eggs and other souvenirs. Eggs were beautifully painted and resistant and can support 100 kilos without cracking. This is one of Cape Town's oldest markets with history dating back to 1696. In 1716, the Burger Watch House was built on the square and is one of the finest examples of Cape Dutch architecture. The Old Town House then replaced it in 1761 and in 1840 it became the first City Hall. In 1961 it was declared a National Monument. Today, it is an art gallery housing the world-renowned Michaelis Collection consisting of early Dutch and Flemish paintings. It has also served as a fruit and vegetable market where slaves used to sell the produce. Ships used this square to trade goods and stock up on produce.

From Green Market it was a short walk to the Company's Garden, which was first built as a refreshment station for the trade route that rounded the tip of Africa between Europe and the east. Ships sent by the Dutch East India Company would stop by after months at sea and stock up on fresh produce grown in the garden, hence the name, "The Company's Garden". It is a large public park and botanical garden set in the heart of Cape Town, home to a rose garden, Japanese garden, fish pond and an aviary.

We walked past the back of Parliament and Tuynhuys, the President's official residence. From here we had a beautiful view of Table Mountain. The tree-lined avenue, with its benches and resident squirrels, forms a pathway between the suburb of gardens and the city centre. There are a number of other important buildings within the garden, the South African

Museum, the Planetarium and the South African Art Gallery. It has its origins in Jan van Riebeeck's vegetable garden, which he grew to feed the original colony as early as 1652. It was declared a National Monument in 1962. It is also the venue of a number of festivals, including the Human Rights Concert and the Youth Festival.

Before we came to Cape Town, there was an apprehension with friends who were with us and some others. They all voiced their concern regarding availability of water in Cape Town. Although we knew that we would be staying in good hotels and it was confirmed that there would be no issue as regards water it was still a matter of worry. Despite good rains in 2013 and 2014, the City of Cape Town began experiencing a drought in 2015, the first of three consecutive years of dry winters brought on possibly by the El Niño weather pattern and perhaps by climate change. Water levels in the City's dams declined from 71.9 percent in 2014 to 50.1 percent in 2015.

Since 2017, the municipality of Cape Town had activated its drought-awareness campaign, publishing weekly updates on regional dam levels and water consumption and using electronic boards on freeways to notify drivers of how many days of water supply Cape Town had left. Then, in January 2018 and with Day Zero looming, the city got more aggressive. The water crisis brought the city to the verge of taps being turned off altogether – a prospect, which at the time was referred to as "day zero." The public awareness campaign around the water crisis led to lasting change in locals' behaviour when it came to water consumption. People have adjusted to using water in a restricted manner. Although water restrictions have been lifted, it has now become a way of life with the local people. Everyone is cautious on use of water. Due to climate change, one cannot predict as to when there could be another water shortage.

Tourism and all other businesses were badly affected because of water shortage. Government ensured that households using high volumes of water faced big fines. The city also significantly hiked tariffs as well as rolling out management devices, which set a daily limit on the water supply to properties. The citizens came together to fight this crisis. On the face of it, we could not see any scarcity of water. Businesses and people seemed to be moving on fine.

In the afternoon we went to take the cable car ride to go up to Table Mountain. Our guide Junaid told us that in case the weather was bad, cable car would not operate. To our good luck the weather was fine. The cableway is 90 years old and it started operating in 1929. It was a five-minute cable car trip to the top of Table Mountain, 1,089 metres above Cape Town. Table Mountain is the icon of the Mother City. It is one of the oldest mountains in the world. From top it was a spectacular view of Cape Town and its surroundings. Since it was a clear sky and good visibility we could see the 12 Apostles, the V&A Waterfront, Robben Island, Mitchell's Plain and the Cape Flats.

We joined a guided walk tour starting from Twelve Apostles Terrace. It was an interesting walk with the guide who told us about the cableway, Table Mountain, its history, inhabitants and flora and fauna.

Table Mountain and the surrounding area was home to the Khoisan people long before the first Europeans arrived. They also gave Table Mountain its first name, *Hoerikwaggo*, or Mountain in the Sea. This later changed when, in 1503, Portuguese explorer, Antonio de Saldanha, hiked the mountain, the first recorded hike in history and renamed it Tabao de Cabo (table of the Cape). The name changed again in 1652, when Dutch settlers started referring to the mountain as *Tafelberg*. Table Mountain consists of sandstone and Cape granite formed by glacial action 520 million years ago. It is reportedly at least six times older than the Himalayas, making it one of the oldest mountains in the world.

There are nicely marked trails to explore Table Mountain. Table Mountain National Park has the richest floristic site in the world. The flora on Table Mountain is very different, all over the mountain. The western side receives more direct sunlight throughout the day and it is a dryer side of the mountain, producing a smaller shrub-like vegetation. The eastern side of Table Mountain is shaded throughout the day and has a wetter terrain, with streamlets, waterfalls, and seeps. This side of the mountain produces an indigenous forest. Most of this forest was planted back in the day when wood was needed for construction. Certain plant species date back to over 60 million years and many of these are endemic to Table Mountain.

Table Mountain plays host to over 1460 of plant species, especially Fynbos. Fynbos consists of four plant groups, the Proteas, Erica's, Restios and Geophytes. Fynbos is a very unique vegetation type and has developed over millions of years. Table Mountain had lost several plant species as a result of fires, human influence, and erosion. Now Cape Floristic Region is helping to maintain some of these plants.

Although Table Mountain is located in the centre of the city, there is plenty of wildlife that still exists here including Rock Hyrax, mongoose, Cape fox, genet, porcupine, caracal, clip springer, Himalayan Tahr and various varieties of lizards and frogs.

The variety of vegetation and topography, attracts a wide range of different bird species like soaring raptors, sugarbirds, Jackal buzzard, Knysna warbler, Paradise flycatcher and many others.

We walked up the steps on top to the light house, which again provided a spectacular view.

Table Mountain offers plenty of adventure activities like bicycle tours, mountain biking, rock climbing, mountaineering and abseiling also known as repelling; we could see some people repelling down steep vertical rocks.

The following day we spent a complete day with the Peninsular Tour which showed the best of the Cape Peninsula. It has been given many names throughout history. It was Sir Francis Drake who gave this south-western most point of Africa the most appropriate name when he in 1579 called it "the fairest Cape in the whole circumference of the globe." Hence it is called the Fairest Cape today.

Of all the drives you can take in Cape Town, few are as beautiful as the one to the Cape Peninsula — a remarkable area to the south of the Mother City. We drove past Sea Point and Camps Bay, past the famous beaches of Clifton and Llandudno, towards Hout Bay. We drove along the Atlantic Seaboard, passing through Noordhoek and Scarborough.

We embarked on one of the boats for the Seal Island cruise from Hout Bay to the magnificent Duiker Island, which is also known as seal island. It is home to a colony of thousands of Cape fur seals; the experienced crew of the boat took us very close to the island to see the seals in their natural habitat. We could also see a number of seabirds flying all over. Due to a large number of seals in the waters around there are plenty of hungry white sharks in the area.

Later we reached the Cape of Good Hope Nature Reserve. Cape of Good Hope, is located at the southern end of Cape Peninsula. It was first sighted by the Portuguese navigator Bartolomeu Dias in 1488 on his return voyage to Portugal after ascertaining the southern limits of the African continent. One historical account says that Dias named it Cape of Storms and that John II of Portugal renamed it Cape of Good Hope (because its discovery was a good omen that India could be reached by sea from Europe); other sources attribute its present name to Dias himself. It was a place we had read about as children in our geography books and seen pictures.

Navigators have over time written a lot about it. Cape of Good Hope is situated at the junction of two major ocean currents, the cold Benguela along the West Coast and the warm Agulhas on the East Coast. Due to markedly differing sea temperatures, the marine life east and west of Cape Point differs. Although the Cape of Good Hope is popularly perceived as the meeting point of the Atlantic and Indian Oceans, they actually meet at Cape Agulhas National Park.

It is rare to see large animals in the Cape of Good Hope, but there are a large number of small animals such as lizards, snakes, tortoises and insects. Other mammals that can be seen here are water mongoose, striped mouse and Cape clawless otter. It is also home to at least 250 species of birds. It is also an integral part of the Cape Floristic Kingdom, the smallest but richest of the world's six floral kingdoms, with almost 1100 varieties of indigenous plants. It is an excellent point to view whales between June and November. We were there in May and unfortunately did not have any luck in sighting them.

It was a momentous occasion to get photographed in front of a board which read: "Cape of Good Hope." This place was busy with everyone wanting take photographs; we really had to sneak in to do so.

We went to Cape Point about a kilometre east of Cape of Good Hope. We took the tram Flying Dutchman named after the legend of a ghost ship haunting the area, to go to the upper lighthouse. The view from the top is exhilarating. There are two lighthouses here, one new and one old. The Old Lighthouse, 238 metres above sea level, is easily accessible from the funicular. The New Lighthouse was constructed in 1919 and electrified in 1936. It is the most powerful light in Africa with a candlepower of 19 million, and used by ships for navigating around that region.

Next place we visited was Boulders Beach located in the Naval town of Simon's Town. It is home to thousands of African Penguins that make a permanent home in these parts, in the penguin colony. It was an alluring sight to see penguins waddling and that too in close proximity and in their natural habitat.

In 1982, a couple of penguins settled on the soft white sand between the large granite boulders that protect the beach from wind and large, stormy waves, and currently, the population is estimated between 2,000 and 3,000 birds. The African penguin has been classified as an endangered species, due to things like over-fishing, habitat destruction, pollution, and irresponsible tourism activities. Boulders and its surrounding beaches now form part of the Table Mountain National Park Marine Protected Area. These African penguins are only found on the coastlines of Southern Africa. African penguins used to be known as Jackass penguins, due to their distinctive braying.

We stopped at the Naval Port of Simon's Town. It is famous for "Just Nuisance", the only dog ever to be officially enlisted in the Royal Navy. He was a Great Dane who between 1939 and 1944 served at HMS Afrikander, a Royal Navy shore establishment in Simon's Town.

At an early age, the pup was sold to Benjamin Chaney who moved to Simon's Town to run the United Services Institute (USI). The USI was frequented mainly by the Royal Navy sailors, the Royal Navy at that time being in charge of the Simon's Town Naval Base. This Great Dane soon grew to be a massive dog and it was here in Simon's Town that he was to become a legend. He was a very friendly dog and considered that all sailors were his friends. Sailors looked after him and fed him.

He could be found all over, with HMS Neptune being one of his favourite vessels. No one could easily get past him and he was loathe to move. The sailors would say, "You're just a nuisance." That is where he got his name from. He would follow the sailors on liberty and on trains. The train conductors were not happy, since he had no ticket. Many letters were written to the Commander-in-Chief of the Navy at that time. After much thought, he decided to enlist him into the Royal Navy. As the dog was enlisted during the war, he was entitled to a free pass on trains!

A proper procedure was followed for his enrolment. After a short while he was promoted from 'Ordinary Seaman' to 'Able Seaman', which entitled him to naval rations. As Just Nuisance had become such a celebrity, he was often required to assist the war effort by attending functions. A marriage between him and Adinda, another Great Dane, was arranged. Five puppies resulted from this union and two of them, Victor and Wilhelmina, arrived to an almost ticker-tape welcome at Cape Town station where they were auctioned by the Mayor of Cape Town for war funds. Just Nuisance died in 1944 at the age of seven years and was buried with full military honours.

Since then, the life and story of Just Nuisance has become so much a part of Simon's Town - a statue on Jubilee Square reminds one of him and his grave on Red Hill is a regular stopping point for visitors.

The following day we drove from Cape Town to Knysna; it was a six hour scenic drive on the Garden Route. Breathtaking, a spectacular natural beauty, a scenic wonderland – these are but some words used to describe the famed Garden Route. It is one of the most beautiful stretches of coastline in the world, a paradise for nature lovers and considered one of the world's greatest coastal drives.

The varied ecosystems of the Garden Route are embraced by ten nature reserves and unique marine reserves, home to soft coral reefs, dolphins, seals and host of other marine life. Various sheltered lagoons and bays along the region are nurseries to the endangered Southern Right Whale which visit annually to calve in the winter and spring seasons.

We reached Knysna, a place diverse in its mix of people and its surroundings; this diversity is reflected in a range of choices of eco-tourism, cultural-tourism and heritage-tourism.

Immediately on reaching Knysna we embarked on a boat cruise on the vast Knysna Lake, which is the country's only National Lake and the largest permanent estuary. It was a scenic cruise, on *MV John Benn*, a double-decker ferry built from yellowwood sourced from the Knsyna region. The boat is named after a legendary pilot of a bygone era. It took us all around the most beautiful scenery in calm waters. The waters of the Indian Ocean channel through two large sandstone cliffs, The Heads, which form the gateway to the old harbour, from where ships carried timber to the far corners of the globe, into the wide lagoon basin. The Heads also guard the sea entrance to Knysna's huge tidal lagoon, and the forests, marshes and pristine beaches surrounding it.

The beautiful town of Knysna is surrounded by the Outeniqua Mountain range, engulfed by indigenous forests and the protected 21 square kilometre marine reserve locally known as the Lagoon. The varying and contrasting habitat found here is a haven for birds. These include marshland, vlei, rushes, fynbos, grassland and farmland. It is also well known as the mecca of indigenous wood furniture. We wished that we had more time to spend in Garden Route, it was so beautiful. There was plenty more to discover on this route.

We started with scenic drive through George and over the Outeniqua Mountains past Oudtshoorn to the Cango Caves, one of the world's great natural wonders sculptured by nature through the ages—a series of dripstone caverns that open into vast halls of towering stalagmite formations.

Cango Caves is located in the Precambrian limestones, a site some 4500 million years old. This is at the foothills of the Swartberg range. These are one of South Africa's best known and most visited caves. Only about a quarter of the caves are open to public. The extensive system of chambers and tunnels run over four kilometres.

We had an experienced and knowlegeable tour guide to take us around. The tours inside have to be undertaken with accredited Caves Guides, one cannot venture on one's own. All tours are supervised. Our guide took us along the magic paths of the world's finest stalactite caves.

The main chambers in the Cango Caves, called Cango 1, contain countless dripstone formations, and Van Zyl's hall, named after its discoverer; the sheer size leaves one breathless. Cleopatra's Needle, which stands 9 metres high and is at least 150,000 years old, is one of the main attractions at the Cango Caves, but the beautiful dark grey roof, with its smoothly sculptured hollows and pendants, comes a close second. Some others are named variously as the bridal couple, glass flower fantasy, the hanging shawl and weird cango candle. We spent more than an hour underground, exploring one of the world's great natural wonders.

It is said that the caves were discovered in 1780. Early visitors had to brave the pitch darkness of the vast caverns from the poor light by carrying self made candles.

After finishing the tour of Cango Caves we reached for lunch at Safari Ostrich Farm by noon. Lunch was delicious and fresh with nice flavours. There were some who ordered Ostrich meat, probably not available in most places. Ostrich meat is a red meat and is the healthiest meat, being low in fat and cholesterol and high in protein.

After a sumptuous lunch our guide took us on a walking tour. Before that we were given a brief about ostriches and visited the Incubator Room and we could see chicks hatching inside incubator. Although ostriches cannot fly, they are strong runners. They can sprint upto 70 kilometres per hour and hold steady speeds of 50 kilometres per hour. One stride can span 3 to 5 metres. When confronted with danger, ostriches can usually outrun any animals posing a threat. They may use their wings as rudders, to help them change direction while running. Their diet consists mainly of roots, leaves, and seeds. Sometimes they consume insects, snakes, lizards, and rodents. They also swallow sand and pebbles which help them grind up their food in their gizzard, a specialized, muscular stomach. Because ostriches have this ability to grind food, they can eat things that other animals cannot digest.

In the farm, we could see ostriches and Emus roaming around freely and had the privilege of seeing some white ostriches. We also got an opportunity to feed them with food in our hands, but were cautioned to be careful while doing so. We were told that an ostrich egg can take the weight of about 220 kg vertically and 120 kg horizontally. There were some eggs kept on the ground; we all stood on them in turn.

We were given a demonstration on carving of Ostrich eggs, leather and various types of Ostrich feathers. As some of us showed keeness to ride ostriches, we were politely told that the practice had been stopped for quite some time.

After spending time with ostriches we reached Cango Wildlife Ranch which was established in 1977. We were all eagerly waiting to start our guided tour, which started at 1500 hrs.

Our tour started in an ancient temple inhabited by giant flying foxes, birds with under-water viewing of dazzling cichlids and giant river turtles. From a Malawian lakeshore home to attractive red river hogs and prehistoric giant water monitors, it could attract curiosity of all! Our guide through themed walk-through experience spoke about modern-day conservation issues our planet is presently threatened with. We saw various animals on the way, including a pygmy hippo.

While walking on an elevated catwalk in Cheetahland, we had a bird's eye-view of some of the world's most endangered and unique big cats—the rare white Bengal tiger, the cheetah and the white lion. Our guide spoke about their habitat and how efforts were being made to preserve this wildlife as we walked above the natural enclosures.

Some of us took the opportunity to get close to cheetahs and take photographs with them under the Natural Encounters programme, being run at the ranch. Encounters can also be enjoyed with tigers, snakes, lorikeets and other animals as and when available. After finishing the guided tour we walked through Kuranda Forest and the Snake Park, which is home to the world's largest venomous snake, the King cobra.

The following day we flew from George, the Heart of the Garden Route and capital of the Southern Cape to Johannesburg. George is the ideal hub from which to explore the diverse scenery and natural wonders of its surrounding areas. We were received at the airport by Tefu, who was to be our guide for rest of the tour.

After a two and a half hours drive from Johannesburg airport we reached Mabula Game Lodge which is located in Mabula Game reserve in the Malaria Free Waterberg region of the Limpopo Province, against the backdrop of the lush green Waterberg Mountains. The 12000 hectare Mabula Game Reserve is home to an abundance of animal and bird life.

We went to our rooms which were traditional with a thatched roof and furnishing tastefully done.

As we arrived a bit late in the evening, we were not able to go for the game drive. We made up for missing the game drive with a lovely meal and a variety of options. Chefs and rest of the staff, made the evening very memorable with great hospitality and service. There were a number of Gujaratis from India, staying here; they had brought an Indian Chef with them. After dinner we joined them for dance and music in a separate hall. Our group also joined them for "Dandiya dance", which is performed in the honour of Goddess Durga.

Next day very early on a chilly morning, wearing our winter jackets, we started the game drive in Safari vehicles, with our professional guide cum driver. As we had missed out our game drive the previous evening, we were now all charged up and extremely excited.

The morning was no disappointment; we saw Wildebeest, Impala, Zebra, Giraffe, Ostrich and four of the big five ie lion, buffalo, elephant and rhino all in a short period. It was like watching a movie of wild animals and everything coming in front of our eye. Mabula is home to some 60 mammals, 300 bird species, 100 plant types and numerous reptile and insect species. It was also a great opportunity to take photographs of animals and birds in their natural habitat.

Mabula Game Reserve has been the home of the award-winning Mabula Ground Hornbill Project. This non-profit conservation project aims to change perceptions and the fortunes of this iconic but endangered species, through multi disciplinary and evidence based conservation techniques.

Following the awesome stay at Mabula we drove for about three hours to reach Johannesburg. Tefu was giving a running commentary throughout the drive and there was no matter that he was not knowledgeable on, be it about flora and fauna, politics, history, geography and people. In the afternoon Tefu took us to the Lion and Safari Park. It is a wild life conservation enclosure mainly for lions.

There is an option to go around the park in a private vehicle or take a game drive organized by the park. We got in the caged safari truck provided by the park, which took us through different enclosures of lion, wild dog and cheetah. During the drive we also saw zebra, ostrich and giraffe.

The lady guide was knowledgeable, gave all the information, answered all the queries with interesting anecdotes and a good sense of humour. When you are in a private vehicle, you are supposed keep the windows closed. It seems some time back an adventurous lady did not pay heed to instructions, kept the window open; she was attacked by a lion and her arm was badly injured. We saw majestic white lions at very close quarters. I told the guide that they really did not look white and probably needed a shower. Prompt came the reply, "you are most welcome to go out and give them a shower!"

After the safari interaction with the cubs was a most interesting experience as they were really cute, full of energy and playfulness, and wanted to get into my jacket. Photographer on site took some amazing photographs, especially those of interaction with cubs. Later some of us fed the giraffes and took photos with them.

The park has well equipped shop with quality items to purchase including toys, clothes, handicrafts, jewellery, books and souvenirs. We bought various items including souvenirs.

We were advised by Tefu that it was not safe to go out alone in Johannesburg. We were thus always in a group. There is quite a high crime rate here, though certain areas are safe. Anyway we did not encounter any safety issues. But the general buzz was that it was not very safe here especially at night.

Johannesburg is also known by the locals as Joburg or Jozi. It is a metropolis like any other with great dining options, shopping, art and culture. It is one of the world's leading financial centres, and the economic hub of South Africa. It produces 16% of South Africa's gross domestic product and accounts for 40% of Gauteng's economic activity.

Later, we visited the Gold Reef City, an amusement park. There are many attractions including water rides, roller coasters and the famous Gold Reef City Casino. It is located on an old gold mine which closed in 1971; the park is themed around the gold rush that started in 1886 on the Witwatersrand. The buildings on the park are designed as a replica of the same period.

Gold mine tour is an interesting part of the Gold Reef City. The theme park surrounds the historically significant no 14 shaft at Crown Mines. This 19th century gold mine produced 1.4 million kilograms of gold before closing, making it the world's richest producer of gold in a span of ninety years. The shaft was opened in 1897, only 11 years after Johannesburg was established and was part of the gold reef stretching 100 kilometres from Boksburg in the east to Randfontein in the west.

This shaft was at its time, one of the deepest gold mines and around 30,000 miners worked here. It was a tough life for miners with a lot of risks involved. Their working conditions were very difficult. They had to live in heat, dampness, darkness and noise and almost always under threat of explosions.

We were taken on a tour down the tunnels; everyone had to wear a hard hat and carry a torch in hand, to experience the life that the miners had to go through. We were advised that as we would be going through restricted spaces, anyone who was claustrophobic could opt-out. Some from the group decided to do so.

On completion of the mine tour, we saw the museum, dedicated to gold mining. In the mine manager's house there was a demonstration of pouring molten gold into gleaming bars of bullion; we could test lifting the bars. Supposedly it is only a demonstration and no real gold is used. At the curio shop a lot of gold mining related souvenirs were being sold ie stones and gold leaves floating in a bottle.

We walked across the road from Gold Reef City to the Apartheid Museum. Either we could book a guided tour or see the museum on our own. We decided to do the latter such that we could move at our own pace and stop where we wanted to. It is a first of its kind museum that illustrates the rise and fall of apartheid. It has photographs, videos, press clips, text panels, personal artifacts and moving anecdotes that gave an insight into the history of apartheid.

In 1995, the South African government set up a process for the granting of casino licenses. The bid documents stipulated that bidders should demonstrate how they would attract tourism and thereby help strengthen the economy and stimulate job creation.

A consortium, called Akani Egoli (Gold Reef City), put in a bid that included the commitment to building a museum. Their bid was successful and the Gold Reef City Casino was built and an adjacent piece of land given for the construction of a museum. The museum opened in 2001.

The Pillars of the Constitution is the first exhibit seen visiting the Apartheid Museum. Located in the courtyard, it includes one pillar for each of the seven values that are enshrined in the South African Constitution ie democracy, equality, reconciliation, diversity, responsibility, respect and freedom.

There are two entrances to the museum white and non white; these tickets are given randomly generated. When walking up there were images on the mirrors of South Africans who descended from the racially mixed community.

There is a detailed coverage of the struggle against apartheid on panels and through short films.

There is a good coverage of Nelson Mandela, who is known for many things but most of all for leading the resistance against South Africa's policy of apartheid in the 20th century. He has been central to every stage of South Africa's epic struggle against apartheid. He was imprisoned for 27 years and served as the first President of Democratic South Africa. He was greatly influenced by Mahatma Gandhi, Walter Sisulu and Albert Lutuli.

In the afternoon we took a short orientation tour of Johannesburg, visiting Hillbrow, Constitution Hill, Central Johannesburg, Braamfontein and Newtown. We started the tour with an introduction to the city and a magnificent view of the 269 metre high Telkom Tower, which is an important land mark of Johannesburg. We visited the inspiring Constitution Hill; it is a living museum that tells the story of South Africa's journey to democracy. The site is a former prison and military fort. Nelson Mandela, Mahatma Gandhi, Joe Slovo, Albertina Sisulu, Winnie Madikizela-Mandela, Fatima Meer, they were all imprisoned here. Today it is home to the country's Constitutional Court, which endorses and protects the rights of all citizens.

On our way to Newtown we passed by the longest southern African bridge, named Nelson Mandela bridge. At Mary Fitzgerald Square we walked on the Jazz Walk of Fame which recognizes nine of South Africa's jazz legends with their names and short inspirational stories about them are engraved in the granite strip.

It was in South Africa Mahatma Gandhi started his non violent movement (Satyagraha) He came here in May 1893 as a barrister after an uninspiring stint in India. He came to assist the lawyer of an Indian merchant in Natal, with the hope of finding better opportunities here.

The incident that changed his life occurred whilst travelling to Pretoria soon after his arrival in Durban; he was thrown off a train, assaulted by a coachman and denied a hotel room in Johannesburg - all because of his colour. These assaults on his dignity, and the knowledge of the humiliations faced by Indians, did not dishearten him but brought out the best in his personality; a strong sense of duty and determination to serve humanity. He decided to dedicate himself to public service and settled in South Africa. After that he spent a couple of years supporting Indians in South Africa.

He left for India on 18 July 1914, where he was to lead millions of people in an epic struggle for independence. He played a major role in the Independence movement of India.

The success of the satyagraha in South Africa and of the independence struggle in India was a source of inspiration to many other peace movements and struggles for human dignity. Dr Martin Luther King and his associates in the movement against racism in the United States and to non-violent revolutions for freedom in Africa and movements for the overthrow of corrupt dictators around the world were all in some way inspired by Mahatma Gandhi.

Mahatma Gandhi also made a great impact on Nelson Mandela, who had become the symbol of resistance to aparthied and this is what he said about Mahatma Gandhi; "The values of tolerance, mutual respect and unity for which he stood and acted had a profound influence on our own liberation movement, and on my own thinking". Gandhian philosophy, he said, had enabled them to mobilize millions of people in the defiance campaign. And this is what Mandela had to say about Gandhi in his message to the international conference on the centenary of Satyagraha in New Delhi in 2007: "In a world driven by violence and force, Gandhi's message of peace and non-violence holds the key to human survival in the 21st century."

Being the last day of our visit, we all went out for dinner and talked about the wonderful time we had in last couple of days. We knew there was much more to see and experience, but it was not possible within the time schedule we had.

A few days spent in South Africa had gone too soon. Tefu was there at the airport to see all of us off and he only left waving at us once he saw us all going through the immigration.

Chapter 20

Kazakhstan: Of Nomads, Horses and Yurts

In September 2019 I travelled to Astana the capital city of Kazakhstan to attend a conference. From the air, Astana appeared dramatically from the empty Kazakh steppe, with its glass and steel buildings. Soon I landed at Nursultan Nazarbayev International Airport in Astana, straddling the Ishim River in the north of the country. From the time I arrived, it was a great experience meeting the very hospitable Kazakhs.

Kazakhstan is believed to have been inhabited as early as the Stone Age, a prehistoric period characterized by the use of stone tools. It was only in the beginning of the 15th century that Kazakh identity came into being and was consolidated into the culture and language of the Kazakhs in the 16th century. After becoming stronger as a people, the Kazakhs fought off a federation of armed Western Mongol tribes in the 17th century, and went on to win major victories over invading forces in the following century.

During the 19th century, however, the vast Russian empire started to expand in Central Asia, ruling most of the countries in the region, including most parts of Kazakhstan which the Russians finally colonized. Following the colonization, some 400,000 Russians immigrated to the country and were followed by one million Slavs, Germans and Jews to establish their residency in the country. This resulted in direct competition between the Kazakhs and the newcomers and in a series of clashes between the natives and the Russians. Superior in strength, Russians prevailed, driving away 300,000 Kazakhs. The famine which started in 1922 worsened the conditions in the country when one million Kazakhs died from starvation. By 1939 the country's population had dropped by 22% because of starvation and emigration. Many years later that is in October 1991, Kazakhstan declared its sovereignty as a member of the Union of Socialist Republics, and its independence from Soviet Union on 16 December 1991. The rest is now part of its modern and current history.

Kazakhstan has a well-articulated culture based on the nomadic pastoral economy of the inhabitants. Animal husbandry was central to the Kazakhs' traditional lifestyle; most of their nomadic practices and customs relate in some way to livestock.

Kazakhstan is located in Central Asia and is the heartland/geographic centre of Eurasia. With a surface area of 2,724,900 square kilometres, Kazakhstan is the ninth largest country in the world, comparable to India and Australia. Its surface is covered by 26% desert, 44% semi-desert, 6% forest and 24% steppe terrain, in addition to a few other landscapes. The South and East have great wild and mostly untouched mountain landscapes with the Tien Shan and Altai being the most prominent. The highest peak in the country is Khan Tengri at 7,013 metres above sea level.

Kazakhstan is famous for its incalculable mineral wealth. Scientists from developed countries consider Kazakhstan to be sixth in the world in terms of abundance of minerals, though this advantage is not being used effectively. The estimated value of the explored areas is 10 trillion US dollars. It is rich in strategic raw resources, primarily, oil and gas deposits.

The historical past of Astana can be retraced with the help of names that changed frequently. The city came into being in 1830 as a result of the construction of Akmola fortress later renamed into Akmolinsk. In 1961 after reaping a record harvest of grain, the city became the centre of Virgin Lands Campaign and in tune with time got the name — Tselinograd. In 1992 it regained the historical name Akmola, after Kazakhstan became a sovereign state. In 1998, it acquired the status of the new capital and was renamed Astana. In 1999 it was awarded the title of the "City of Peace" by UNESCO for the successful development of social, ecological and cultural spheres of life.

Although Russian and Kazakh are widely spoken, language is no barrier, especially with the helping nature of most local people. In hotels and restaurants communicating in English is not an issue. The following day we took a tour of the modern and well laid out city. Our guide Gulnazim picked us up from the hotel for a tour of Astana. Gulnazim said about the city; "Today it is the city of new opportunities. Also it is the main educational and scientific platform of the country where the leading educational institutions and research laboratories are concentrated".

Our first stop was at the Bayterek Tower. The height of Beyterek monument is 97 metres, which corresponds to the year 1997, the year in which Astana was proclaimed as the capital of Kazakhstan. The tower's top is adorned with a huge ball of glass with a diameter of 22 metres weighing 300 tonnes that changes colours depending on the light incidence. Bayterek is one of the most visited monuments in Astana. Bayterek is not just an artistic design, but its image reflects the mythology of ancient nomads. On the top floor of Bayaterek one can place one's hand in the "Ayalyalakan", a gilded hand print of the head of state N. Nazarbayev and according to the established tradition one can make a wish.

Later, we visited the Palace of Peace and Reconciliation, a pyramid shaped building, a modern pyramid unlike the ancient pyramids of Egypt. It was specially built to host the Congress of Leaders of World and Traditional Religions. The construction of the pyramid is based on the principle of the Fibonacci Sequence and Golden Ratio. It is a symbol of religious tolerance. Its top is decorated with a stained glass painting of 130 doves that symbolize nationalities living in Kazakhstan.

Soon we arrived at the Independence Square and walked across to Hazrat Sultan Mosque, the largest in Central Asia, named in honour of the Eastern thinker and philosopher Khoja Akhmet Yassawi. The mosque is strikingly beautiful and imposing. The weather this time of the year was pleasant and Gulnezim told me that during the winters from November to March the temperatures are below freezing and can go down to minus fifty degrees centigrade. The reason that even in winters life goes on fine, is that the city has a huge team responsible for clearing the roads and some wonderful pieces of machinery to help them along. During the tour we drove past Nazarbayev centre; its shape is in the form of a huge eye, looking upto the sky. Then there is the Triumphal Arch, which welcomes guests at the entry to Astana. There is also an observation deck on top of the Arch.

We visited Expo 2017 grounds. Astana had the honour of hosting Expo 2017, the World Fair. The theme was "Future Energy" and more than 100 countries had set up national pavilions showcasing the very best of their technology, art, and culture. The site is centred on a vast glass globe, the largest spherical building in the world, the entire surface of which is photovoltaic, generating electricity from the sun, while the top of the building is equipped with two soft-running wind turbines with a 20 kW capacity. The eight-storey Nur-Alem is 80 metres in diameter and 100 metres high. It is mounted on a 5000 square metre platform. The remaining floors accommodate the Museum of Future Energy.

A visit to Astana would be incomplete in case one did not visit the National Museum. It is the youngest and largest museum in Central Asia. I told Gulnezim to leave me here as I wanted to see it at my pace and I would find my way back. She left a word at the reception of the museum for them to help me get a taxi back to the hotel.

I was welcomed into the grandiose entry hall and commencement of the mesmerizing show of the giant golden eagle soaring over a vast map of the country. The Ethnography hall is of particular interest as it showcases Kazakh musical instruments, products made of felt, wood, leather and jewellery. The Golden Hall has outstanding collections of Kazakh jewellery and items made of gold. Also on display is a yurt, the traditional felt dwelling and its interior design.

The People of Kazakhstan is an interesting area to look at the diverse ethnicities who call the country their home, largely as a result of Stalin era deportations, while 20th century history displays are more sobering, looking at Soviet-era repressions and WWII losses. The contemporary art section shows off Kazakh contributions in the 20th and 21st centuries.

After spending some time inside the museum, I contacted the reception and they were kind enough to book a taxi for me. Typical of the Kazakh hospitality, the young girl on duty came down and accompanied me to the taxi. She gave instructions to the driver to take me back to the hotel.

After spending some time in a new and modern city the following day, B.J. Mikklesen (or BJ) my friend from New York and I flew down to Almaty. BJ and I had organized to undertake this trip together after the conference. We were received at the Almaty Airport by Irina, who was to be our guide for rest of the trip.

We spent some time driving through Almaty, the cultural capital of Kazakhstan. "Alma" means apple in Kazakh. At one time Almaty was filled with apple orchards and now one can see them in the outskirts only. Before Kazakhstan became an independent country, its former capital city, Almaty went by another name Alma-Ata, meaning 'Grandfather of the Apple'. Celebrated as the birthplace of the apple, the notion of Alma-Ata evokes nostalgic images. Almaty was the capital of Kazakhstan until 1997 when it was moved to Astana. One of the reasons given for the move was that Almaty was too close to China.

We drove through Almaty, which has beautiful streets, lined with trees. The parks are mature and well kept. The buildings are of the Soviet era. It remains Kazakhstan's trading and cultural hub.

After some time we were in Kaskelen town starting our beautiful journey of Kaskelen mountain gorge. The serrated mountains loomed in the distance as we moved towards them. The silence that followed was spine chilling. The heaven-touching apex of the mountain was drenched in brilliant light. We stopped on the way and started a short hike in the mountains, in the picturesque Ushkonyr plateau. The average height above sea level is about 2000 metres. We could see a number of hang gliders in the sky and taking off from top of the mountains in the valley. Ushkonyr is one of the main hang-gliding places near Almaty.

Whilst hiking we visited the Elk farm. Elk farming is an agricultural industry for the production of elk as livestock or for the sport of hunting. Elk have a variety of uses. The velvet antler or, the antler in the premature stages of growth, has been found useful in medicinal purposes, as well as the venison industry. Elks were freely roaming around.

Lunch was served. My friend BJ had "Kuyrdak", made of Elk, supposedly the national dish of Kazakhstan. Since Irina already knew my dietary requirement, I had some soup and vegetables.

We reached Nomad Ethnic Centre located at the foothills of Ushkonyr plateau, to spend the night here and experience the local way of life. It is a unique historical and an ethnographic complex. The foundation of its creation is based on the centuries-old traditions, culture and life of the nomadic tribes of the Great Steppe — Sakas, Usuns, Kangyus, Turks, Kazakhs and many others.

We checked into a yurt. This is something that we were looking forward to staying in; it is one of the oldest and greatest inventions of Eurasian nomads. Yurts for centuries have been a practical and convenient, portable accommodation. I had met a college going Kazakh in Astana, whom I had mentioned that I would be staying in a yurt. He did tell me then that I was punishing myself. Obviously, for people staying in the city it was something very ancient and perhaps commonplace.

The dinner was prepared by local women, which was fine and some dishes were specially made for me. It was quite an experience for someone like me, who has been used to drinking only cow or buffalo milk. We were offered sweets made of camel milk. I was offered a glass of horse milk after dinner and Irina told me all good things about it. It is common here to be drinking horse milk. I politely refused and told Irina that I could ride a horse, but would not drink horse milk. I had refused it for no other reason other than that I had never had it before.

At night the sky was clear, not a cloud could be seen anywhere. The sky was a mixture of dark midnight blue and purple. The stars just decorated the sky. It looked as if someone took a handful of glitter and just threw it up to the sky.

At night it was quite cold. The day had been quite hectic. I went to sleep in no time, with oblique thoughts and mini dreams. I slept like a log. I got up in the morning with a view from my yurt overlooking the valley and beautiful serene surroundings watching Hang Gliders in the sky.

This Nomad Ethnic Centre has plenty of activities like archery master class, horse riding, craft workshops on pottery, carpet weaving, embroidery, cooking lessons and class on yurt assembling.

We visited a traditional yurt in the premises kept for demonstration. We were given a complete briefing on yurt. A traditional yurt is a portable, round tent covered with skins or felt and used as a dwelling by nomads in the steppes of Central Asia. The Kazakh yurt is easy to assemble and disassemble. It retains heat well and protects from the wind, as well as from the excessive heat in the summer. When it is hot, felt flooring is removed to make the inside cooler. For the winter, the yurts are insulated with double covers, surrounded with snow. It has a complete facility for staying, cooking, saddles etc. It is kept open from top during the day, depending on the weather and closed at night. We could see the moon from the opening on top and a clear sky.

Yurt has three main parts which include Shanyrak—top of the yurt, Kerege—walls carcass and Uwyk—a carcass part from Kerege to the Shanyrak. The carcass is usually covered with pieces of felt from outside and decorated with carpets from inside. Shanyrak is extremely valuable for Kazakhs and is considered to be a sacred symbol of family wellbeing and peace.

Yurt usually does not have rooms in it, and it was a common practice to have a separate yurt as a bedroom, separate one as a kitchen, guesthouse, etc as long as people could afford that. A nomad made the yurt easy for assembling and disassembling, and with the help of one camel and two horses the entire construction of the yurt and decorations of the interior were easily transported.

Researchers and scientists found evidences that 5,500 years ago people of the steppes of modern Kazakhstan were the first to domesticate horses, specifically the people of Botai. Kazakh nomads tamed a wild horse, eventually using it for its milk, transportation and maybe for its meat.

There was a spectacular display of horsemanship. It started with Jigitovka (trick riding) which involved vaulting, standing on galloping horse and saluting; in a way it was acrobatics on horseback. While riding they used the bow and arrow to hit a target.

There was a game of Kokpar; it is one of the most popular games of Central Asia, Kazakhstan and Afghanistan. Even in the time of Genghis Khan, the Kokpar was favourite game of nomads. This game consisted of two teams of horse riders. The history of Kokpar is many centuries old. Physical strength is one of the important components of the game; it is necessary to lift the goat carcass with one hand. The objective is for the team to gather a goat carcass and bring it to their part of the playing field, past a designated line. Each team tries to do this as many times as a possible to gain points. This is followed by Audyryspak; the objective of this game is quite simple; two horsemen must wrestle and attempt to push the other off of the saddle.

After the spectacular show I went for a horse ride in the foothills, with Soliya the daughter of the couple who ran this place.

After the momentous stay at the Nomad Ethnic Centre, it was time to go back to Almaty for the journey back after completing the last agenda on our list which was visiting Sunkar Falcon Farm.

Sunkar Falcon farm was originally established to protect the saker falcon, whose numbers dropped alarmingly in the 80s and 90s, when a thriving market developed to export the birds to Arabia for big money. Habitat degradation and the impact of agrochemicals are other big issues confronting almost all birds of prey in Kazakhstan.

Sunkar has around 400 birds; it is taking care of some 15 species of owl, eagle, lammergeier, vulture, hawk and falcon. The birds at the centre have all been rescued and cannot be released anymore into the wild as they would not survive. However, a breeding project to release birds back into the wild does release golden eagles and saker falcons.

Since we reached a bit early, we went around looking at birds in cages and also some Kazakh hunting dogs that are kept by the centre. When hunting the Kazakhs usually took a horse, an eagle and a hunter dog (tazy) with them.

The show included elements of falconry and eagle hunting, with eagle, owls, golden eagles, saker falcons and even a griffon vulture all displaying their prowess. Pavel Pfander, Sunkar's Kazakhstani-German bird trainer, ornithologist and falconer, put on a highly entertaining and educational show. It was quite impressive to see these birds of prey unfold their massive wings very close to us and responding to the commands of the trainer.

It was again time to say goodbye to our guide Irina and Kazakhstan. BJ had decided to stay back for a couple of days more. After leaving him at the hotel, I went straight to the airport to take the flight back home.

Chapter 21

Kenya: The East Africa Experience

In late January 2020, I along with family visited Kenya with a group of friends from different walks of life.

Kenya is located in East Africa and is surrounded by Indian Ocean, Tanzania, Uganda, Sudan , Ethiopia, and Somalia. Lake Victoria is shared between Uganda, Tanzania, and Kenya.

The capital of Kenya is Nairobi. Major towns include Mombasa and Kisumu, followed by Nakuru, Eldoret, Lamu, Kitale and others. The total area of Kenya is 58,000 square kilometres and the population is estimated to be 52 million. It is the 47th largest country in the world.

There are over 40 different ethnic groups in Kenya. Mount Kenya is the second highest mountain in Africa and the country takes its name from the mountain. The earliest inhabitants of Kenya were hunter-gatherers but from about 2,000 BC herders came to the region. Then from about 800 AD Arabs sailed to Kenya. Some settled and intermarried and they created the Swahili culture along the coast. The first European to reach Kenya was Vasco da Gama in 1498.

The colonial history of Kenya dates from the Berlin Conference of 1885 when the European powers first partitioned East Africa into spheres of influence. In 1895, the UK Government established the East African Protectorate and, soon after, opened the fertile highlands to white settlers. Kenya attained her independence in 1963 from the British colonial rule and gained internal self-rule on 12 December 1963. It became a republic twelve months later on 12 December 1964, with the late Jomo Kenyatta being the first Kenyan President.

The economy of Kenya is a market-based economy with a liberalized external trade system and a few state enterprises. Major industries include agriculture, forestry, fishing, mining, manufacturing, energy, tourism and financial services. Estimated GDP is USD 99 billion and per capita GDP of USD 2,010 making it the 62nd largest economy in the world. Kenya's national currency is the Kenyan Shilling although foreign currencies such as US dollars are widely accepted.

The climate of Kenya varies by location; along the coast it is tropical. This means rainfall and temperatures are higher throughout the year. At the coastal cities, Mombasa, Lamu and Malindi, the air changes from cool to hot, almost every day. The climate is temperate inland. Nairobi has a very pleasant climate throughout the year due to its altitude.

Swahili and English are widely spoken. They serve as the two official working languages. Swahili is of Bantu (African) origin. It has borrowed words from other languages such as Arabic. As regards the formation of the Swahili culture and language, some scholars attribute these phenomena to the interaction of African and Asiatic people on the coast of East Africa.

Mombasa was the first place that I had been to abroad; it was after covering a distance of 2400 nautical miles as a cadet on an Indian Naval ship and spending over a fortnight at sea. The next visit to Kenya was after well over four decades and this time we were there in a few hours, flying from Mumbai to Nairobi across Indian Ocean and Arabian Sea.

Immediately after landing at Jomo Kenyatta International Airport in Nairobi and loading our bags in the Land Cruisers, we were on our way to Amboseli National Park. It was a five hour scenic drive with stops en route for tea and snacks. There were vendors en route selling mangoes and oranges, filled in bags. We bought some from them and moved on. Even before we were close to Amboseli we sited Towers of Giraffes; they looked fabulous and lofty, quite powerful but docile. In the evening we reached Amboseli Sopa Lodge, set in 200 acres of private land, and with a rustic charm of its own. Everyone wished us by saying *Jambo*, meaning hello.

Amboseli National Park is located in Loitoktok District in the Rift Valley Province of Kenya. The park is 392 square kilometres in size at the core of an 8,000 square kilometres ecosystem that spreads across the Kenya-Tanzania border.

Amboseli is synonymous with two particular things; majestic herds of elephant and a glorious view of Mount Kilimanjaro in neighbouring

Tanzania. Amboseli National Park is Kenya's second most popular national park after the Masai Mara National Reserve. Amboseli was declared a UNESCO-Mab Biosphere Reserve in 1991. Amboseli is in the foot hills of Kilimanjaro. Kilimanjaro is 19,340 feet high; it is the highest free-standing mountain in the world and is also commonly known as the roof of Africa, as it towers over East Africa, and the whole continent for that matter.

Next day early in the morning and in the evening we went on Safaris in the Park in our Land Cruisers. Even before we entered the park, we could see giraffes, zebras, wildebeests and other animals.

We entered the park through the Kimana gate. At the entrance to the park rules are written: "Maximun speed limit is 40 kmph. If you speed, elephants will flag you down." This was apart from other rules. Amboseli National Park is home to a variety of wild animals. We got an opportunity to see the African elephant, wildebeest, giraffes, zebras, impalas and ostriches

We saw herds of elephants. The biggest can be up to 7.5 metre long, 3.3 metre high at the shoulder, and 6 tonnes in weight. Tusks, which are large modified incisors that grow throughout an elephant's lifetime, occur in both males and females and are used in fights and for marking, feeding, and digging. The other notable feature of African elephants is their very large ears, which allow them to radiate excess heat. We stopped a number of times to watch them as they crossed a few metres in front of our land cruisers.

We saw a host of Kenyan birds of various types and sizes, both large and small. Dan our Safari driver and guide was knowledgeable on all kinds of birds, animals and about Kenya and adjoining countries. He would stop to explain every time he saw a new variety of bird. The low level swamps and seasonal waters of Amboseli are a big attraction for the birds. Here we saw ducks, cranes and hundreds of pink flamingos, apart from other varieties of birds.

We saw a lot of Maasai people. They are an indigenous ethnic group in Africa of semi-nomadic people. Due to their distinct traditions, customs and dress and their residence near the many national game parks, they are known internationally because of their links to the national parks and reserves. They live by herding cattle and goats. There are 43 tribes in Kenya with different languages and cultures. Kenyan Asians are officially recognised as the 44th tribe of Kenya.

We visited a Maasai village; although it was an optional excursion, everyone volunteered to visit the village. There is a fee paid to the village chief; as per him the amount is spent on education, health and betterment of Maasais. We were welcomed by a large number of Maasais as soon as we got off the vehicle. They were singing in Maa language and dancing and asked us to join them. We all danced with them. They performed *adumu*, a jumping dance, jumping several feet high in the air, as if they had some built-in springs in their legs. Except for some elders living in rural areas, most Maasai people speak the official languages of Kenya Swahili and English.

Maasai wear the colour red because it symbolizes their culture and they believe it scares away lions. Also, most of the men wear a *shuka*, which is a red robe. The women wear clothes that are colorful and decorated with beads.

We were escorted to their village and given an introduction on their way of life. We were shown their houses, called *bomas*, made of mud ash and cow dung. These are small structures with thatched roofs; it is the job of the Maasai women to build these sturdy dwellings. These huts are constructed in a wide circle so that their livestock can stay in the middle protected from predators like lions and cheetahs. The huts are surrounded by thick thorny fences as an added protection. There was a village doctor who was there with herbs for medicinal use. We were told about the use of these herbs to cure some ailments. They drink cow milk as also blood of cows, by making a hole in the neck. It is considered to be high in protein and is considered beneficial for people with the weakened immune system. They answered all our queries and some of them spoke good English.

Maasais do not believe in after life. Most dead bodies are simply thrown to the wild forests for scavengers. Burials are believed to harm the soil and is reserved only for some chiefs. In fact, on some occasions, the dead would be smeared with fat so as to easily attract wild animals to eat the bodies.

After a tour of the Maasai village, we were ushered to their local marketplace behind the village. Women in their colourful attire were selling garments, beaded necklaces, bracelets, local jewellery, and handicrafts. Outside the village there were some children on their way home back from school, smiling and waving at us.

Pran Mehta, a Rotarian who was travelling with us and spends a lot of his time on education, was very keen to visit the local school; unfortunately he could not do so since children were already on their way home. He became friendly with the Maasai Chief, who was ready to walk with him to the hotel, which was a bit distant. We did not want to take a chance, lest he be attacked on the way by some wild animals!

In the evening we were all sitting down in the restaurant for dinner and suddenly the lights were switched off. We all thought that there was a power failure. To our surprise there was the restaurant staff dancing and singing a birthday song for Pran Mehta on his birthday. It was a lovely surprise for him.

The following day we travelled to our next destination Naivasha; it was a six hour drive, through the 'Great Rift Valley' originally given the name by British Explorer John Walter Gregory. The Rift Valley is a geographic stretch extending 6,000 kilometres across the Middle East and Africa from Jordan to Mozambique. The valley encapsulates tremendous changes in topographic diversity with its scarps and volcanoes, lakes, ancient granitic hills, flat desert landscapes and coral reefs and islets. Lions, leopards, African elephants, rhinos, buffaloes, cheetahs, giraffes, antelopes, zebras and primates ranging from mountain gorillas to chimpanzees all find a home in the Rift Valley.

We arrived a bit late in the afternoon at Lake Naivasha Sopa Lodge. The hotel staff were waiting to serve us lunch. Naivasha is a small town and the gateway to Lake Naivasha.

It was a mesmerizing resort, set in one hundred and fifty acres of grassland studded with Acacia bushes and trees; the resort is not only home to resident giraffe, waterbuck, zebras but also Vervet and Colobus monkeys. At night we were escorted to our rooms by the hotel security due to wild animals in the area. Some of us were lucky to see hippos grazing in front of our rooms, which seems was quite common. Also to walk to the lake any time of the day, we had to be escorted by security staff. It was a great opportunity to take photographs with animals very close to us.

After lunch, we took a boat ride in Lake Naivasha. It is unpredictable with rainy weather. We were lucky at least when we started our boat ride it was not raining at all, though in between there was slight drizzle. To our relief, we were given orange coloured life jackets and before too long we were cruising along the tranquil waters of Lake Naivasha.

Lake Naivasha is a freshwater lake northwest of the capital Nairobi and it is the highest of the Rift Valley lakes which is 1884 metres above sea level. Its waters are shallow with an average depth of five metres. Freshwater shores fringed with papyrus and yellow acacias, hippos frolicking in the shallows and the cacophony of twittering birds, created a lasting impression of Lake Naivasha. We saw herds of hippos in the lake. Hippos are unique amphibious mammals and are the third largest land animals on earth. It suddenly started pouring heavily and our boat drivers came back with full speed.

The following day we started our journey for Masai Mara National Reserve and reached there after over a six-hour road journey. At the entrance to Masai Mara there were colourfuly dressed Maasai men and women selling handicrafts. We checked in at the Masai Mara Sopa Lodge. It is located high on the slopes of the Oloolaimutia Hills. It was one of the first safari lodges to be built in the Masai Mara Game Reserve, a reason why its gardens and trees are so lush and mature. All the buildings follow the design of traditional African round houses with conical roofs, and these stretch along the line of the hills with the impressively large public area buildings.

Masai Mara is one of Africa's greatest wildlife reserves. Together with the Serengeti National Park in Tanzania it forms Africa's most diverse, incredible and most spectacular eco-systems and possibly the world's top safari big game viewing eco-system. The Reserve is popular for its large animal migration, which occurs every year as a routine ritual. Herds of animals, about 1.4 million wildebeests, about 200,000 zebras and more than 500,000 gazelles migrate to Masai Mara Conservancy in search of grass by negotiating through the dangerous crocodile rich river. This show of migration recurs every year during July to the last week of October. The Conservancy spans over 1,800 square kilometres. December to February is a great time as it is dryer and good for the big cats. There have been some 95 species of mammals, amphibians and reptiles and over 400 birds species recorded on the reserve.

There are four main types of terrain in the Mara – the Ngama Hills to the east with sandy soil and leafy bushes favoured by black rhino, Oloololo Escarpment forming the western boundary and rising to a magnificent plateau, Mara Triangle bordering the Mara River with lush grassland and acacia woodlands supporting masses of game especially migrating wildebeest and the Central Plains, forming the largest part of the reserve with scattered bushes and boulders on rolling grasslands favoured by the plains game.

We spent one evening and the next full day in the Reserve. The roads were so bumpy and my iphone showed that I had walked over 20000 steps; may be every bump was being recorded as a step !! Our Kenyan driver guides made sure that we did not miss out on sighting any wild animal. We saw the big five - cape buffalo, elephant, leopard, lion and rhino. We also saw wildebeests, zebras, Thomson's gazelles, cheetah, impalas, giraffes, fox, ostriches, hippos and some other animals.

It was a sight to see cheetah playing with his cubs. Cubs came very close to our vehicle and were playing underneath our vehicle. We saw a lion and lioness walking majestically and mating, a leopard hiding in grass under a tree, and elephants protecting and moving gracefully with baby elephants. While adult males enjoy their solitude, female elephants live in groups with young ones, and are led by a matriarch. Cape buffalos are territorial and protective and can charge at great speed when they feel threatened. We could see them moving in a large herd grazing. Wildebeest prefer grassy plains and open woodlands, are active at day and night and like to travel in large herds, grazing round the clock.

It was a most memorable sight to see hundreds of animals in the close vicinity; the lions were alert and made a protective circle around their young ones to save them from predators. One has got to be there to see so many animals in one area. This undoubtedly was the highlight of our visit. After such wonderful sightings, when we were on our way back, we kept admiring all varieties of animals that we had seen. As a matter of fact we had seen so much of wildlife, there was not much excitement left. Not that we did not enjoy viewing every animal that we saw on the way. There was a lady in the group, who repeatedly wanted to get out of the vehicle to take photos. After seeing the wild animals, she did not utter a word about getting down from the vehicle.

The safari would not have been so exciting but for our driver guides who were really very well informed and filled in with the most fascinating and interesting facts about the most curious of creatures, both big and small. Their knowledge of the country was enormous. We could ask them any question and there always was a well informed answer.

The finale of our stay in Masai Mara Sopa Lodge was a dance performance in the evening by the Maasai people in their colourful attire, dancing with their warrior shouts. Grunts followed chants and the pounding of feet in harmony, and rhythm of heartbeats. There were no drums, only voices replicating the sound of instruments and rhythm.

The following day, we drove to Nairobi. It was again over a six-hour drive. By now we had got used to long drives from one place to another, but every drive was worth it.

Nairobi city and its surrounding area also form the Nairobi County. The name Nairobi comes from the Maasai phrase, *Enkare Nyrobi*, which translates to cool water. The area Nairobi currently occupies was essentially an uninhabited swamp until a supply depot of the Uganda Railway was built by the British in 1899 linking Mombasa to Uganda. The location of the camp was chosen due to its central position between Mombasa and Kampala. It was also chosen because its network of rivers could supply the camp with water and its elevation would make it cool enough for residential purposes for not only the thousands of Indian labourers who came to Kenya to work on the railway line, but also for the British settlers. With such a strategic location, it had soon grown big enough to become the railway's headquarters.

Once we entered Nairobi, the traffic slowed down and it gave a feeling of entering a busy metropolis. We stayed at Emara Ole-Sereni, a brand new hotel, located at a convenient location with proximity to both local and international airports and to Nairobi's Central Business District. Ole Sereni is a premium wildlife resort in Nairobi, overlooking the Nairobi National Game Park. From the balcony of our rooms we could view wildlife.

As we had the day at our disposal and wanted to make the best of it, we visited Daphne Sheldrick's Elephant Orphanage which is located in the Nairobi Game Park and was originally started by David Sheldrick. Orphaned baby elephants from all over Kenya are looked after here. Visitors are allowed daily from 1100 hrs to 1200 hrs.

Driving through the resident area of Langata, we visited the Giraffe Centre where Daisy, the famous Rothschild giraffe can be seen and fed at the beautiful home overlooking the Ngong Hills.

Driving through the city we saw the Parliament Buildings and the Kenyatta International Conference Centre, Nairobi National Museum and Snake Park. Museum is located at the Museum Hill, a short drive from city centre. It was built in 1929 and is the flagship museum for the National Museums of Kenya. A guide from the museum took us around. It houses celebrated collections of Kenya's history, nature, culture and contemporary art. The artworks and materials used in the fabrication of outdoor sculptures, the landscaping and the botanic gardens, link to the four pillars of Kenya's national heritage i.e. nature, culture, history and contemporary art.

Snake Park is located adjacent to the National Museum. It houses various varieties of snakes, fishes and reptiles. It also offers services such as rescue and rehabilitation centre for reptiles ie abandoned, confiscated and illegal collection. Information on aquarium fishes and reptiles is given here and specialized talks are also organized. Even today the Snake Park has continued assisting the city residents of Nairobi by removing spotted house snakes and as well as giving advice on how to reduce possible snakebites within their homesteads. The Park also provides snake identification service.

Inspite of the busy day we found time to visit the Maasai Market, which moves to different places all seven days of the week. Luckily, it was open at Capital Centre located not far from the hotel. It is a place to shop for not so expensive, beautiful and colourful souvenirs to take back home. A lot of bargaining goes on here. It is an open air market with a wide variety of items to shop including African pots and pans, African paintings, African materials, curios, jewellery, shoes, bags, clothes, and utensils among other things. There is a keenness among all vendors to sell their merchandise.

Africans are a generally friendly people. Kenyans embody this culture to the fullest. A special mention can be made of Asians' contribution to Kenya. The first person to openly demand independence in Kenya was the Asian trade unionist Makhan Singh. For that he was detained for 11 years. The firebrand Leftist political strategist Pio Gama Pinto and many other members of the Asian community made tremendous contributions to Kenya. The University of Nairobi, Kenya's premier institution of higher learning was intended to be a memorial for Mahatma Gandhi and the initial funding for it came from the Asian community.

Kenyan Indians, or Wahindi as they are known in Swahili, have come to epitomise trade across the country. From small shops in towns all over Kenya, selling basic household commodities, to massive manufacturing companies, the Wahindi dominate. What is even more interesting is that, in a country of 40 million people, there are only 100,000 Wahindi – less than a quarter of a percent of the total population. But their contribution to the economy far outstrips their numbers. Asians run many businesses from small shops to sprawling multinationals. They own workshops and contracting firms. They build roads and control hotels.

There have been many famous Kenyans; Wangari Muta Maathai was a renowned Kenyan social, environmental and political activist and the first African woman to win the Nobel Prize. Maathai founded the Green Belt Movement, an environmental non-governmental organization focused on the planting of trees, environmental conservation, and women's rights. In 1984, she was awarded the Right Livelihood Award in 2004. Jomo Kenyatta was the first President. American President Barack Obama's father was Kenyan. Kenya has produced famous writers such as Grace Ogot, Meja Mwangi, Margaret Ogola, and Binyavanga Wainaina.

After a wonderful visit with a great group, we came back home carrying memories of a beautiful country, animals roaming free in the wild and amazing people.

Postscript

COVID-19 Changing the world and New Normal

Over the centuries the world has faced wars, natural disasters, and disease. War has destroyed communities and families and disrupted social and economic fabric of nations. Natural disasters like cyclones, floods, earthquakes, landslides, tsunami, avalanches and volcanic eruptions have destroyed human habitations, environment and properties. Diseases have been responsible for loss of life and even damaged crops. Illnesses have indeed become a part of human suffering, though advances in modern medicine has made a big difference.

One of the major infectious diseases that has brought human activity to a standstill in recent times is COVID-19; it is the worst crisis since World War II. It is also like its earlier manifestation mainly a respiratory disease. The first known severe respiratory illness caused by a coronavirus emerged with the 2003 Severe Acute Respiratory Syndrome (SARS) epidemic in China. A second outbreak of severe illness began in 2012 in Saudi Arabia with the Middle East Respiratory Syndrome (MERS). COVID-19 being a totally new virus created a lot of confusion with doctors trying out various antivirals and other drugs to save patients. As time has passed better knowledge and understanding of the virus has improved outcomes, especially in serious hospitalized cases all over the world.

On 31 December 2019, Chinese authorities alerted the World Health Organization (WHO) of an outbreak of a novel strain of coronavirus causing severe illness, which was subsequently named SARS-CoV-2 and COVID-19 by the World Health Organization. However, the Chinese authorities hid the information on human to human transmission for a few weeks which subsequently created a backlash of blame and resentment from the global community as the virus spread rapidly to over 200 countries. Many countries in the western Europe were badly affected but U.S. remains the worst affected till date leading in both total population affected and mortality figures. No wonder the Trump administration is highly critical of China and also WHO for failing to warn the world about the virus in late December 2019 when Wuhan saw a huge spike in cases and the fact of human to human transmission was abundantly clear.

The disease appears to have originated from a Wuhan seafood market where wild animals, including marmots, birds, rabbits, bats and snakes, are traded illegally. Coronaviruses are known to jump from animals to humans, so it's thought that the first people infected with the disease,a group primarily made up of stallholders from the seafood market contracted it from contact with animals.

All countries started taking precautions as deemed necessary as COVID-19 had started spreading all over the world. At the start of the outbreak most countries had cancelled flights to China and were not allowing Chinese carriers to operate in their country. Gradually countries started putting restrictions and not allowing passengers to enter the country from affected countries. Flights were cancelled and the borders closed.

As reported by World Health Organization on 30 October 2020, a total of 44,888,869 cases were confirmed in more than 227 countries and territories. There were 1,178,475 deaths.

With both national and international travel coming to a total halt the travel and tourism industry has been the sector worst affected. The World Travel and Tourism Council stated that COVID-19 could cut 50 million jobs worldwide in the travel and tourism industry. Asia is expected to be the worst affected. Once the outbreak is over, it could take up to 10 months for the industry to recover.

According to United Nations Secretary-General, Antonio Guterres USD 5 trillion had been mobilized; most of that money was pumped in by the developed world, including USD 2 trillion in the United States, to support their own economies from the consequences of the pandemic.

On 25 March 2020 in India, a three-week nationwide lockdown was declared as it was felt that social distancing was the only way to break the cycle of infection. India did start taking precautions well in time even before the lockdown. Movement of all trains, buses and flights were cancelled. In spite of the lockdown labour who had come to big cities started moving back to the villages in large numbers. It was a difficult job for the government to control that. Labourers probably felt that it was better to be with their families in villages and normal survival would at least be possible. Lot of shelters were set up for the poor, food was being provided and financial aid given.

Future outlook

The worldwide outbreak of of this novel pandemic has brought the world to a standstill. The world is in the midst of the deepest recession in peacetime history over the past 150 years. As the World Bank's Global Economic Prospects and the latest Economic Outlook from the OECD demonstrate, the impact is devastating all over. Tourism has been the worst affected of all major economic sectors. Travel business in particular is in the dumps with no movements taking place and modes of transport shut.

On closing of International borders there were a lot of tourists, students, professionals, workers and others who were stuck abroad. Diplomatic missions had stopped giving visas. Travel agents spent a lot time cancelling travel arrangements, advising and helping out their clients. Many people all over the world were caught in the midst of a foreign visit and the Indian government went about bringing them back from countries such as China, Italy, Spain, UK and many others.

With the advance of technology and internet, even during lock down, one could be in touch with people and could perform a lot of tasks. Companies were doing virtual meetings, video conferences and interviews. Live charity concerts and virtual house parties were being organized. On News channels news presenters were broadcasting from home. Reporters were reporting and interviewing on skype. Lot of training programmes and seminars were being organized online. It is the younger generation that would remember this period, when children had to stay at home. They attended virtual classes from home wearing uniform.

During this pandemic, in India there has been a commendable contribution by doctors, nurses, health staff in hospitals, military, para-military, police, sanitation staff, shops, local vendors and all those who kept the supply chain going on to look after the health and survival of others. Unfortunately, India lost some five hundred frontline doctors and medical staff to this virus.

As per World Travel & Tourism Council (WTTC), under the worst-case scenario, prolonged travel restrictions could put more than 197 million jobs under threat and cause a loss of more than USD 5.5 trillion to global Travel & Tourism GDP.

Travel particularly domestic travel has restarted since mid-July in some countries including India but in a phased manner. In India now various ministries are involved like Home, Health, Aviation, Tourism and security agencies to make rules and give clearances for people to travel. It is going to be a complex scenario.

Gradually some international flights have started operating though initially to bring their citizens back. Subsequently "air bridges" and "travel bubbles" are being created, that allow for non-essential travel depending on the country where COVID-19 virus appears to be under control .

Although people and are taking flights with a lot of apprehension, the risk of catching an infection on an aircraft is typically lower than in a shopping centre or a closed office environment. However, one needs to take basic precautions like wearing a mask and sanitizing of hands. Modern aircraft have high efficiency air filters similar to those used in top hospital operating rooms. They capture more than 99.9% of the airborne microbes in the filtered air. Some countries have started asking for COVID clearance tests to be done before travel as a precautionary measure.

There may not be mass tourism for some time but people would travel for business sooner than later. But ultimately people will want to relax, explore and travel again be it for professional, social, recreational and humanitarian purposes. May be people would travel less frequently while investing in top quality and personal experiences. The impact of the pandemic on travel and tourism has also been covered extensively by the media particularly print media in India. A recent report in the *Times of India* (1 August 2020) captioned "Wings clipped, travel's all about discovery of India now", details how tourism organizations are ramping up the prospects of domestic sector, designating new spots and creating facilities, encouraging self drive tours and even providing insurance coverage to tourists for COVID treatment. However, it's still a challenge as different states in the country have imposed their own protocols which have to be followed.

Ultimately there is likely to be a vaccine or therapeutic cure to fight COVID-19. It would take years to understand the significance and the happenings of 2020. COVID-19 has accelerated high speed digital connectivity, linking people in businesses, schools, doctors, healthcare, shops and changed our entire way of life. COVID-19 crisis has been a global turning point, when many of the fundamentals of our social and economic life will be remade and a new normal established for quite some time. On the social front it is said that the Indian Namaste, or a wave of the hand from a distance may become the norm instead of the handshake for years to come.